I0800127

POSTCARD HISTORY SERIES

Orlando

IN VINTAGE POSTCARDS

POSTCARD HISTORY SERIES

Orlando

IN VINTAGE POSTCARDS

Lynn M. Homan and Thomas Reilly

ARCADIA
PUBLISHING

ISBN 978-0-7385-1381-2

Published by Arcadia Publishing
Charleston, South Carolina

Printed in the United States of America

Library of Congress Catalog Card Number: 2001092298

For all general information contact Arcadia Publishing at:
Telephone 843-853-2070
Fax 843-853-0044
E-Mail sales@arcadiapublishing.com
For customer service and orders:
Toll-Free 1-888-313-2665

Visit us on the Internet at www.arcadiapublishing.com

Contents

Acknowledgments

Postcards often present a different view of a particular area than photographs show. Most photos feature the people and places important to the individual taking the picture. Postcards, on the other hand, have been prepared commercially to present the scenes and subjects most important to the community and its visitors. *Orlando in Vintage Postcards* shows readers that story through postcards drawn primarily from two sources. Paul Camp, Special Collections, University of South Florida, assisted us in our use of the extensive postcard collection housed there. In Micanopy, Florida, Larry Roberts graciously offered us postcards from both his personal collection as well as those for sale in his shop, Larry Roberts Antiques. In addition to the information on the postcards themselves, several books on Orlando also provided important information. *From Florida Sand to "The City Beautiful": A Historical Record of Orlando, Florida* by E.H. Gore and *Orlando: A Centennial History* by Eve Bacon offer detailed histories of the area and its residents. *Orlando History in Architecture* by the Orlando Preservation Board contains photographs of some of the city's architectural treasures, while Jerrel H. Shofner's *Orlando: The City Beautiful* spotlights the Orlando of both past and present.

INTRODUCTION

A destination for millions of visitors from all over the world, Orlando is best known today as home to America's most famous theme parks. That is only a recent event, however—before the 1970s, today's vast pleasure emporiums didn't even exist. Nevertheless, just as tourists today mail off thousands of postcards depicting their Orlando vacations, earlier visitors also recorded their trips with postcards. Covering the period from the late 1800s through the mid-1960s, these views relate a story of a vastly different Orlando. They tell of a small, but steadily growing central Florida community peopled by cattle ranchers and citrus growers, polo-playing English expatriates and real estate speculators, military personnel and ordinary people seeking a home or vacation in the warm Florida sunshine.

Orlando had much the same beginning as many other Florida towns. At the conclusion of the Second Seminole War, homesteaders seeking free land joined the handful of hardy pioneers already in central Florida, earning a living in agriculture and cattle ranching. Following Florida statehood in 1845, the gigantic and somewhat ominously named Mosquito County was rechristened Orange County.

By the mid-1850s, Jernigan, a small settlement near Fort Gatlin, had been transformed into the town of Orlando. According to local history, Judge J.D. Spear led the movement to relocate the county seat from Enterprise to Orlando in 1856. He may also have played a role in the naming of the community—some sources cite Judge Spear's fondness for Shakespeare's play *As You Like It* as the origin of the community's name. Still others tie the name to Orlando Reeves, a soldier killed in an 1835 Indian attack, or to an early settler in the area, Orlando Rees. While the exact origin will probably never be known, residents voted to incorporate a municipality named Orlando on July 31, 1875. Citrus planted in the early 1870s began to bear fruit. Bringing both people and goods with its arrival in 1880 and subsequent expansion, the railroad linked Orlando with the rest of the state. Census records showed an increase from 200 to 2,481 residents between 1880 and 1890.

Unfortunately Mother Nature had other ideas. Although cold waves had periodically damaged crops, winter took on new meaning for residents in late 1894 and early 1895. Known as the Big Freeze, plummeting temperatures devastated the citrus industry, wreaking havoc with the area's economy. While several growers replanted their groves, others turned to cattle ranching, celery growing, or turpentining the forests of central Florida. One grower converted his citrus packinghouse into a skating rink complete with picnic facilities. Some gave up completely and moved back North.

The freeze of 1894–1895 had destroyed the economy. As the population declined, the *Daily Record*'s references to Orlando as "The Phenomenal City" ceased. By 1905, however, Orlando's economy was rebounding. As newcomers arrived, both the business and residential districts expanded, giving the town a different, more permanent appearance. Orlando was becoming a metropolis. Although Albert Gallatin Branham had planted approximately 400 oak trees in 1885, an additional 5,000 live and water oaks had been added during the ensuing years. In 1908, a landscaping campaign that included the planting of hundreds of palms, azaleas, and flowering shrubs throughout the town gave rise to a new appellation—"The City Beautiful."

When America entered World War I, Orlandoans did their part. More than 700 residents registered for military service; Lester LoBean was the first to land in France. Randolph Cobb was the first local soldier to be awarded the Croix de Guerre. Civilians also joined the effort; Liberty Loan and Red Cross drives never failed to meet their quotas during the war years.

Orlando set a precedent when women received the right to vote in municipal elections in April 1919. The Board of Trade also began a concentrated effort to make the state, and especially Orlando, America's new winter home. By 1920, the organization, renaming itself the Chamber of Commerce, had posted highway signs advertising Orlando as far north as New England. Civic clubs, railroads, bus lines, and real estate promoters joined the campaign to attract Northern visitors as well as businesses looking for branch office locations.

The Florida land boom had begun. By August 1920, real estate had become the most popular occupation—occupational licenses had been issued to nearly 150 real estate operators in Orlando alone. Subdivisions were platted; land auction extravaganzas attracted buyers. Although the developments often consisted of nothing more than sets of fancy entrance gates and a lot of hope on the part of the promoter, many sold out immediately. Property changed hands on a daily or even an hourly basis, as speculators gambled on ever increasing prices. One of Orlando's most ardent proponents, Carl Dann, later commented, "It finally became nothing more than a gambling machine, each man buying on a shoestring, betting dollars a bigger fool would come along and buy his option."

By 1926, speculation had reached an all-time high—and then the bubble burst. As out-of-state newspapers issued warnings of risky Florida land purchases, banks became increasingly wary of real estate loans. A September 1926 hurricane spared Orlando but further dampened the Florida land boom. By 1928, the crash that still awaited the American stock market had already hit Orlando. Not until just prior to America's entrance into World War II would the economy improve substantially.

In 1940, the federal government established a pilot training facility, the Army Air Corps Center, at Orlando's municipal airport; adjacent land was leased for military housing. Pine Castle, a second air base, was quickly constructed just south of the city. Aircraft companies opened new facilities, spurring additional growth. Placed on standby status after the war, the bases saw reactivation during the Korean Conflict. When Orlando Air Base was eventually taken over by the U.S. Navy as a training center in the late 1960s, the city would once again feel a strong military presence. Meanwhile, in 1956, the Glenn L. Martin Company announced plans for a missile plant at Orlando. America entered the space race from nearby Brevard County's Cape Canaveral two years later, further intensifying the expansion of technology-based industry.

In 1961 city leaders asked permission for commercial jets serving Orlando to share jet runways at McCoy (formerly Pine Castle) Air Base. The Air Force agreed, and in 1965, expanded the plan to full civilian/military use. That same year also saw the completion of both the Beeline Expressway and Interstate 4 through Orlando. These aviation and highway improvements not only facilitated commerce, but also meant easier access for visitors. Orlando quickly adopted a new nickname—"The Action Center of Florida."

In terms of growth, however, the most significant event of that year, and perhaps even the years to come, took place on November 15, 1965, when spokesmen revealed the buyer of large tracts of land just to the west of the city. According to the announcement, by its opening in 1971, "The $100-million Walt Disney World would be similar to California's Disneyland, but 'bigger and better', offering total entertainment for the millions of Americans it was sure to attract. The second phase, an Environmental Prototype Community of Tomorrow (EPCOT), would be built later." Life in Orlando would never be the same again—but that's a different era and another story.

One

"The City Beautiful"

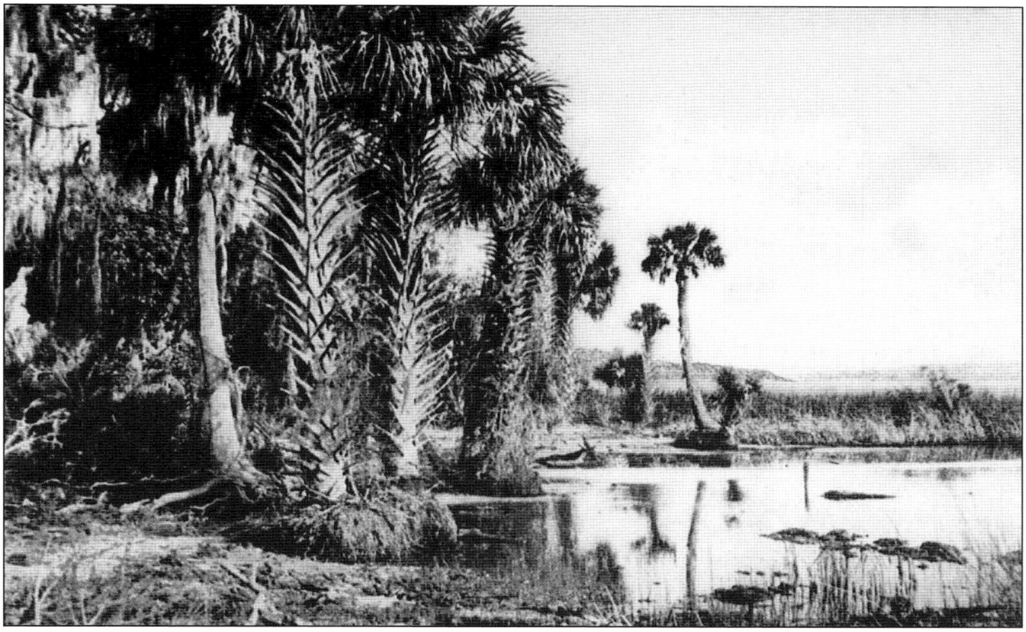

What better postcard with which to begin a pictorial account of Orlando than one that depicts the tropical flora and fauna of the area. Tall trees draped with trailing Spanish moss and cabbage palms surround one of the many shallow lakes in Orange County. Rising from the water is a suspicious-looking object that in all probability is an alligator. Off in the distance are visible the superb grazing lands that made Florida one of the leading cattle ranching states in the nation. When homesteaders moved into central Florida at the end of the Second Seminole War, cattle ranching and agricultural pursuits, including the growing of cotton, became the primary ways of earning a living. Citrus growing would take the place of cotton following the Civil War. And then of course there were the tourists. Almost from the beginning and certainly continuing into the present day, visitors have been part of Orlando's story. Written on this postcard were the words, "Beautiful weather here. When are you coming?" (University of South Florida Special Collections.)

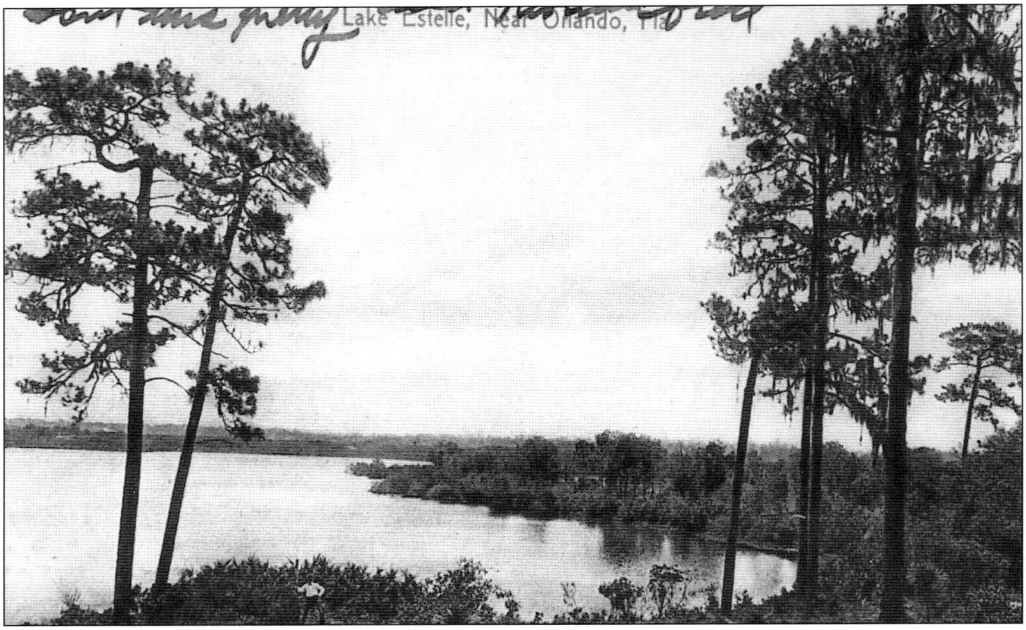

Just as tourists do today, early visitors sent postcards to friends and families back home encouraging them to come to Orlando. In 1906, one of her friends sent this view of Lake Estelle to Miss A.S. Peck of Jordan, New York. Written across the top is the question, "Isn't this pretty and Floridified?" The Board of Trade would have heartily endorsed such sentiments! (University of South Florida Special Collections.)

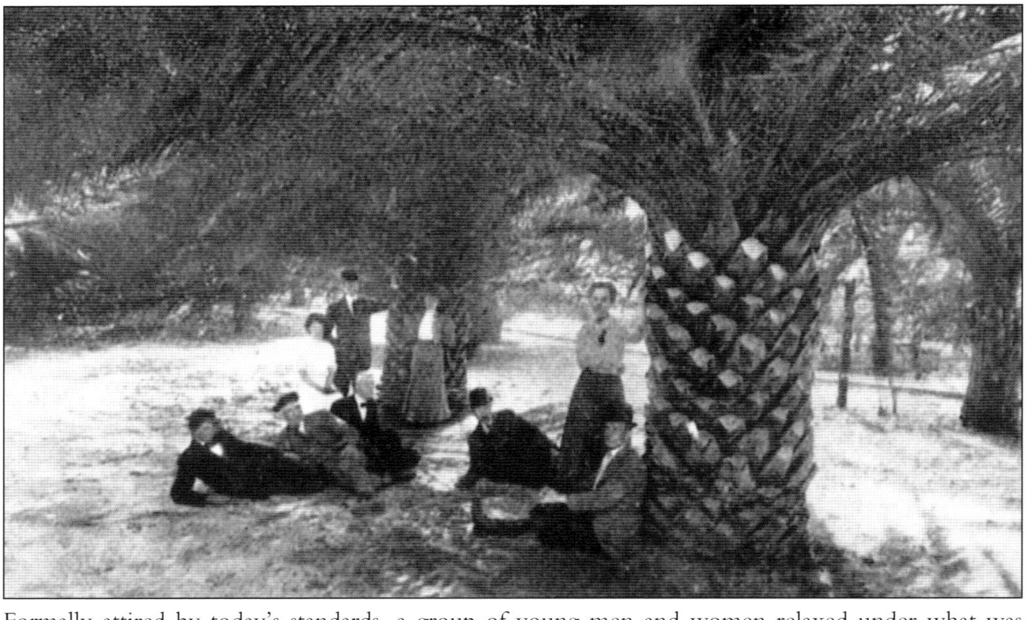

Formally attired by today's standards, a group of young men and women relaxed under what was known as a Phoenix or date palm. The 1908 postcard included a description of the tree, terming it "another species of the palm family which grows to a prodigious size with enormous long feathery leaves or branches. These beautiful trees may be seen on the grounds of many residences of Orlando." (University of South Florida Special Collections.)

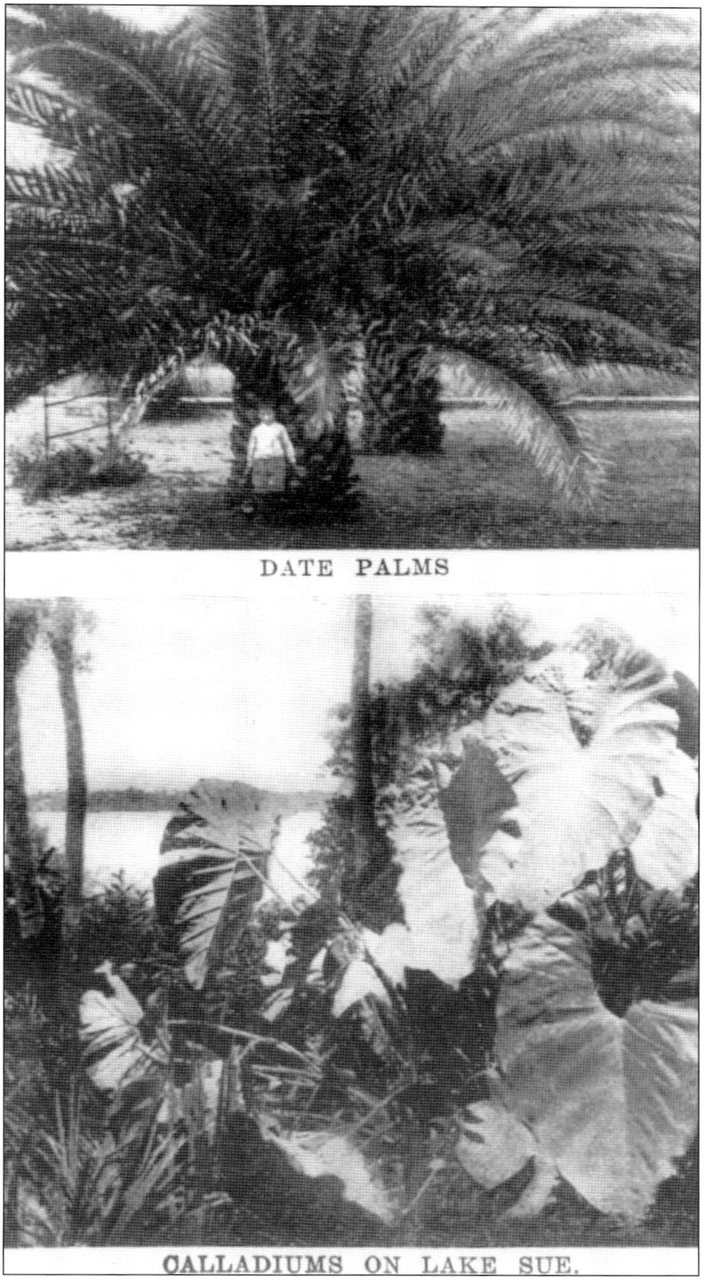

Numerous lakes, ranging in depth and size, dotted the Orlando area. Several, such as Lake Dot and Lake Greenwood, were sinkholes that had formed when the soil gave way to reveal water-filled caverns beneath the surface. Early settlers named many of the lakes for family members; other lakes were named for their appearance. Lake Dot, for example, resembled a small round dot, not to mention the fact that the new name sounded more attractive than its former appellation—"the mud hole with the alligator." Making reference to the caladiums and date palms planted near Lake Sue, this particular postcard stated that the vegetation grew to enormous size because of the long growing season. It also referred to the gardens in the area where hundreds of thousands of such plants were grown for market. (University of South Florida Special Collections.)

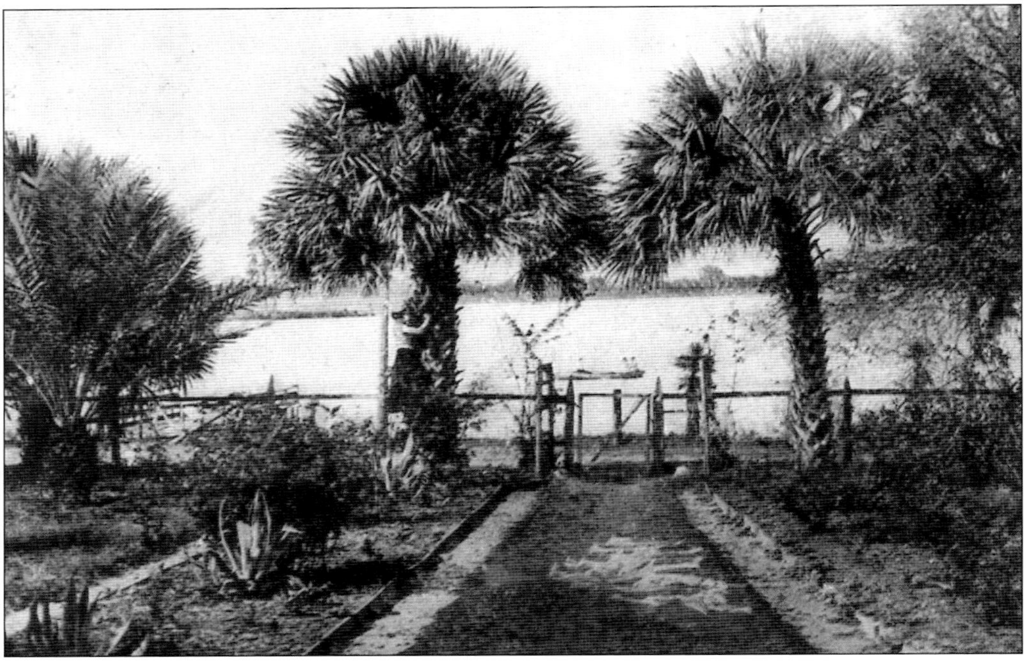

Tropical foliage was a popular topic for postcard manufacturers. A scene featuring Rock Lake, named for a large underwater rock formation on its east side, described two varieties of palm trees—the date and cabbage palm. The two trees flanking the walkway are cabbage palms, while the one on the left side is a date palm. (University of South Florida Special Collections.)

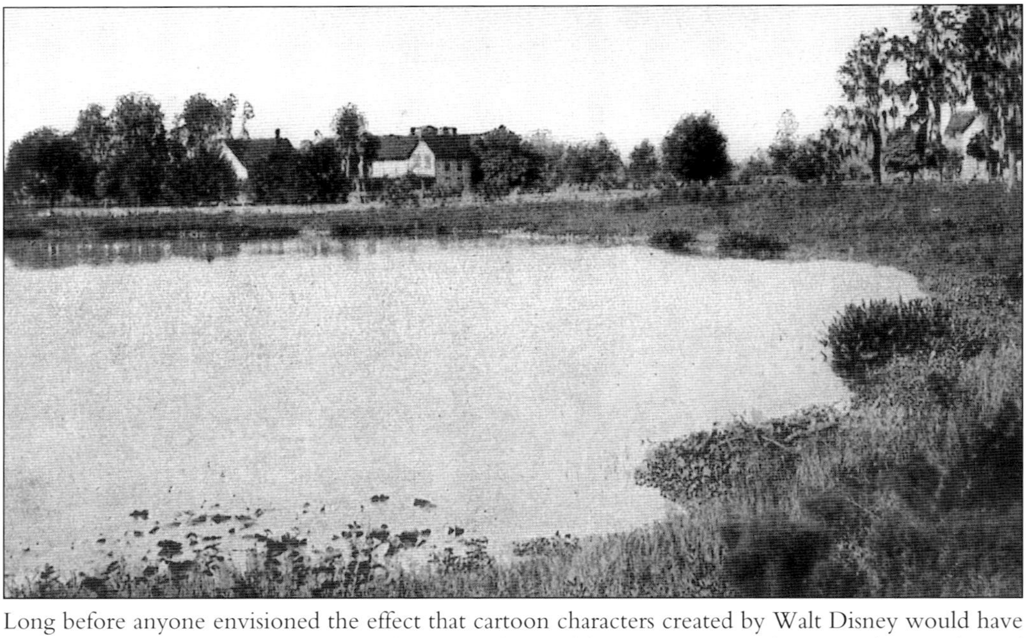

Long before anyone envisioned the effect that cartoon characters created by Walt Disney would have on the Orlando area, a local spot bore the name of one of the Disney mice. This pastoral scene showed a few of the early homes built on the shores of Lake Minnie. Originally named Lake Eva, the lake would become the site of several of the earliest and finest homes in Orlando. (University of South Florida Special Collections.)

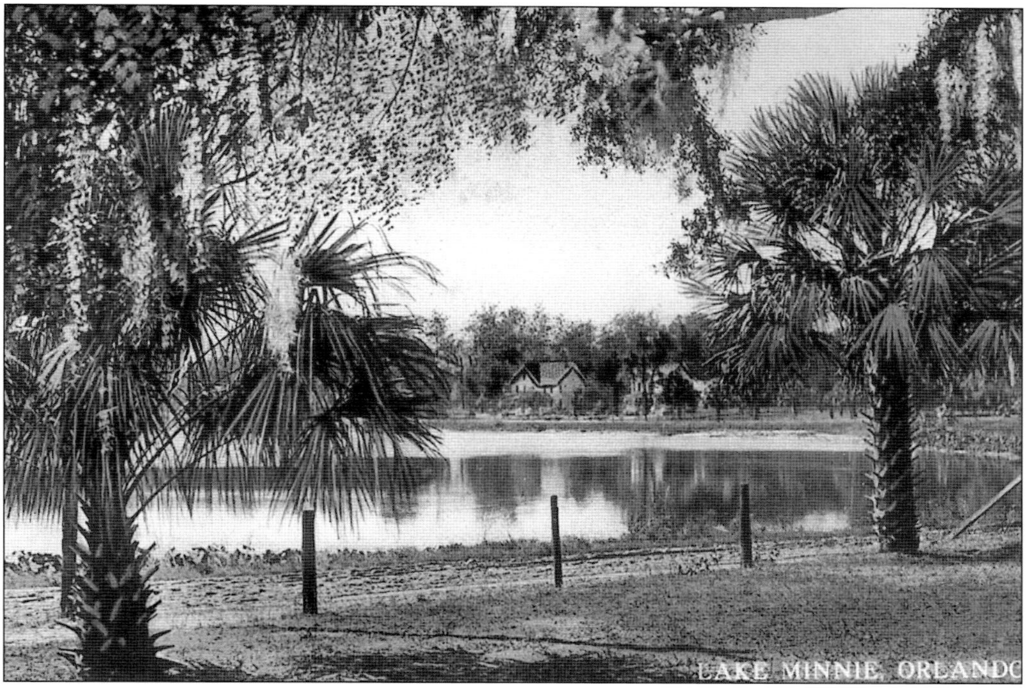

During the 1870s, Minnie Hall, daughter of Dr. Fergus S. Hall, and her sister Fannie married two brothers, Oliver and John Poyntz, both of whom were involved in numerous local businesses, including banking and real estate. When John Poyntz built a home on the shores of Lake Eva, the lake was renamed in honor of his wife, Minnie. With four residences, all inhabited by newly married couples, built on the banks of the lake, the area was quickly nicknamed "Honeymoon Row." By 1918, however, the *Morning Sentinel* contained an article discussing improvements to the once-again-renamed body of water. "On Lake Cherokee a row of light posts have been placed on the west side and the west shore has been graded." (University of South Florida Special Collections.)

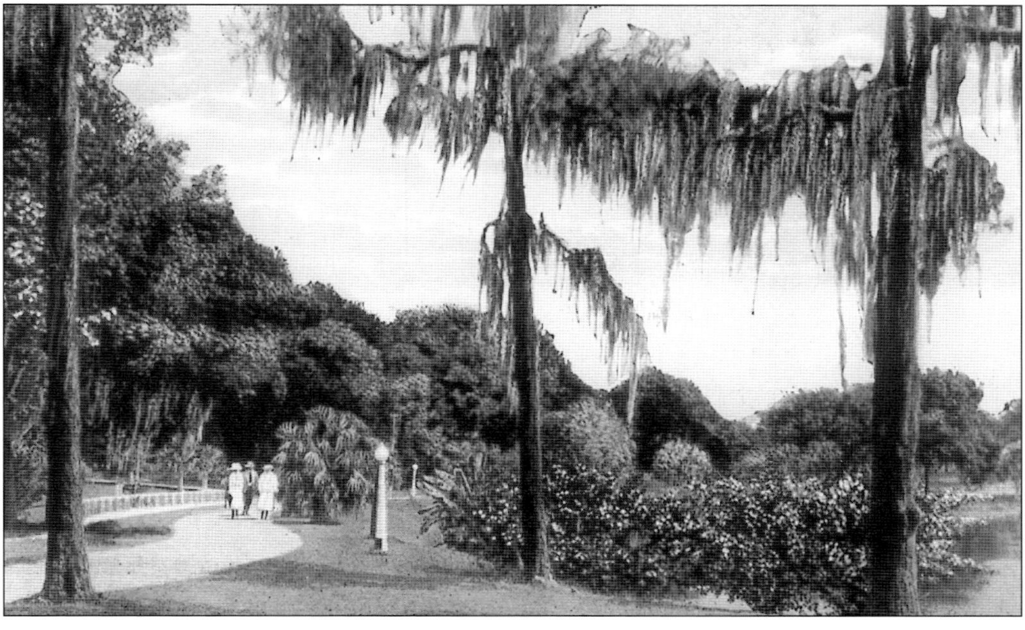

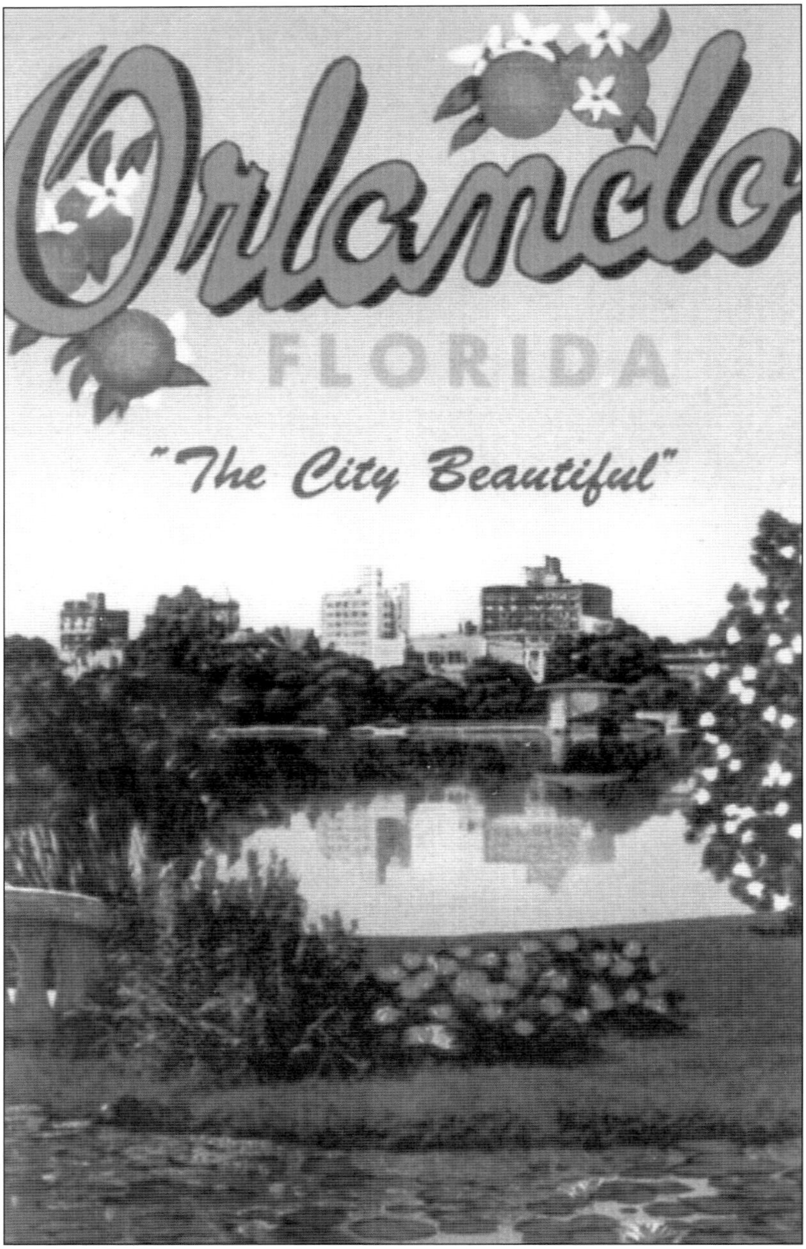

Although this particular postcard dates from a somewhat later period, it prominently features the slogan by which Orlando would come to be known for many years. In 1887, a local newspaper, the *Daily Record*, described the community as "The Phenomenal City." This title was proudly proclaimed until the disastrous freeze of 1894–1895 devastated not only the citrus crop, but the rest of the economy as well. By 1908, however, the population was growing and the economic situation was improving—the city needed a new slogan. Mrs. W.S. Branch Sr. suggested "The City Beautiful," based upon a recent campaign to beautify the city by planting palms, azaleas, and flowering shrubs. Selected from a variety of choices including "The Queen City," "The Magic City," "The Picturesque City," and "The Health City," the new nickname was quickly adopted and soon appeared on all types of promotional literature describing Orlando. (Florida State Archives.)

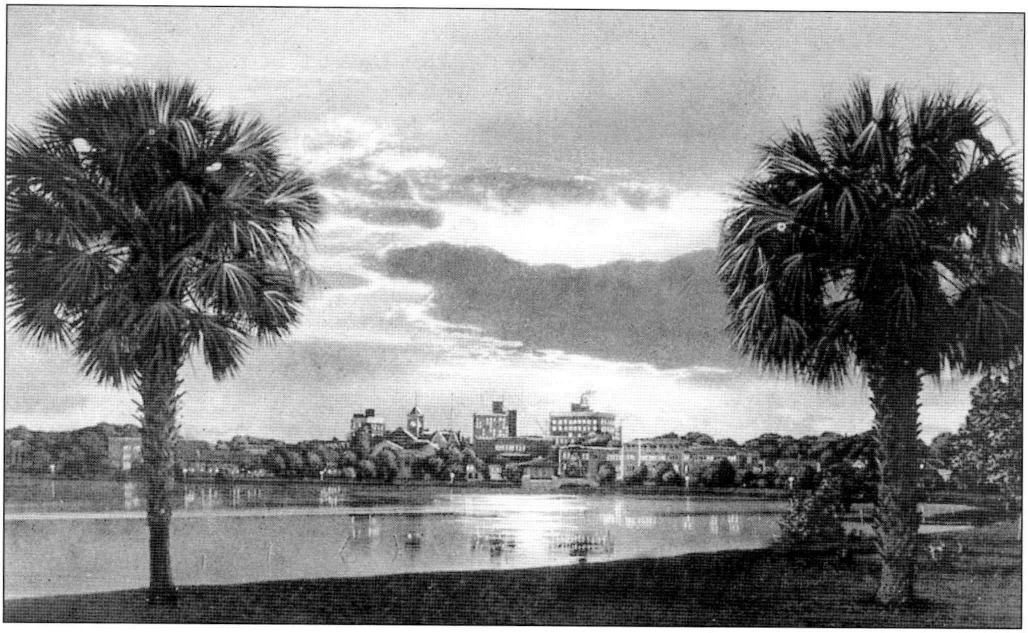

For more than 50 years, Orlando would be known officially as "The City Beautiful." Millions of postcards bearing the designation wended their way north in the hope of luring winter visitors to an area soon to be known for its warm weather and gorgeous tropical foliage. Included in many views were scenes of Orlando's lakes, both by moonlight and in daylight. The *Sentinel-Star* promoted the city in 1941 by saying, "Thousands of sea gulls fly to Orlando's 33 lakes every day and will feed tamely from the hand of the visitor. A large variety of wild ducks, swans and geese, and occasionally herons and cranes from the Florida Everglades visit the city's lakes." Frequently featuring the growing city's skyline in the background, the postcards could be dated by the different buildings shown. (University of South Florida Special Collections.)

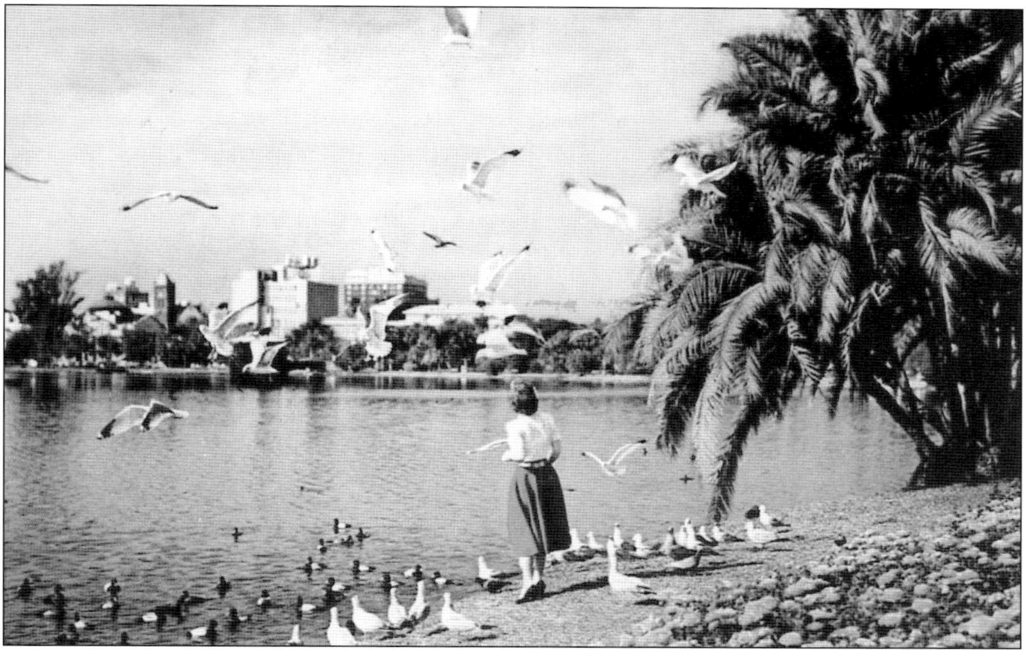

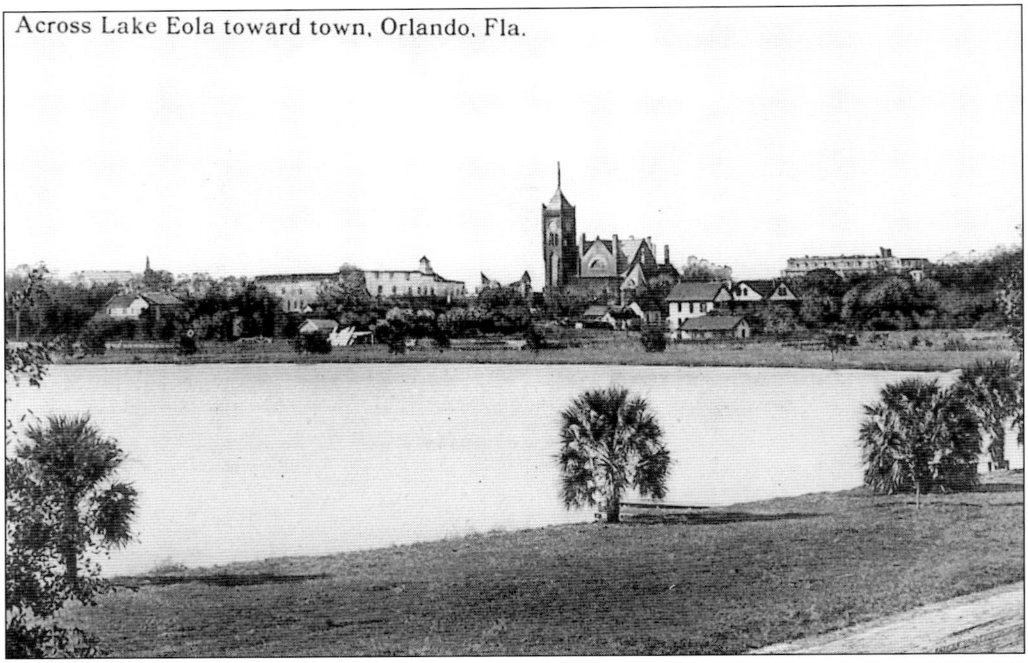

Even without a postmark, the early date of this postcard can be discerned by the dearth of buildings visible from across Lake Eola. Most prominent in the center of the skyline is the 1892 brick courthouse. The road running along the shoreline is also unpaved. (University of South Florida Special Collections.)

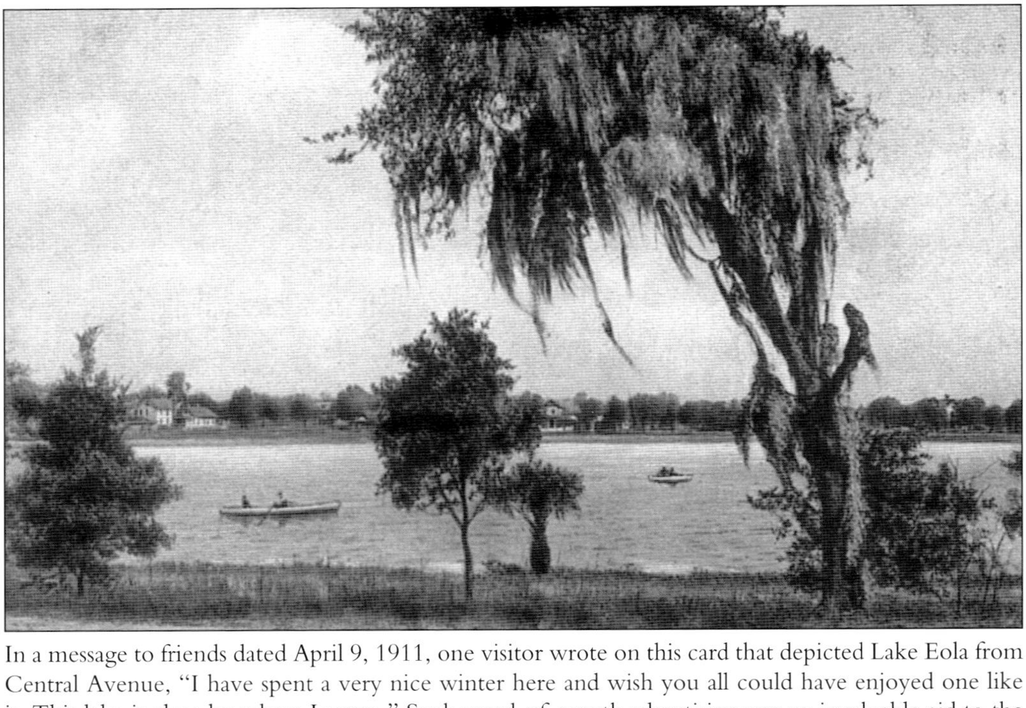

In a message to friends dated April 9, 1911, one visitor wrote on this card that depicted Lake Eola from Central Avenue, "I have spent a very nice winter here and wish you all could have enjoyed one like it. This lake is close by where I room." Such word-of-mouth advertising was an invaluable aid to the Board of Trade as it sought to attract winter visitors. (Larry Roberts Antiques.)

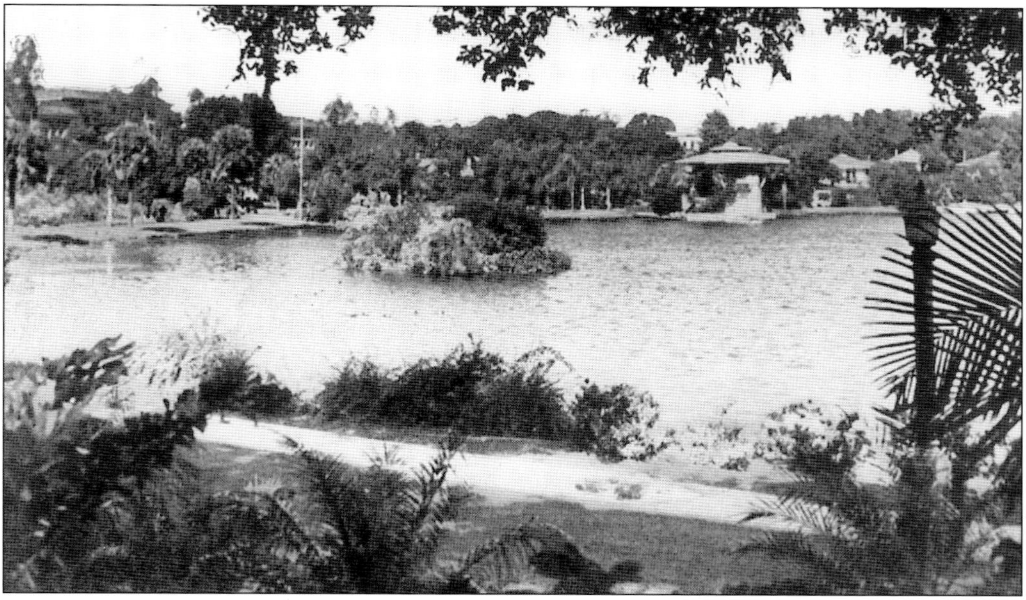

Orlando pioneer Jacob Summerlin purchased several hundred acres of land that included all of Lake Eola in 1873. In addition to allowing local residents to use the spring-fed lake as a water source, Summerlin further demonstrated his civic generosity in 1883 when he donated a strip of land encircling the lake to the city on the condition that it be made a public park. (University of South Florida Special Collections.)

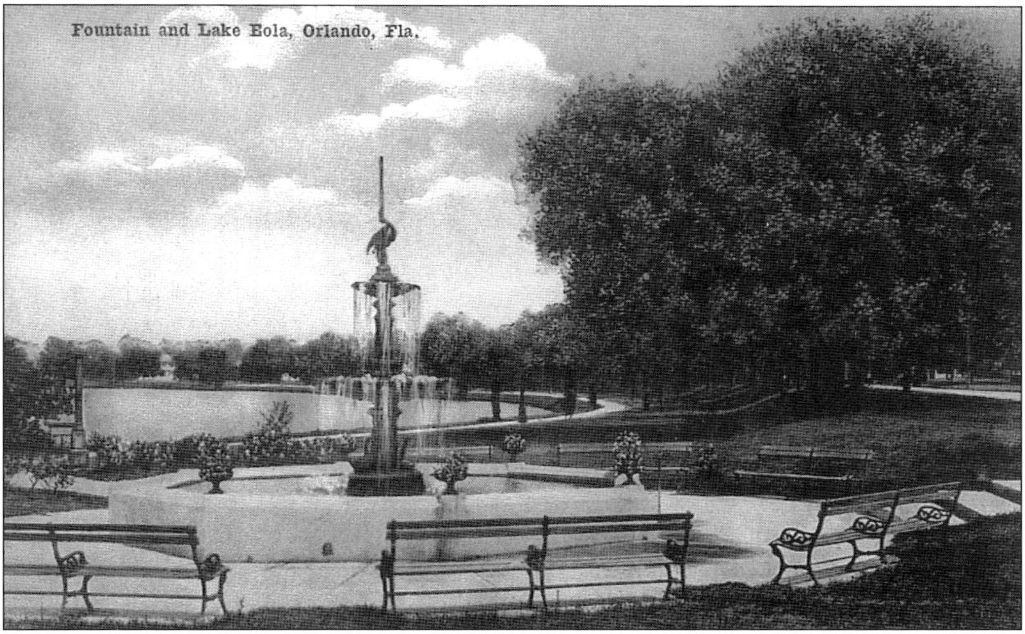

In 1913, E.F. Sperry, a member of Orlando's first park board, contributed $2,000 to fund construction of a fountain in Eola Park. Facing Central Avenue, the wrought-iron fountain consisted of "a large acanthus leaf with a duck base surmounted by a bittern set in an octagonal masonry basin with eight vases." Years later, in 1957, Orlando's far more elaborate Centennial Fountain would be placed in the center of the lake. (Larry Roberts Antiques.)

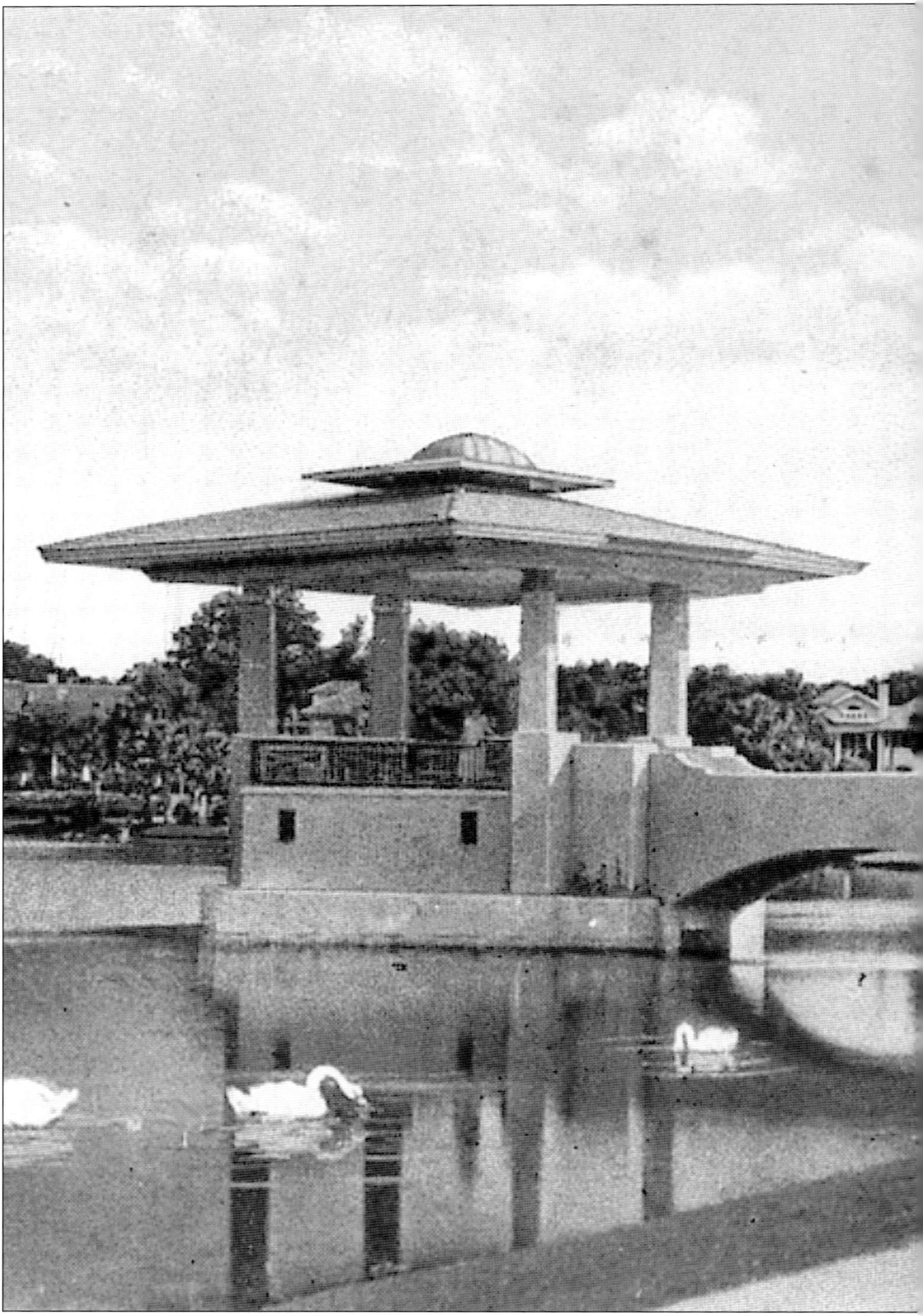

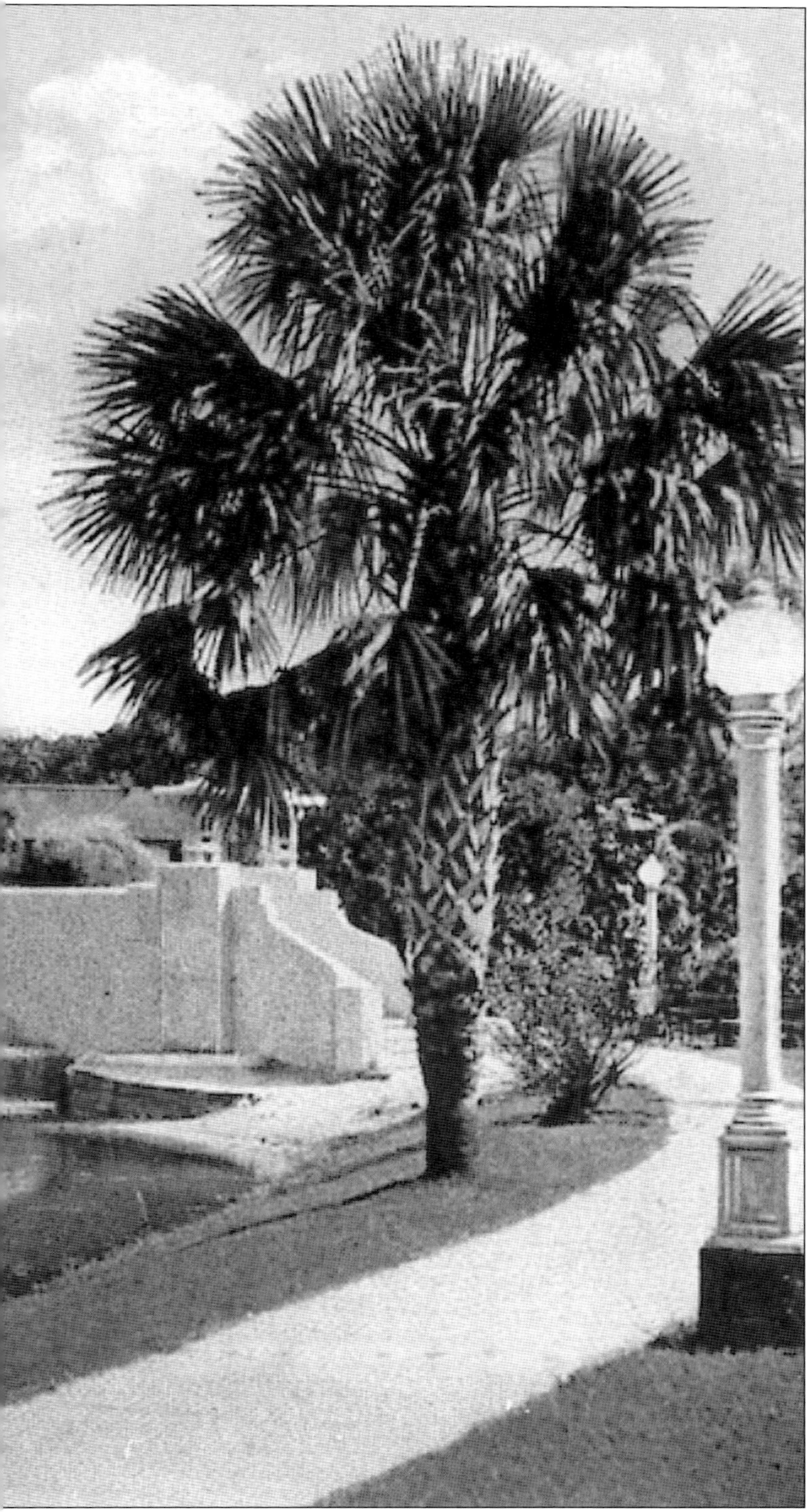

Musical performances at Lake Eola were one of the most popular forms of entertainment in town for residents and visitors alike. Erected in 1919, a bandstand provided the site for a seasonal six-week concert series that included two daily performances. The band committee charged a minimal fee of 10¢ per seat. On Christmas Eve in 1922, some 8,000 people celebrated the occasion at the Municipal Christmas Tree in Eola Park. Following a concert by the Knights of Pythias band, carols were sung and two Santa Clauses offered boxes of candy to children in the audience. The following year, the old bandstand was termed an eyesore and was replaced by this more elegant one. (University of South Florida Special Collections.)

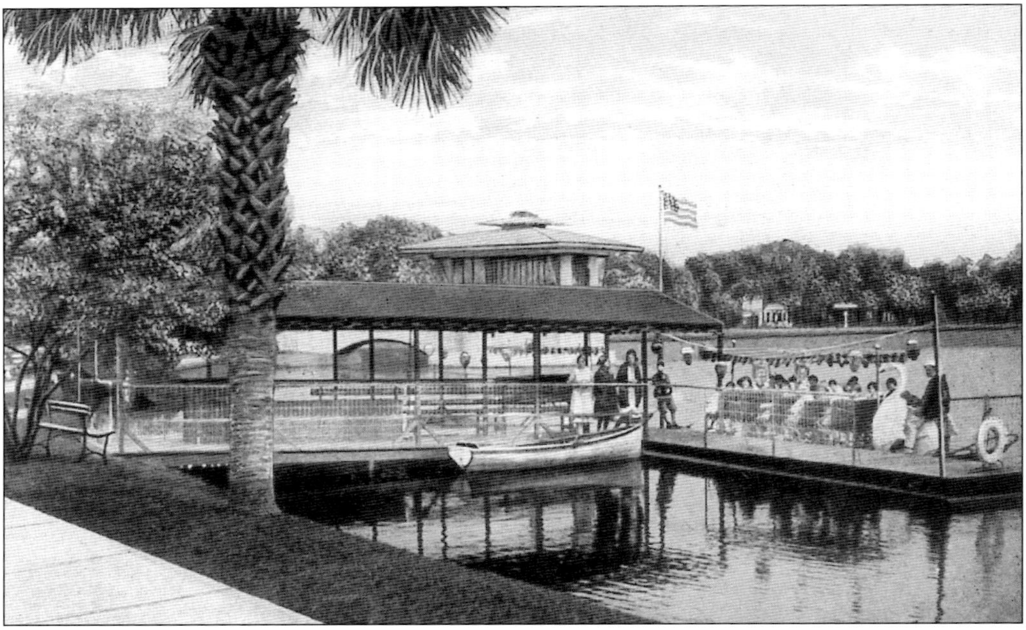

Boating on Lake Eola was also a popular form of recreation. From a landing near the bandstand, an enterprising resident rented canoes to pleasure-seekers. Those looking for less strenuous aquatic activity could cruise the lake as passengers on tour boats that were gaily decorated with carved swans and shaded by striped canvas awnings. (University of South Florida Special Collections.)

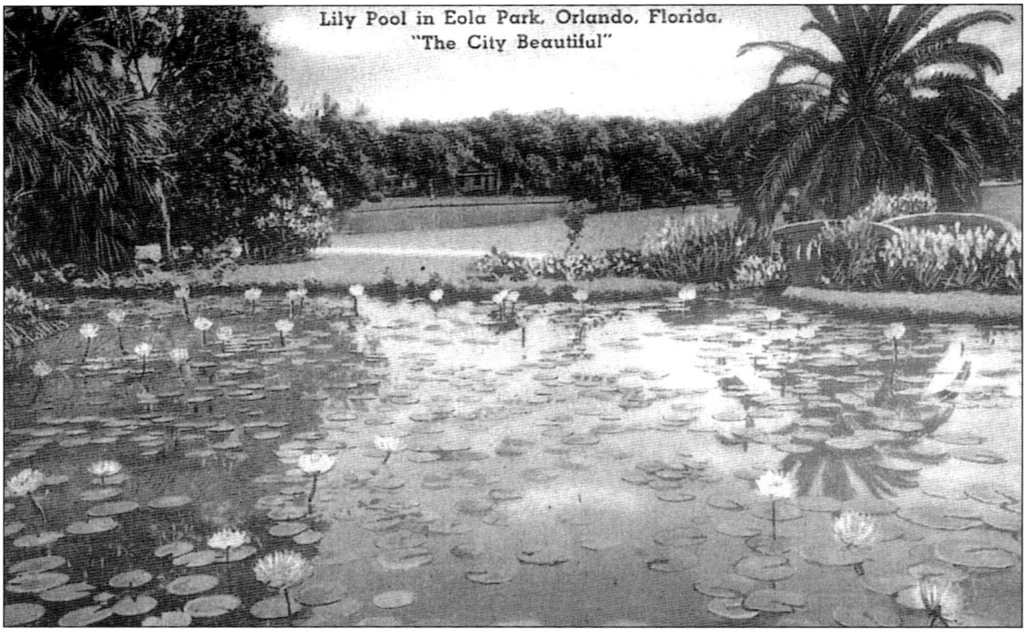

Orlando did an excellent job of living up to its name as "The City Beautiful" with its citywide beautification projects. Views such as this one of the lily pool in Eola Park proclaimed, "Scores of rare and exotic water plants add to the tropical beauty of Eola Park, regarded as one of Florida's most beautiful spots. Floodlights illuminate the pool from dusk to dawn for many of the rare specimens bloom while most of the citizens sleep." (Larry Roberts Antiques.)

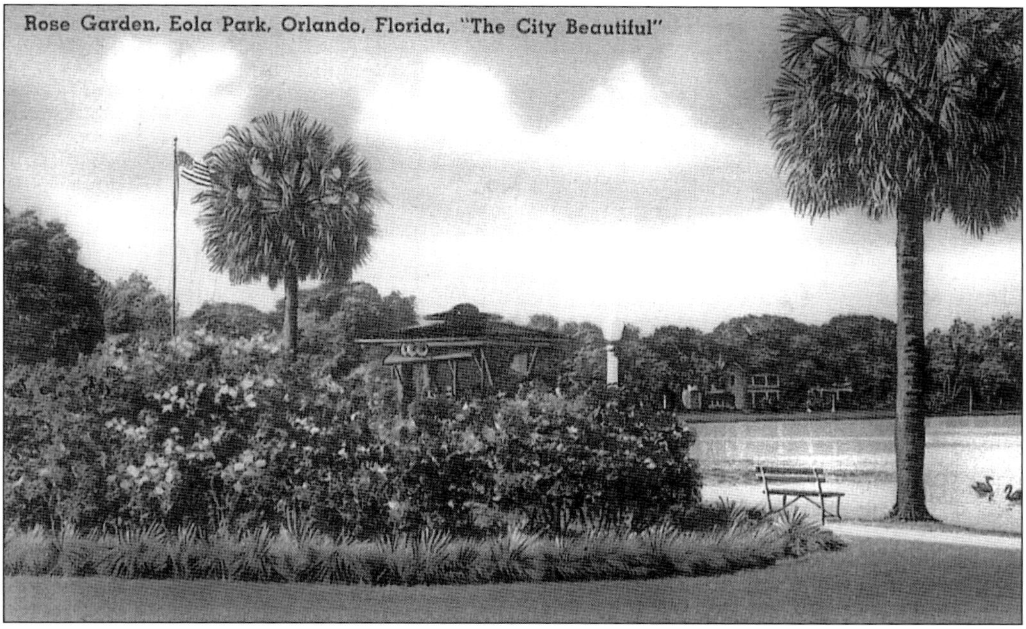

In 1914, the Civic League of Orlando contributed to the beautification effort when its members donated 100 rose bushes to begin the Rose Garden in Lake Eola Park. Other donations followed, and in January 1918, the newspaper reported, "Lack of a water system in Eola Park made necessary the purchase of a gasoline pump for watering plants, shrubs, and the six hundred rose bushes." (Larry Roberts Antiques.)

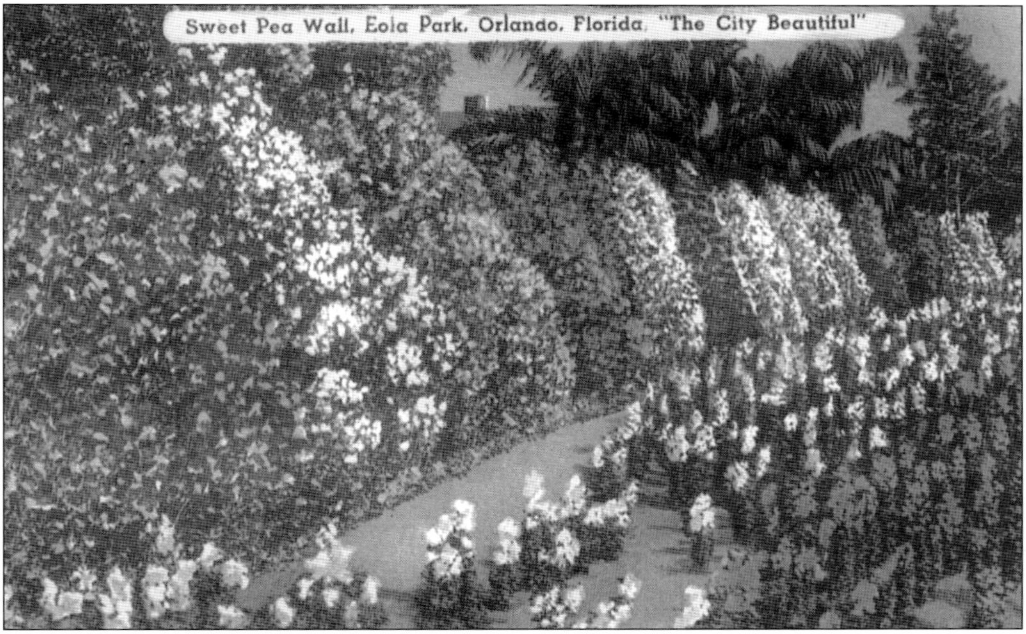

One of the most spectacular floral sights in Eola Park was the famous sweet pea wall. Blooming from December until late February, the varicolored flowering vines reached a height of nine feet. Since floodlights illuminated the display, visitors could stroll along pathways surrounded by colorful flowers at any time of the day or night. (Larry Roberts Antiques.)

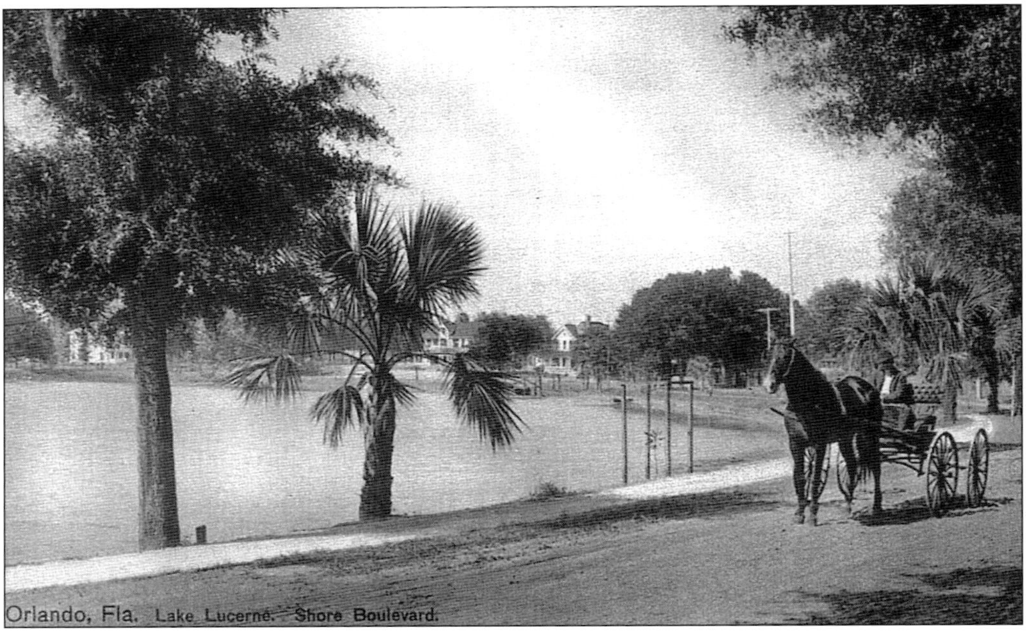

Originally called Lake Lucindy in recognition of an early resident living along its west side and later renamed for the Swiss lake it was thought to resemble, Lake Lucerne was another of Orlando's more than 30 lakes. Located to the south of Lake Eola, Lucerne's shoreline had become an upscale residential area by the early 1900s. (Larry Roberts Antiques.)

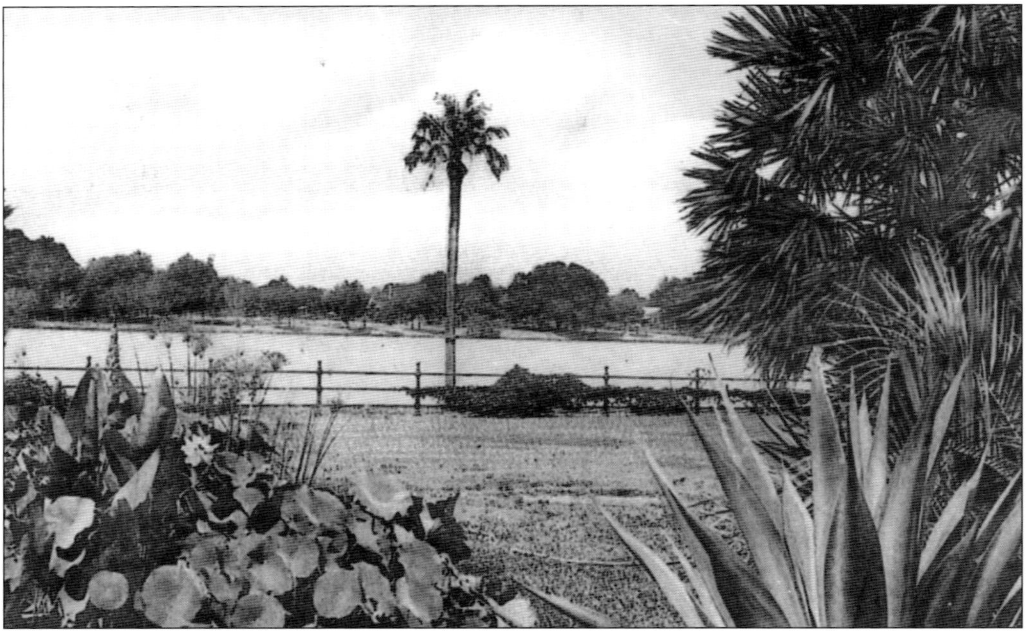

Like Lake Eola, Lake Lucerne was frequently the scene of recreational activities, both informal as well as organized. In 1911, a young woman swam around the lake five times to set a long-distance swimming record. One visitor inscribed this postcard with the message, "Remember the water carnival? It was under the tall palm tree that we sat and watched. Hope you are both well." (University of South Florida Special Collections.)

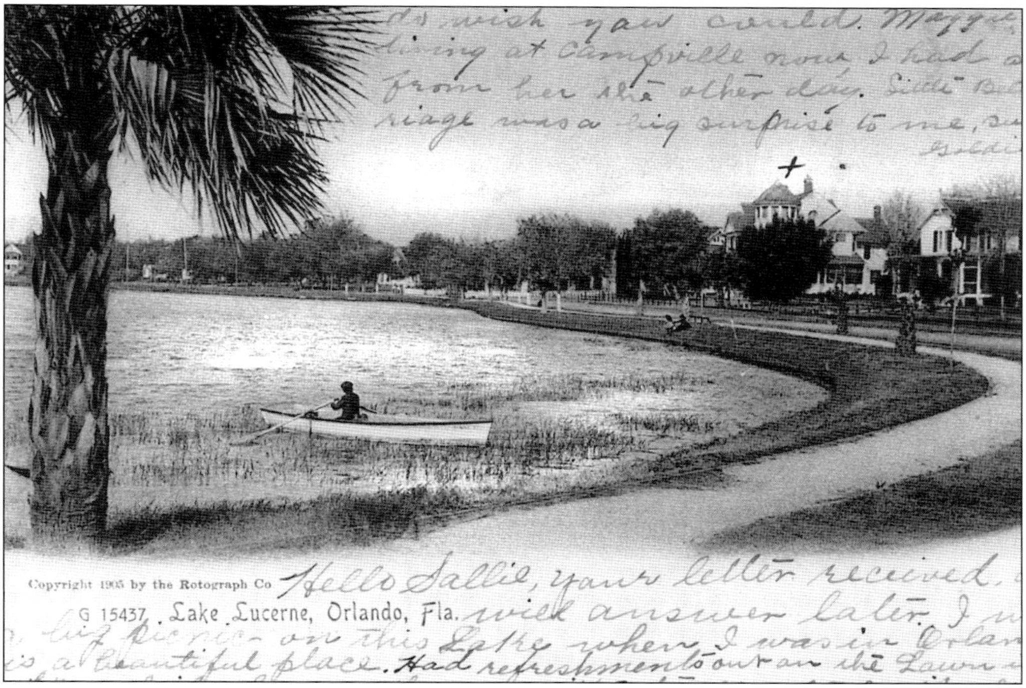

While picturing a boater on Lake Lucerne, the upper postcard's most interesting feature lies in the message sent to Sallie by her friend Goldie. "I was at a big picnic on this lake when I was in Orlando. It is a beautiful place. Had refreshments out on the lawn in front of Mr. Giles house, the one with the cross over it." The lower card provides a better view of the same house, a Victorian residential showplace belonging to James L. Giles, a real estate developer, businessman, and civic leader who served several terms as mayor of Orlando. With its four-acre site on Lake Lucerne, the home was the scene of a reception for 800 guests in 1916. (University of South Florida Special Collections.)

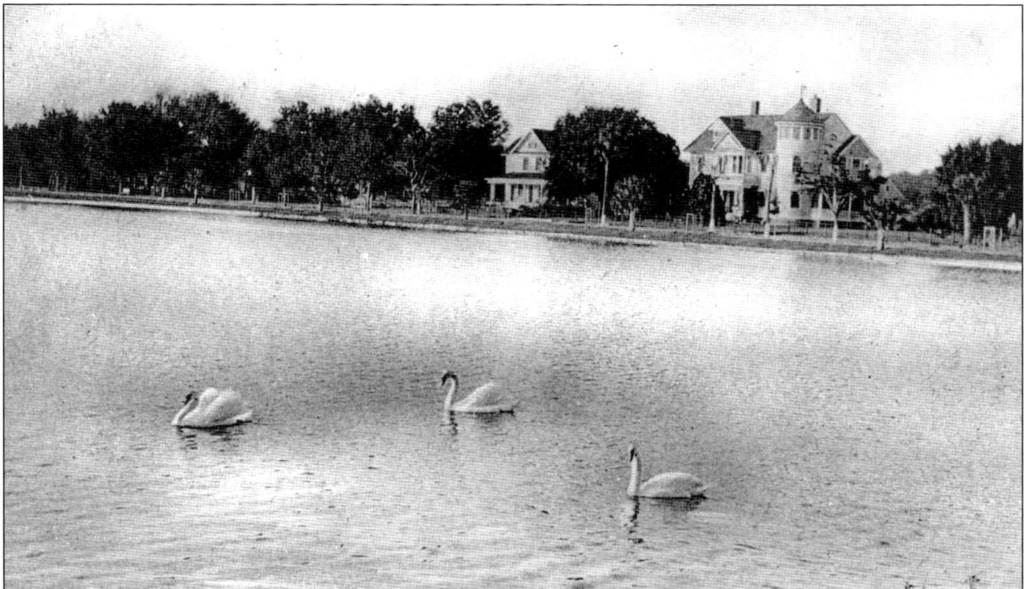

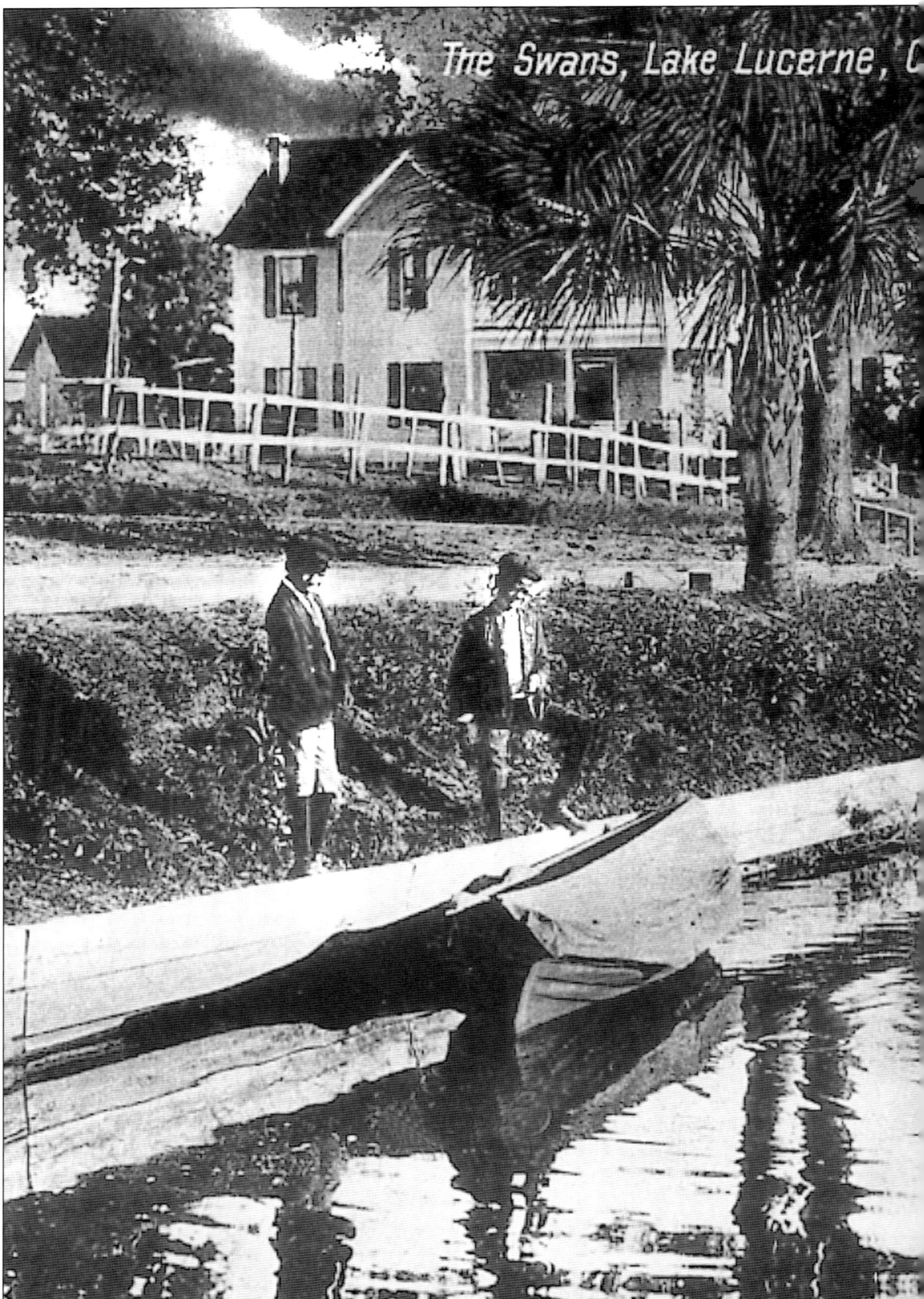
The Swans, Lake Lucerne, C

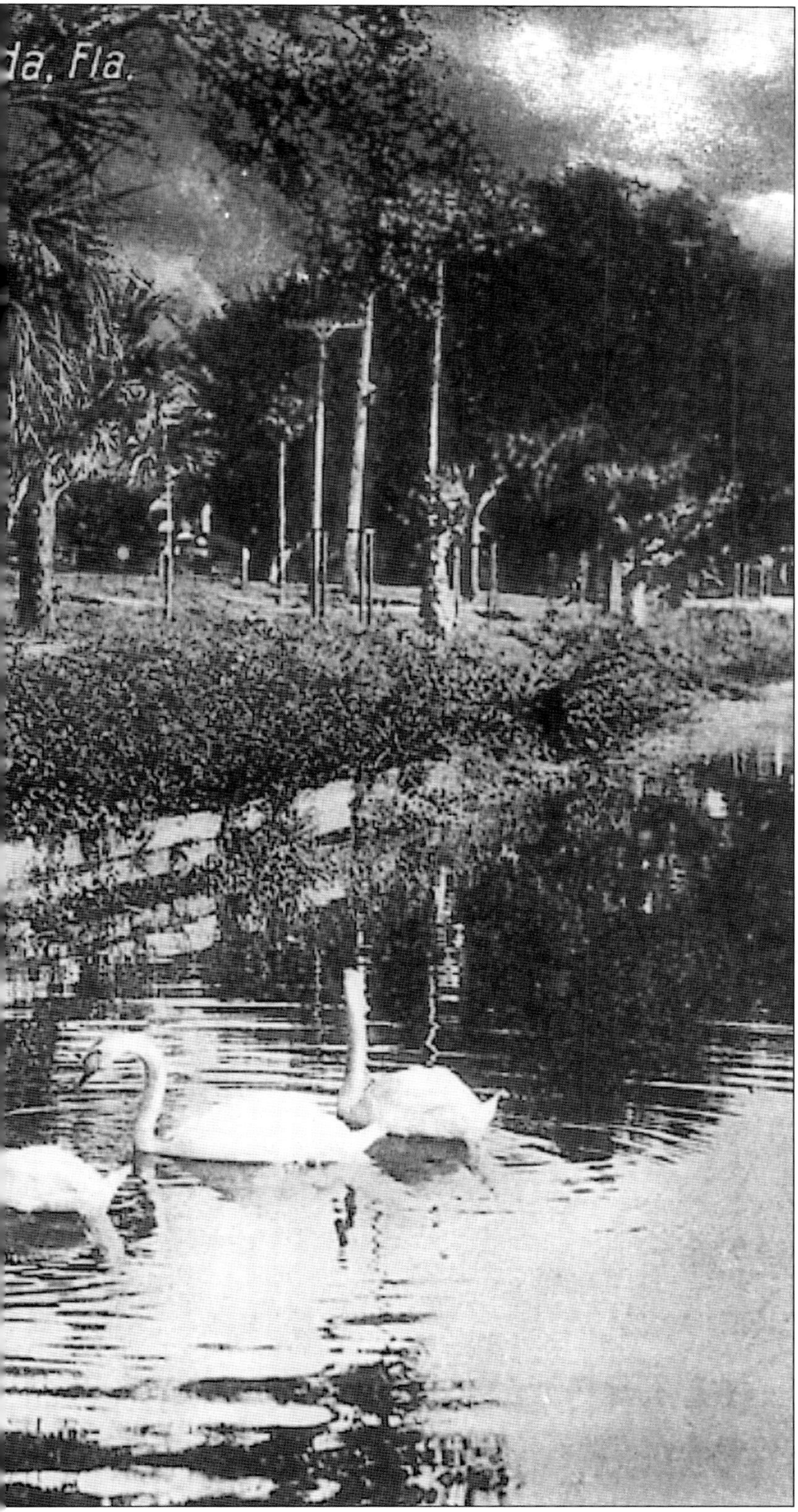

Lake Lucerne was famous for its swans. Charles E. Lord, whose home was located on the west side of the lake, made a trip to England in 1910. There he purchased two pairs of swans, one white and one black, which he shipped back to Orlando. The swans thrived, eventually populating not only Lake Lucerne but other Orlando lakes as well. In fact, the swans did so well that the report of the Orlando Park Commission for 1917 stated, "The number of swans increased to twenty-seven in the spring, and having an offer of $80 for four of them, we sold them to a Northern dealer. It may surprise you to know that since the advance in the price of grain, it costs us nearly $15 a month to feed the twenty-three swans." (University of South Florida Special Collections.)

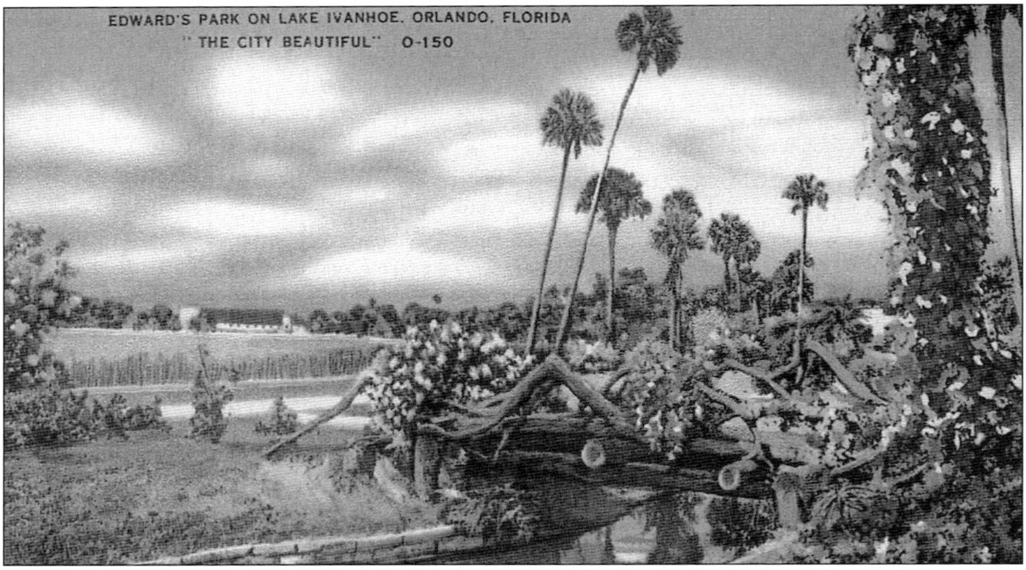

Situated along Lake Ivanhoe, this park was rededicated in 1935 to honor one of Orlando's civic leaders and physicians, Dr. Gaston Edwards. With a depth of 20 feet and named for a character in Sir Walter Scott's novel, Lake Ivanhoe had been the site in 1910 of an amusement and recreational spot known as Russell Point. The largest of Orlando's lakes, Lake Ivanhoe would be substantially altered by the construction of Interstate 4. (Larry Roberts Antiques.)

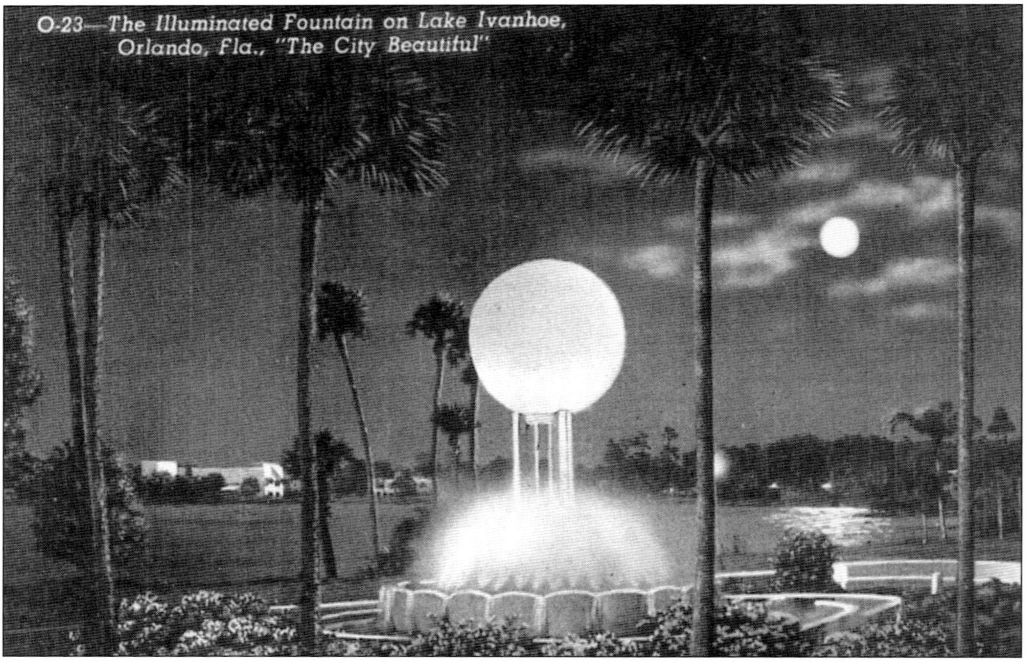

The illuminated fountain on Lake Ivanhoe was a federal Works Progress Administration project. Not everyone found it acceptable, however. Orlando's comptroller and tax collector W.C. Lanier referred to it as "that fountain they put down there, that thing with the ball on top, down at the lake" and complained that although it was supposed to cost $5,000, the final expenditure was actually $9,000. (University of South Florida Special Collections.)

Although many people, including residents, WPA workers, and members of civic clubs, took part in Orlando's beautification efforts, A.C. Coith, superintendent of the parks department, certainly played a major role. Coith was the creator of the famous sweet pea wall at Lake Eola, as well as many of the beautiful flowering displays in other city parks. The huge azaleas in the park at Lake Ivanhoe, for example, dwarfed this woman and her companion. Likewise, jacaranda trees covered "The City Beautiful" with a carpet of bluish-violet flowers each spring. (University of South Florida Special Collections.)

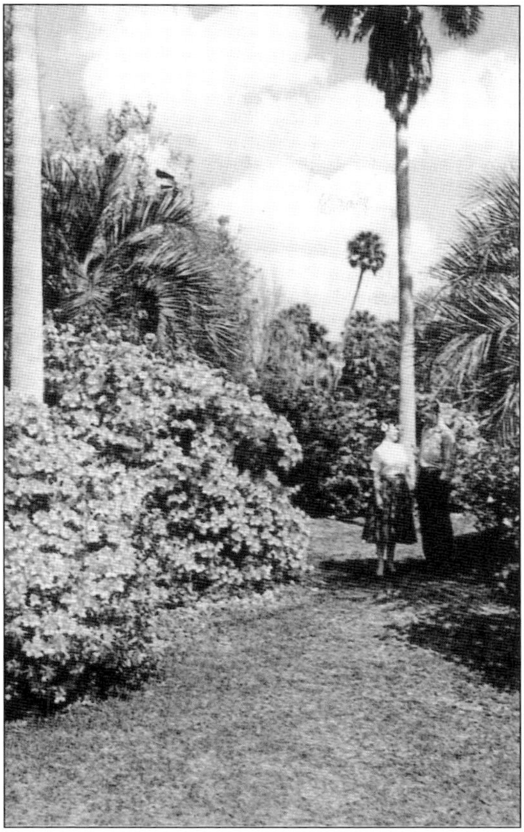

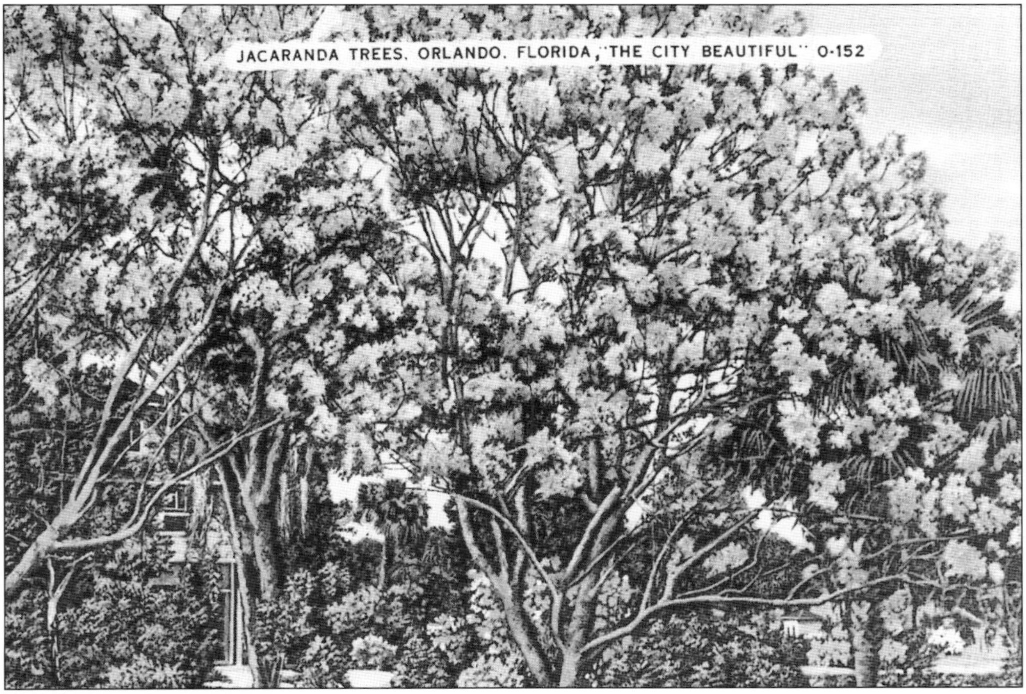

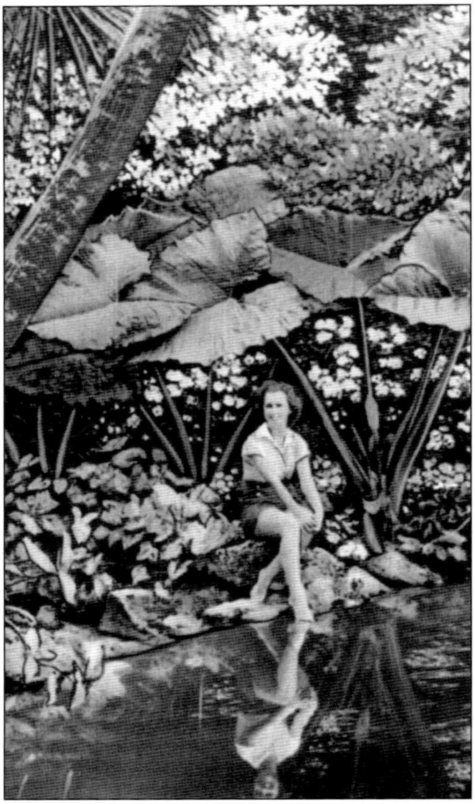

If the floral displays in city parks and on the grounds of private homes in Orlando weren't enough to satisfy nature lovers, there were also other opportunities. The 55-acre Mead Botanical Garden advertised that its main entrance was situated in Orlando, although the remainder of the garden was located in nearby Winter Park. This 1940s-era postcard pictured a visitor surrounded by tropical foliage. (University of South Florida Special Collections.)

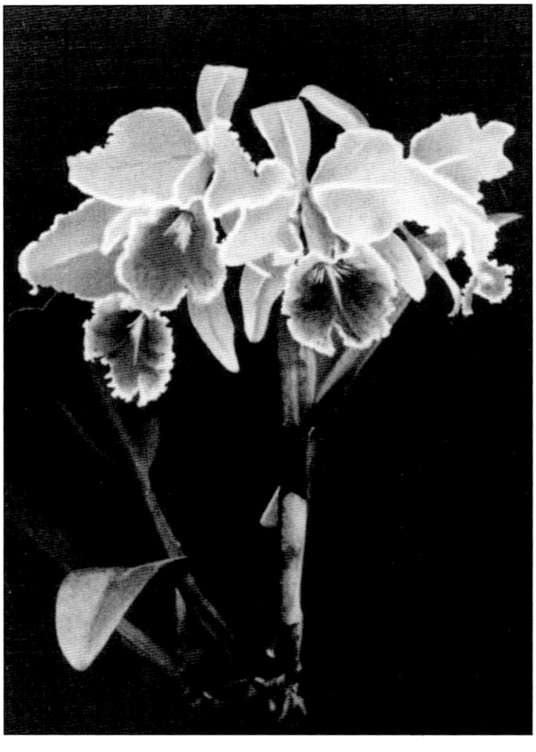

Five greenhouses at the garden contained not only thousands of rare orchids, but also gardenias, camellias, and tropical palms, while a small lake offered a rookery for nesting herons and egrets. It also provided a home to a family of alligators. A 1941 mail-away edition of the *Sentinel-Star* newspaper reported, "Orlando's public and privately planted palms are augmented by those at the Mead Botanical Gardens and Daetwyler Azalea Gardens." (University of South Florida Special Collections.)

Two

Around Town

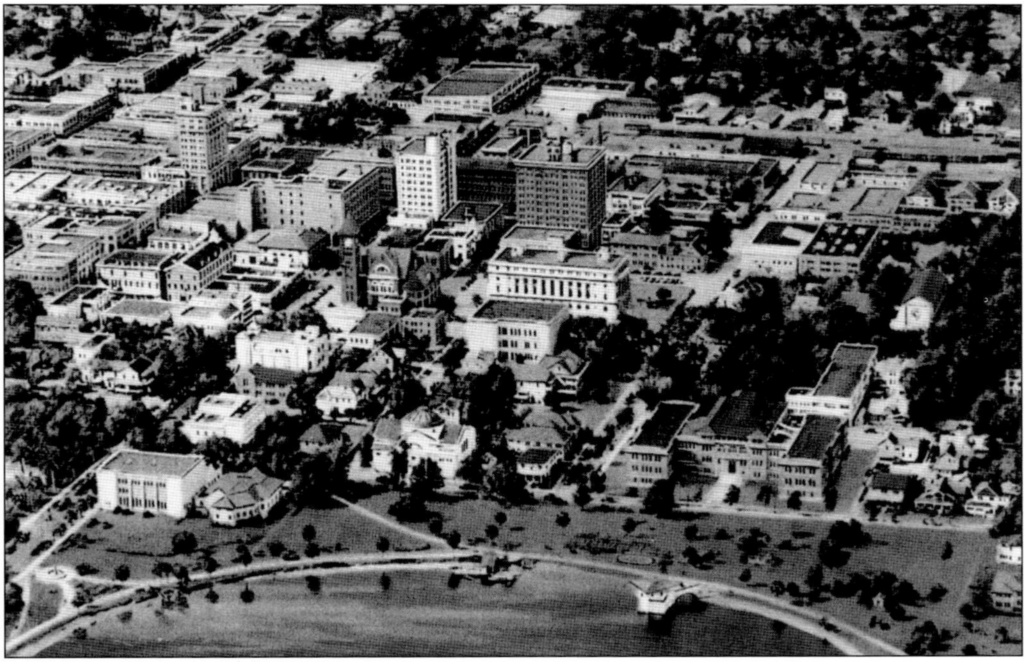

In 1919, the Orlando Board of Trade, soon to become the Chamber of Commerce, published a promotional brochure, *Orlando, Florida, from the Air.* It touted Orlando as inland Florida's largest city, as well as the seventh largest city in the state. It also bragged of 33 miles of brick streets, 35 miles of sidewalks, 2 daily newspapers, and 150 real estate agents. The community that had been platted at the time of its incorporation in 1875 with boundaries of one mile in each direction had expanded considerably. With the exception of the decade following the devastation of the citrus industry in 1894–1895, "The City Beautiful" exhibited a steady population growth that would continue for years to come. Postcards such as this view of Orlando in the second quarter of the 20th century provided a bird's-eye view of the evolving downtown business section. (University of South Florida Special Collections.)

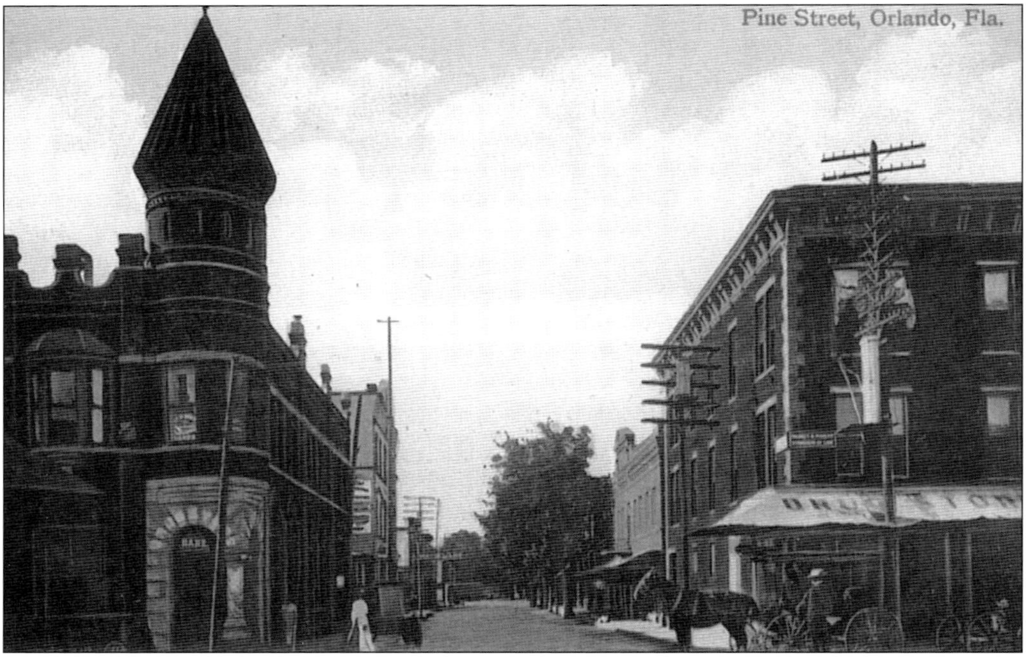

Two major fires in the years just after the town's incorporation convinced Orlando's businessmen to rebuild with brick rather than wood as a building material. A view of Pine Street showed several businesses, including a bank, land sales office, hardware store, attorney's office, and a drugstore. At the same time, a look in the opposite direction along Orange Avenue would reveal similar kinds of businesses housed in buildings that sported much the same architectural style. As horse-drawn wagons churned the unpaved streets into sandy ruts, female shoppers tried in vain to keep their long skirts clean. (Larry Roberts Antiques.)

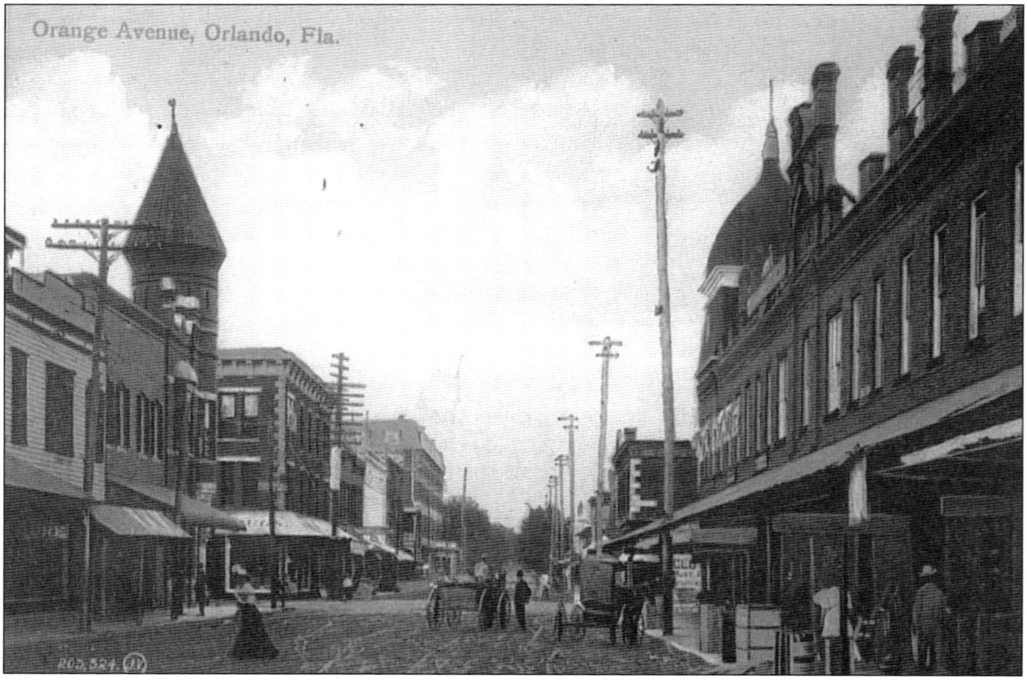

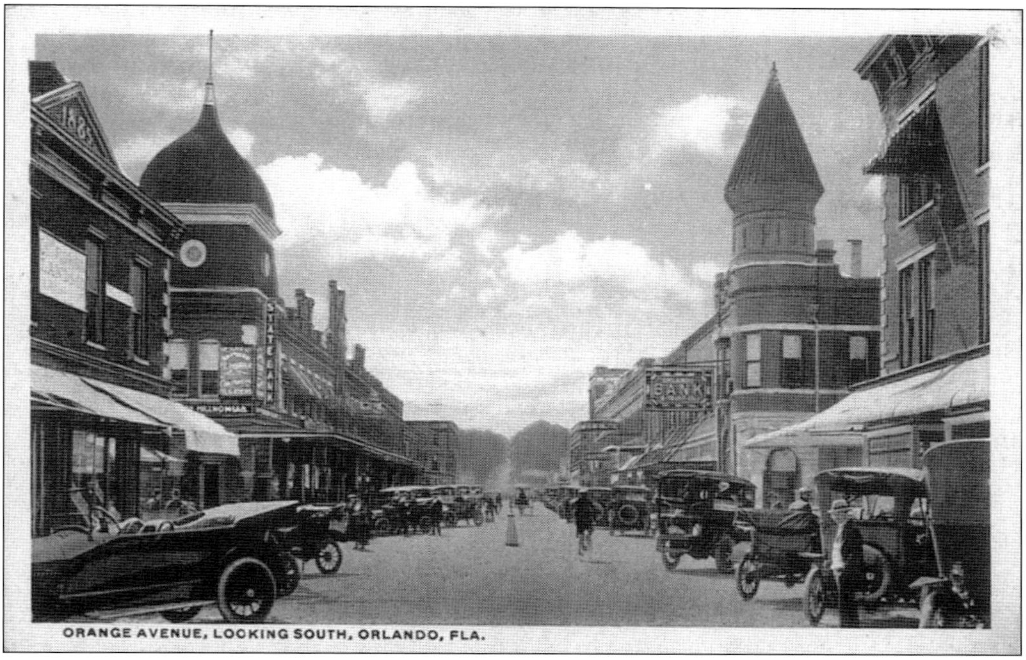

Just a few years later, the same location presented a different view. While the occasional horse was visible, dozens of automobiles now lined the brick-paved streets. The Watkins Block, at the corner of Pine and Orange, contained such enterprises as the State Bank, McCrory's 5 & 10 Cent Store, and the Hammond-Bunch Company, as well as offices of the A.L. Beck Lumber Company and Southern Fertilizer Company. In 1914, at a cost of $17,000, Colonel T.J. Watkins added 20 additional rooms to his Watkins Block. In 1920, he sold the building for the grand sum of $200,000.
(Larry Roberts Antiques and University of South Florida Special Collections.)

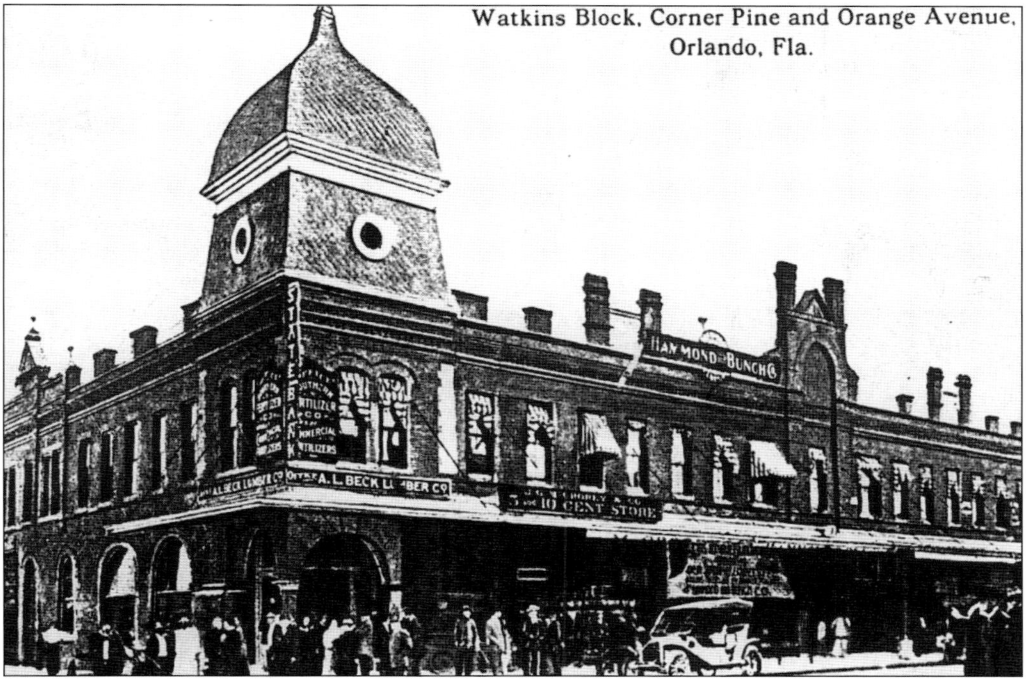

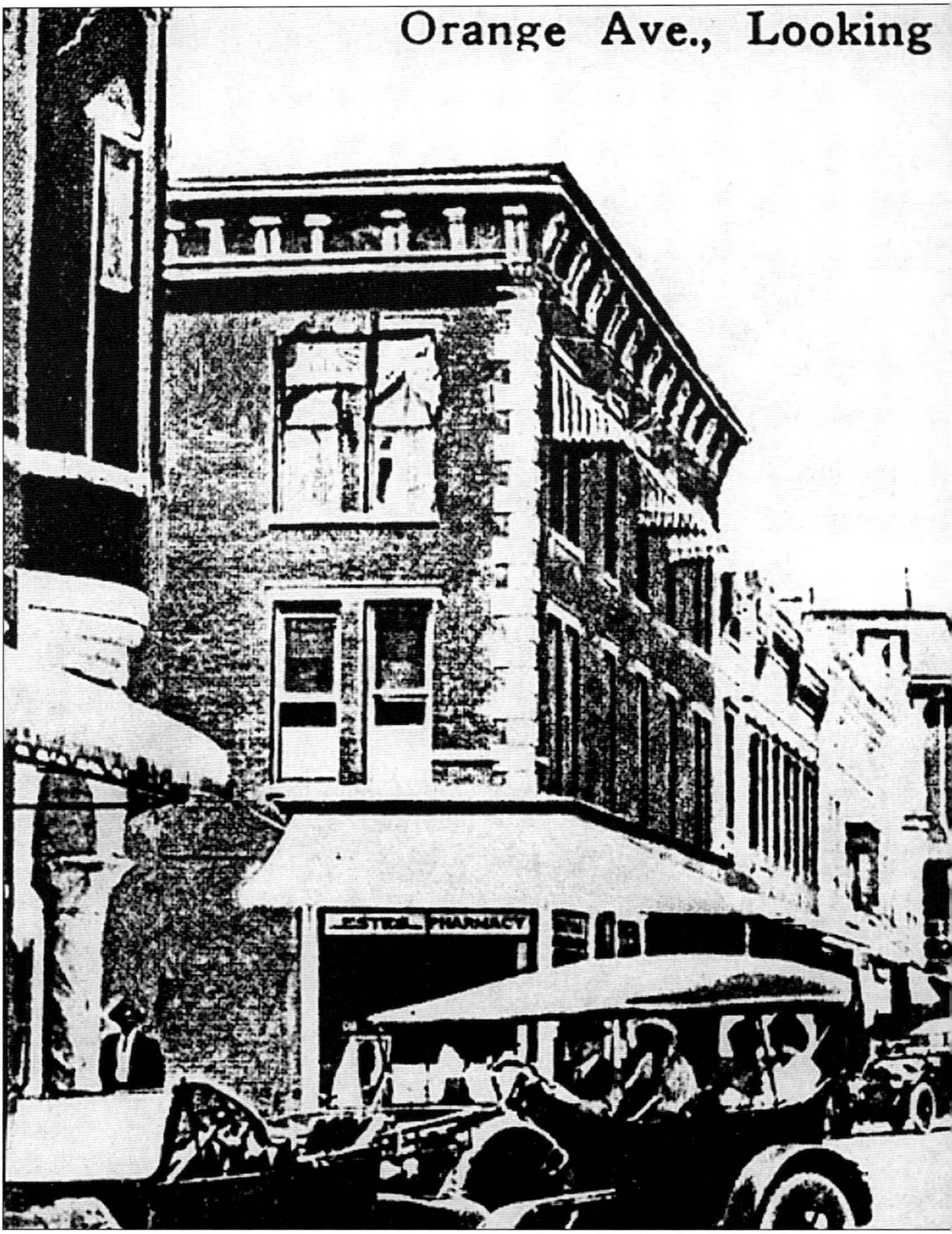

Orange Avenue was considered to be the major thoroughfare in Orlando in the early 1900s. According to one local historian, Orange Avenue received its name from T.J. Shine, who played an active role as a bank director, Board of Trade officer, and organizer of the Orlando Guards. In 1879, Shine built a magnificent home having both indoor plumbing and a tennis court on the northwest corner of streets he named Orange Avenue and Jefferson Street. The names were selected because

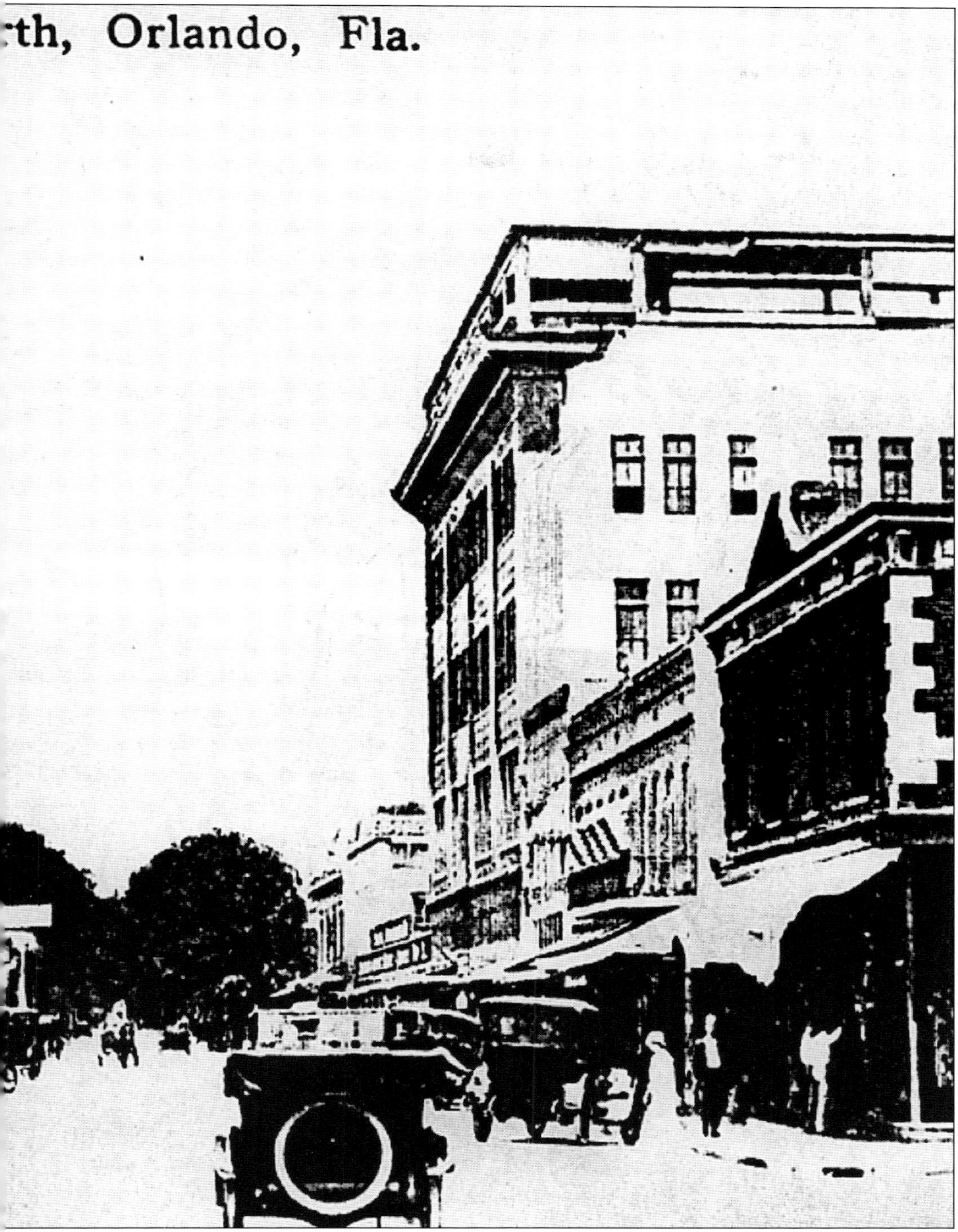

Orange Avenue terminated in an orange grove at its northern end and Thomas Jefferson had been his wife's great-grandfather. Little did Thomas Shine realize that in less than 100 years, the last of the many orange groves lining Orange Avenue would fall victim to a developer's bulldozer. (University of South Florida Special Collections.)

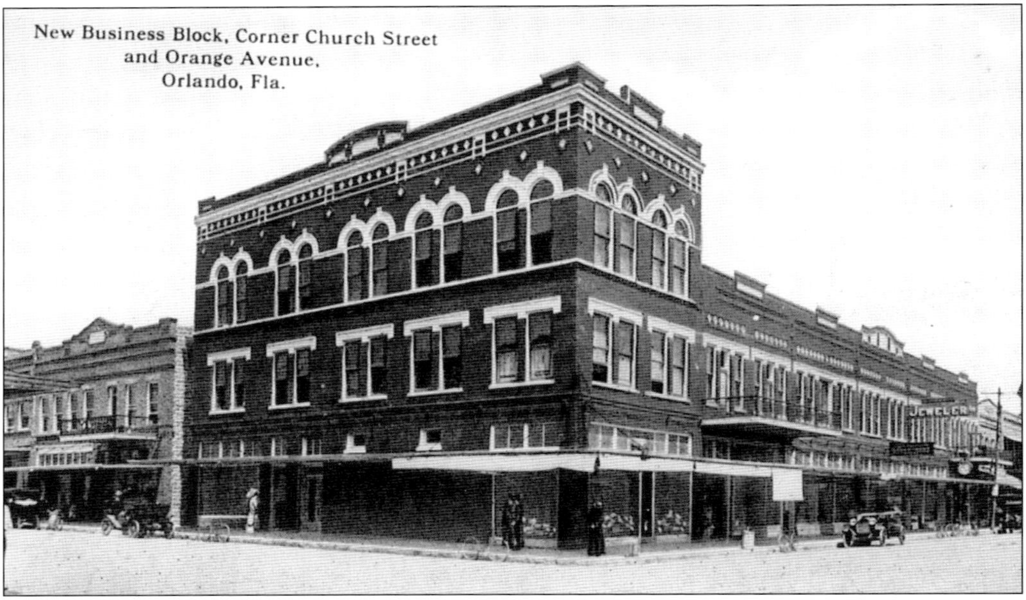

In 1880, Church Street had formed the southern boundary of the Orlando business district, but that would soon change as the city continued to expand until 1895 and the Big Freeze, paused long enough for residents to regroup financially, and then continued to expand. Orlando's commercial buildings of the late 19th and early 20th century featured brick construction with elaborate cornices, arched windows, and stone ornamentation. (University of South Florida Special Collections.)

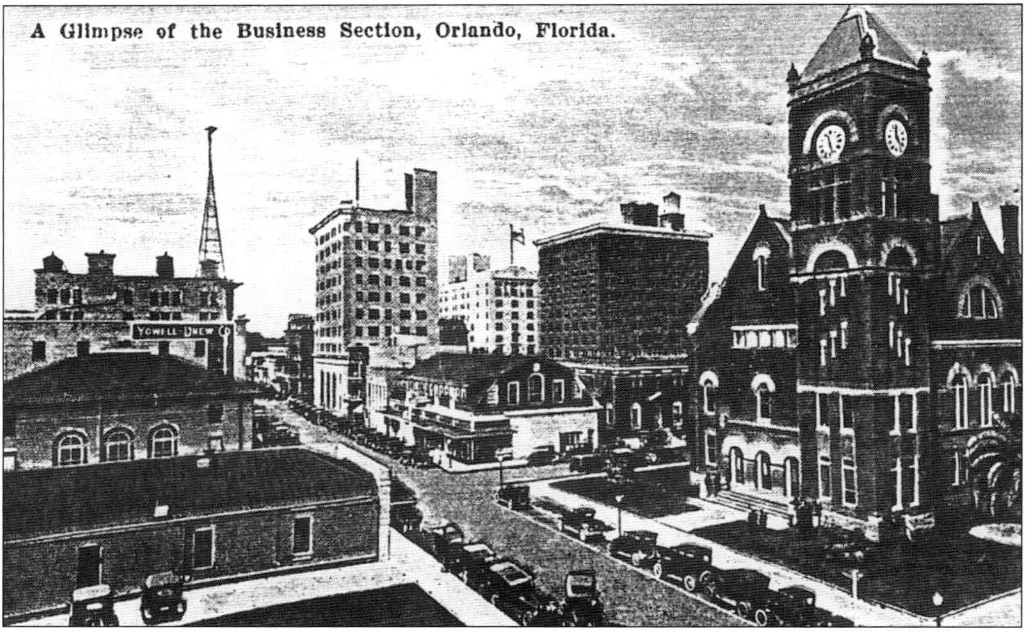

Termed "A Glimpse of the Business Section," this postcard showed just that. On the right-hand side, it prominently featured the 1892 Victorian-style county courthouse on the corner of Central Avenue, the dividing line at that time between north and south Orlando, and what was then known as Main Street. Several hotels, stores, and the 1917 post office were also visible. (University of South Florida Special Collections.)

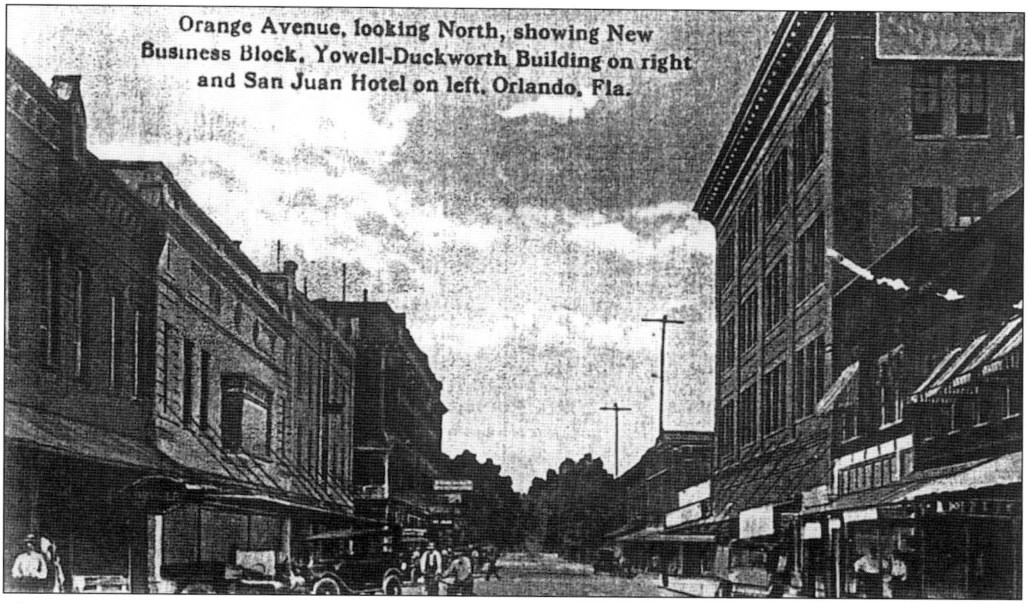

These two views of Orange Avenue were separated by just a few decades, but the increased development was readily apparent. In 1941, the *Sentinel-Star* ran the lower postcard with the following description: "North on Orange Avenue—An international thoroughfare traveled by many of the world's greatest personages who live in Orlando and vicinity during the winter season or year round. Here is commerce, industry, business, life, and unending color. Orlando's business district is among the most modern in the South and compares with the finest in the North. Three financial institutions of Orlando last June reported deposits of nearly twenty million dollars, a record unparalleled for any city of its size. Orange Avenue is a spacious 40-foot-wide boulevard that is nearly six miles long, connecting Orlando and Winter Park." (Larry Roberts Antiques.)

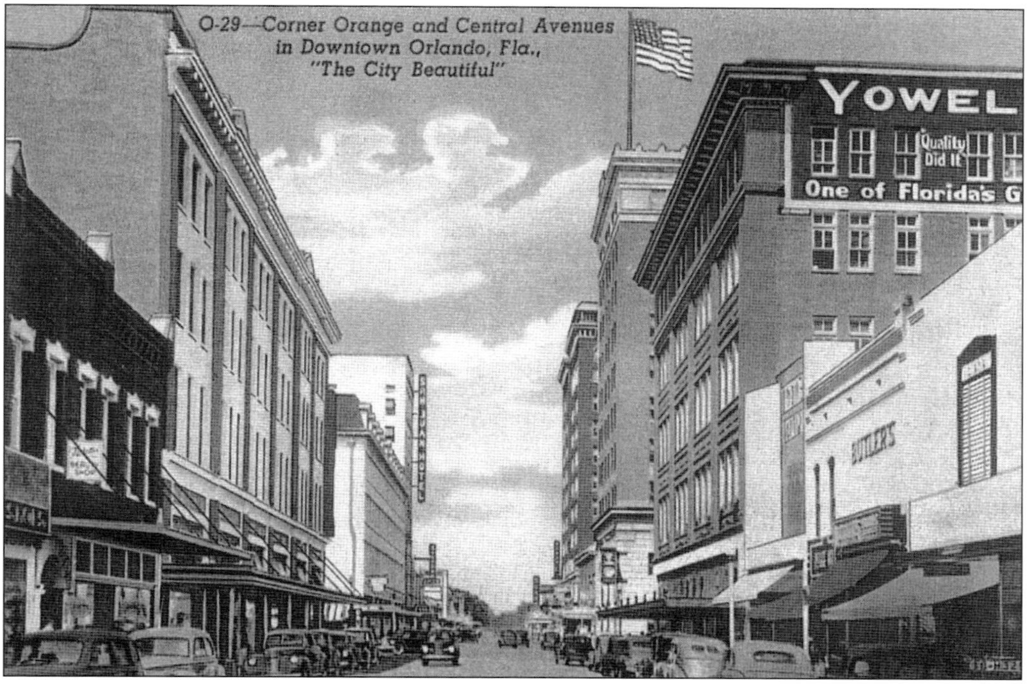

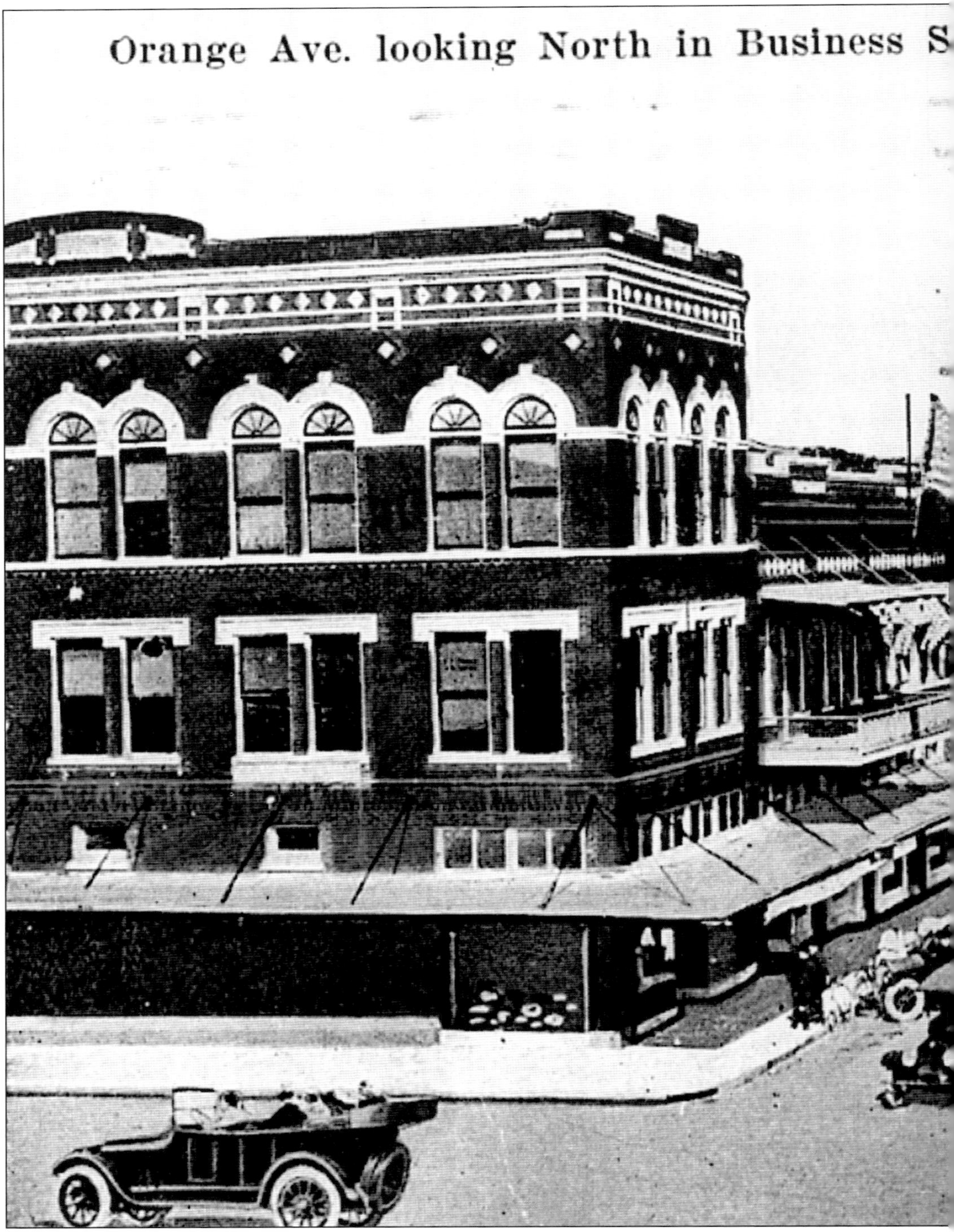

This postcard, dated 1920, shows the business portion of Orange Avenue with many of the buildings that date from the late 1800s. As is apparent by the increased automobile traffic, however, big changes were about to take place. In Orlando, as in all of Florida, the real estate boom was beginning; some of the city's most dramatic growth was about to occur. Advertising as far north as New England, the Board of Trade had begun a concentrated effort to make the state, and especially Orlando, America's

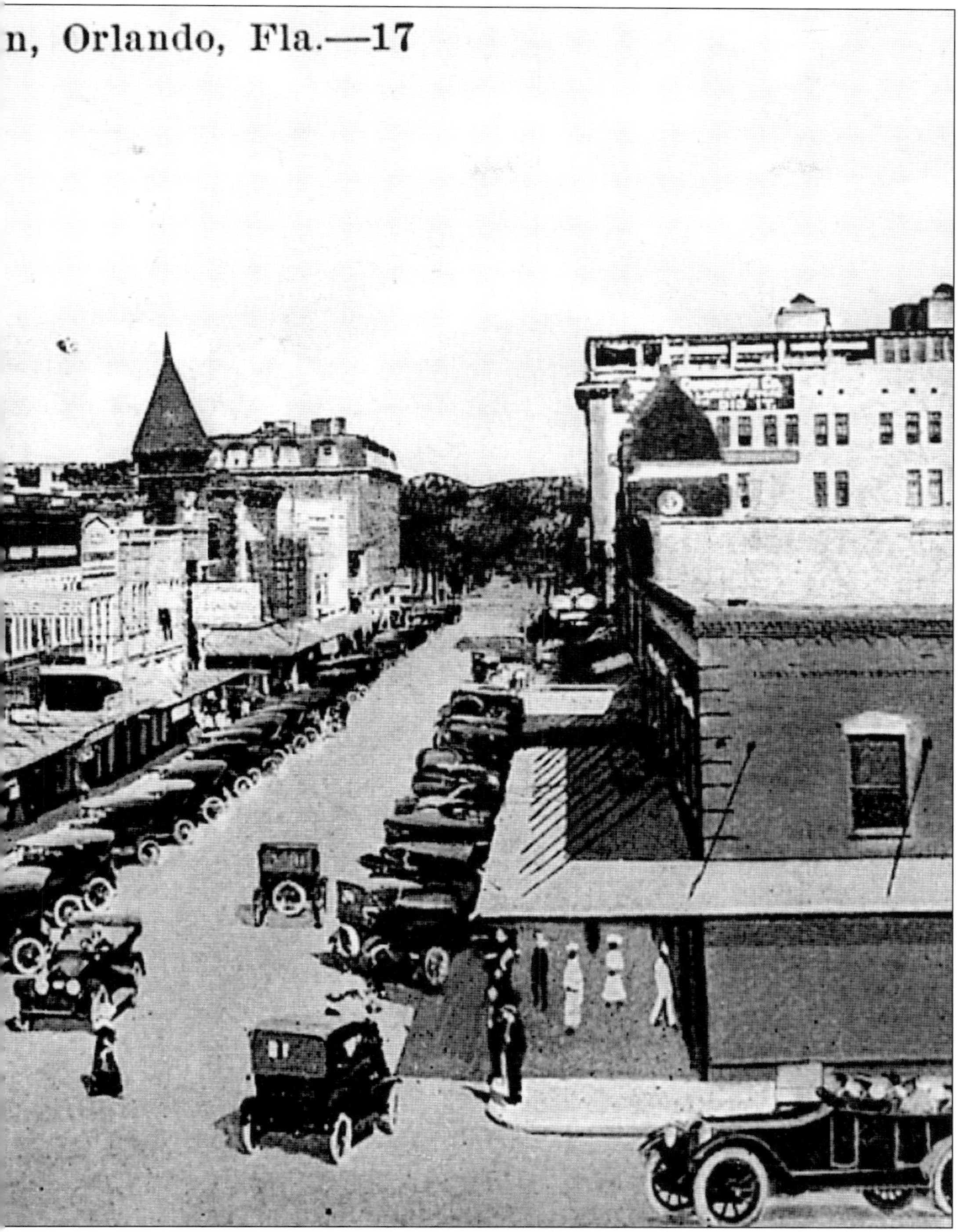

new winter home. Civic clubs, railroads, bus lines, and real estate promoters joined the campaign to attract Northern visitors as well as businesses looking for branch office locations. By August 1920, real estate had become the most popular occupation—occupational licenses had been issued to nearly 150 real estate operators in Orlando alone. (University of South Florida Special Collections.)

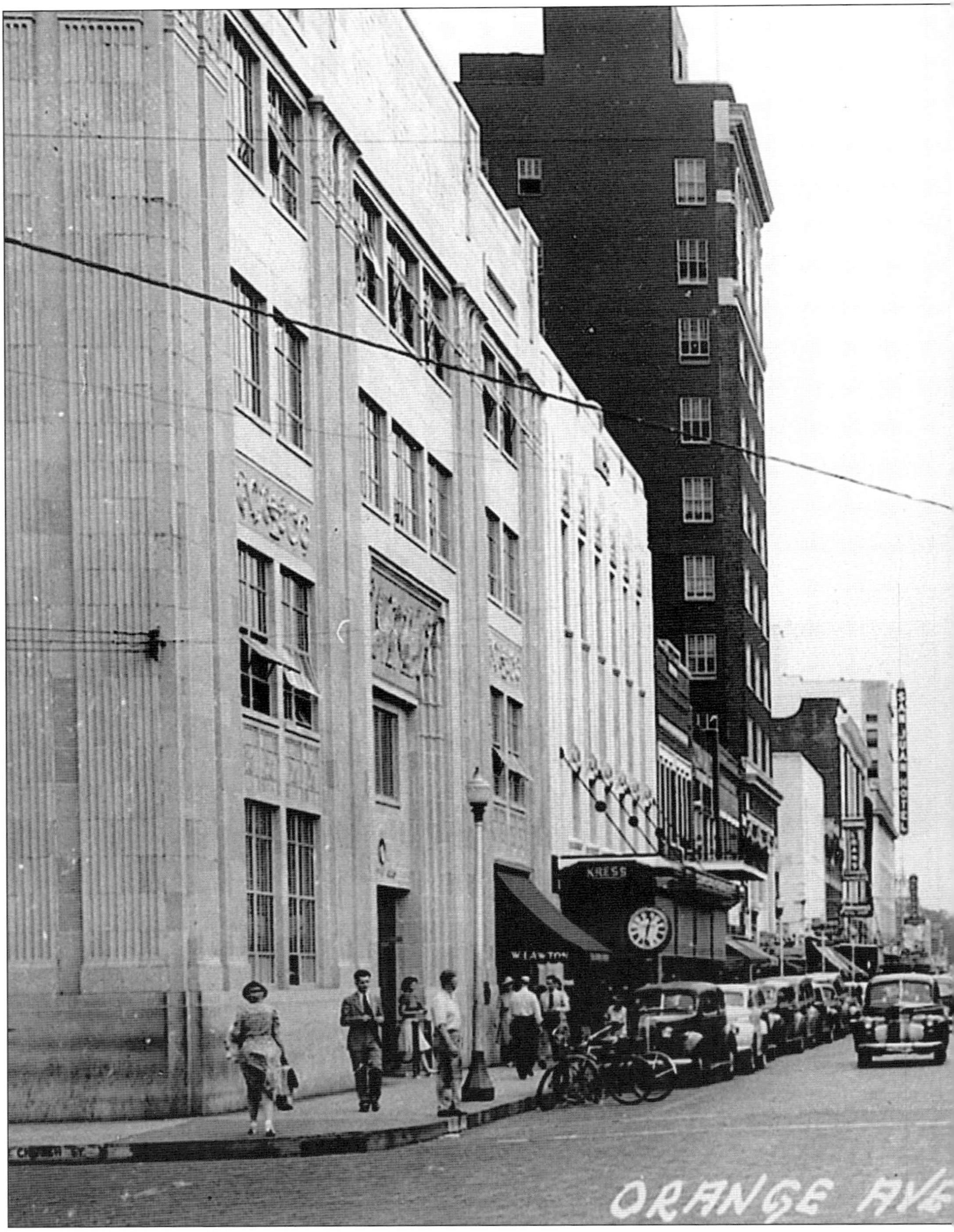

During the real estate boom of the 1920s, property changed hands on a daily or even an hourly basis, as speculators gambled on ever increasing prices. Even to the most cautious, the future appeared rosy. As this later postcard shows, the appearance of the same block of Orange Avenue had changed dramatically. New buildings were constructed. Older structures were remodeled and expanded. By 1926, speculation had reached an all-time high—and then the bubble burst. As out-of-state newspapers

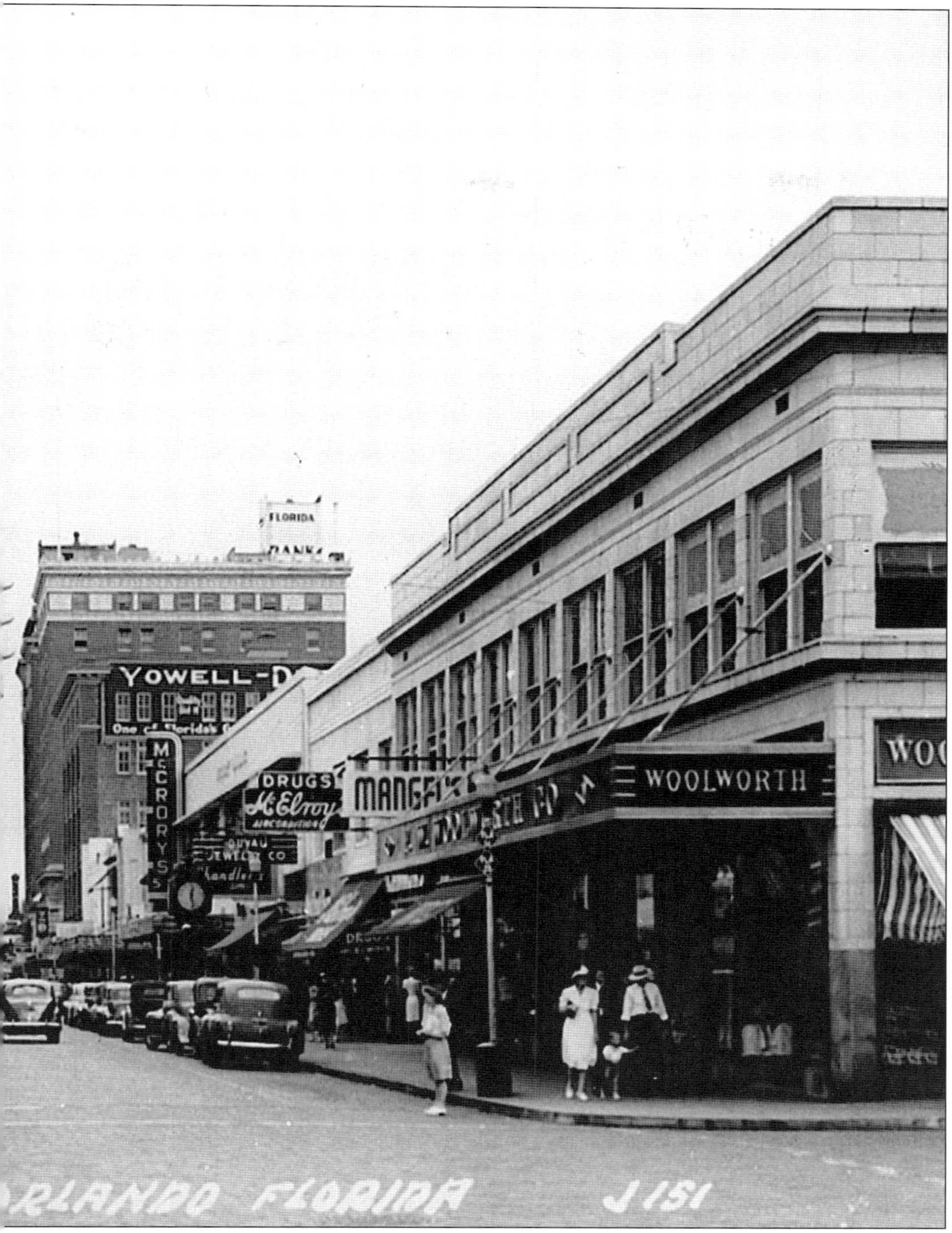

issued warnings of risky Florida land purchases, banks became increasingly wary of real estate loans. A September 1926 hurricane spared Orlando but further dampened the Florida land boom. By 1928, the crash that still awaited the nation's stock market had already hit Orlando. Not until just before World War II would Orlando's economy rebound. (University of South Florida Special Collections.)

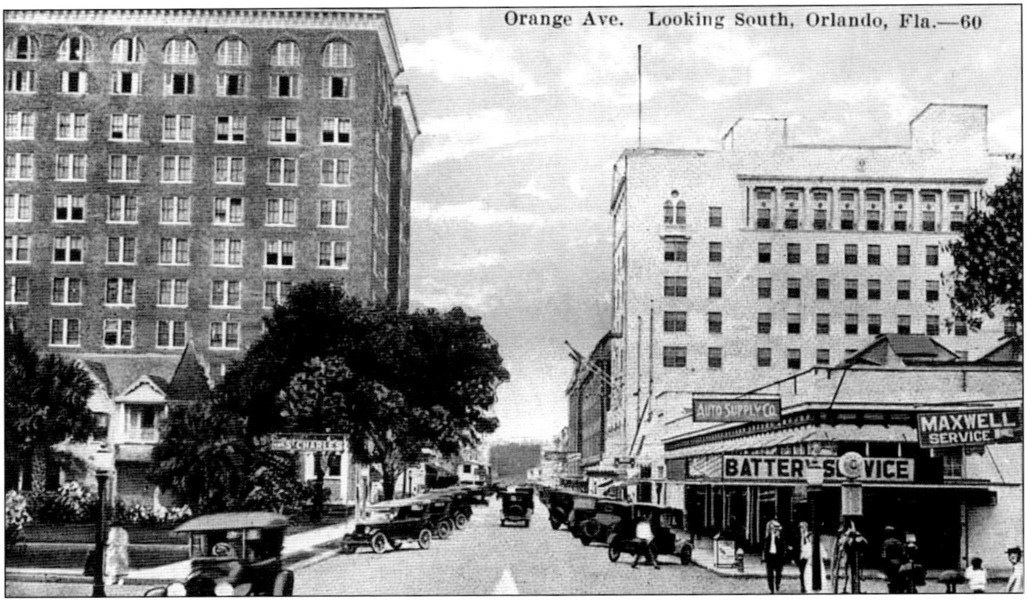

These two postcards provide excellent examples of both the advantages and disadvantages inherent in the use of postcards as research tools. The photographic content can be an invaluable way to document time periods, architectural styles, and even the presence of particular buildings or businesses. For example, careful examination of the upper card shows the St. Charles Hotel just to the left of the tall structure that is the Angebilt Hotel. Across the street, the Auto Supply Company advertises battery service. The lower card pictures the same scene a few years later. Unfortunately, while the first card is captioned "Orange Avenue, Looking South," the second is labeled "Orange Avenue, Looking North. Since both postcards have an identical perspective, either the buildings have exchanged places or the text is erroneous. (University of South Florida Special Collections.)

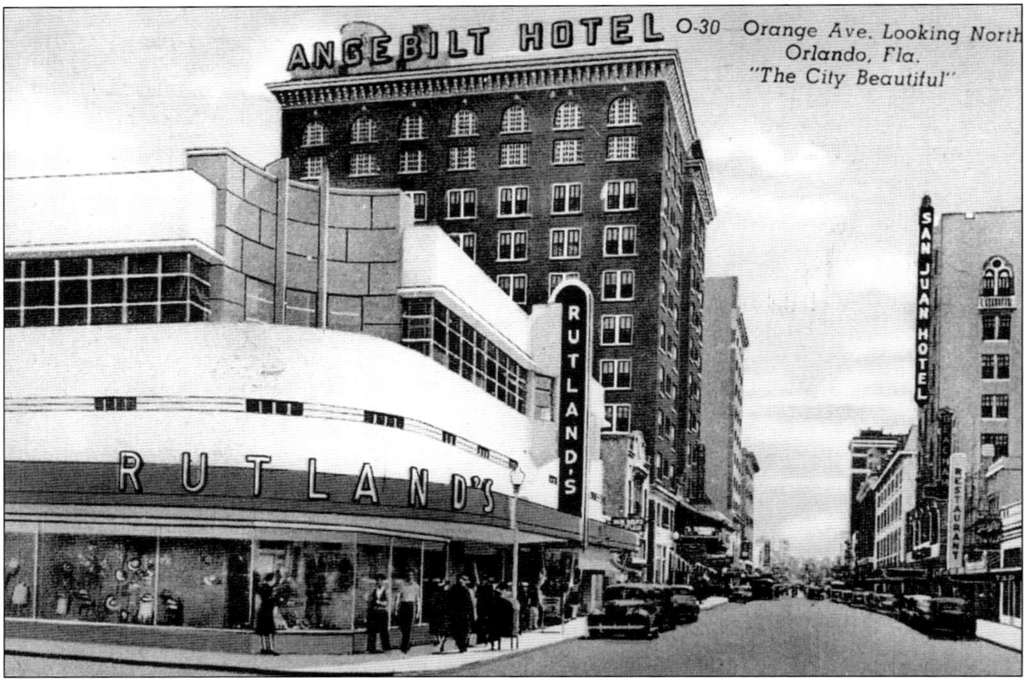

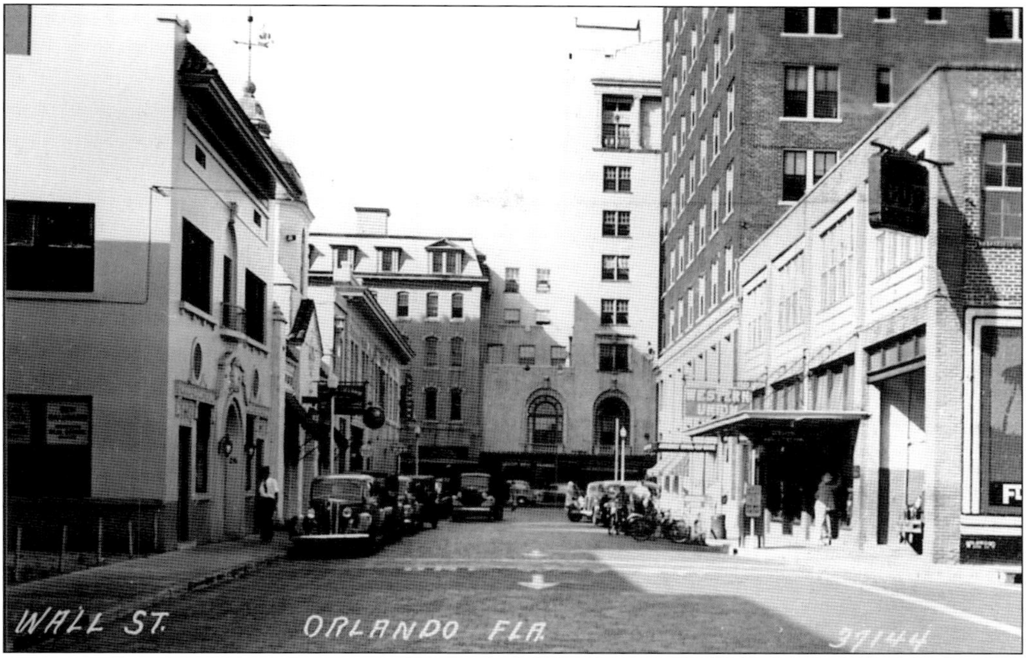

These two postcards also indicate another potential pitfall for researchers. Over the years, streets are often renamed; addresses are renumbered. Author Eve Bacon devotes four pages in the appendix of her two-volume Orlando centennial history to a listing of the many streets that have been known by a variety of names. Wall Street, a short thoroughfare running east and west between Magnolia and Rosalind Avenues, is a prime example, since it was originally known as Oak Street for the grove of live oak trees along its border. To add to the confusion, in the 1960s Magnolia Avenue was extended to include what was formerly known as Main Street. (University of South Florida Special Collections.)

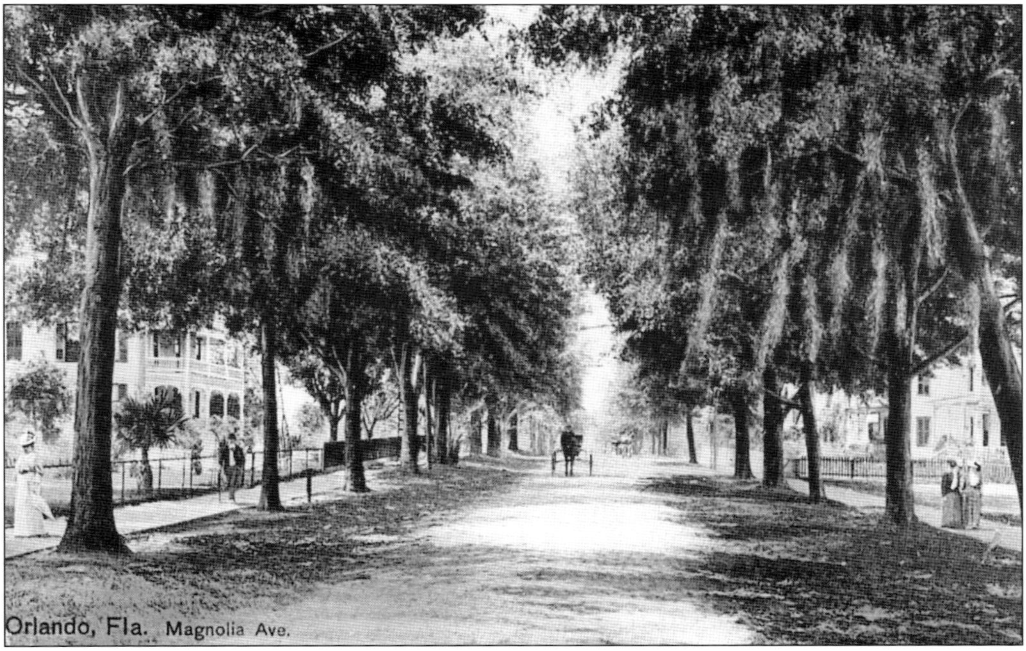

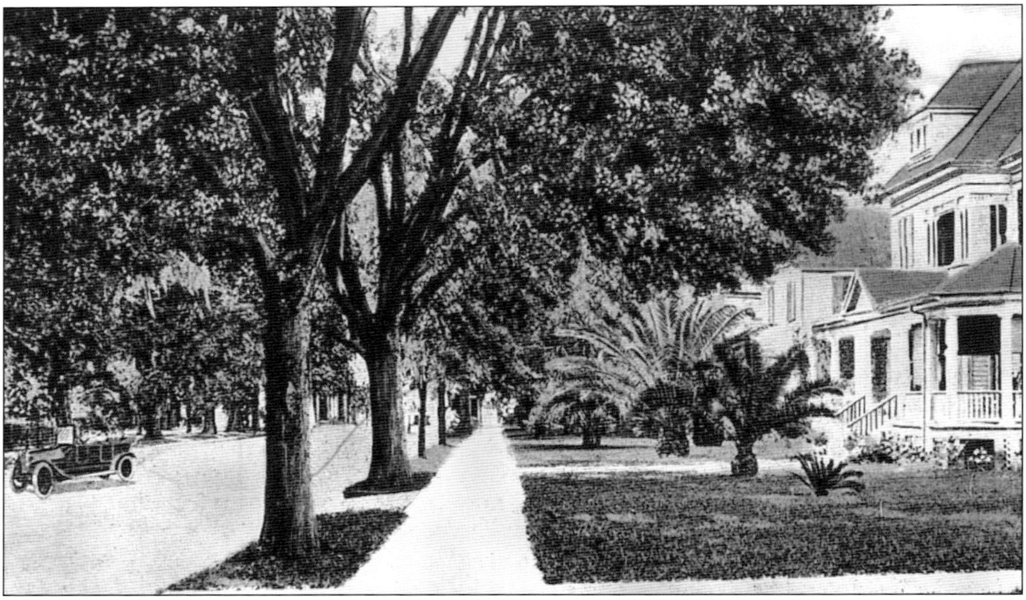

In the 1880s, many downtown businesses, including dry goods, hardware, and furniture stores, listed their addresses as South Orange Avenue. It would be dangerous for a researcher to assume, however, that the thoroughfare was entirely commercial in nature. This postcard reveals that South Orange Avenue was also home for many Orlando citizens. In fact, in the 1890s, from Church Street south, Orange Avenue was one of the newest residential neighborhoods. (University of South Florida Special Collections.)

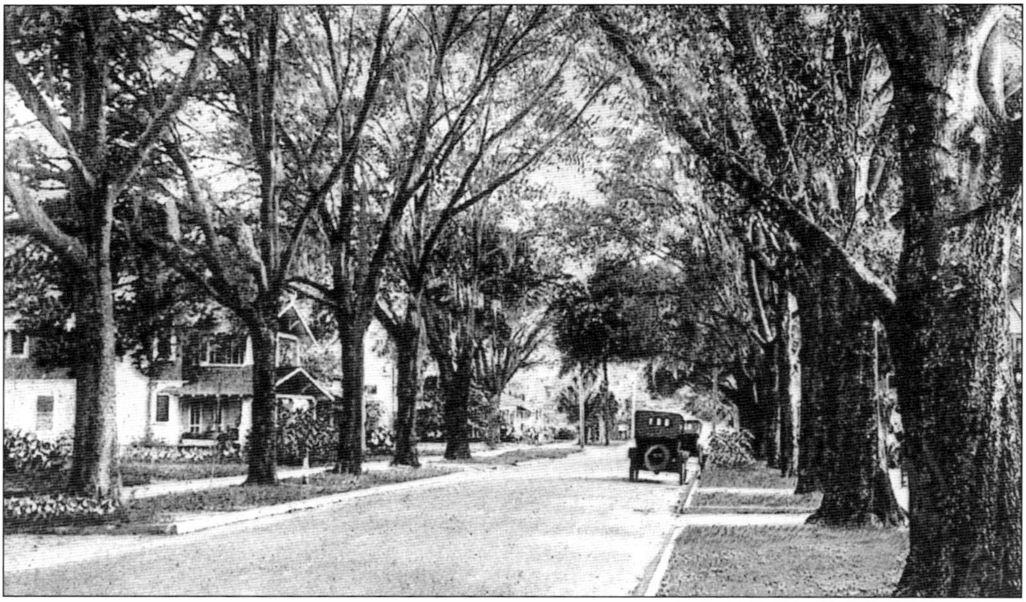

Rosalind Avenue provides still another example of name changes. First named West Street because it marked the western boundary of property belonging to Orlando pioneer Jacob Summerlin, it was renamed Rosalind Avenue in 1919. This action was taken at the request of members of the Rosalind Club, one of Orlando's premier social organizations for women. (University of South Florida Special Collections.)

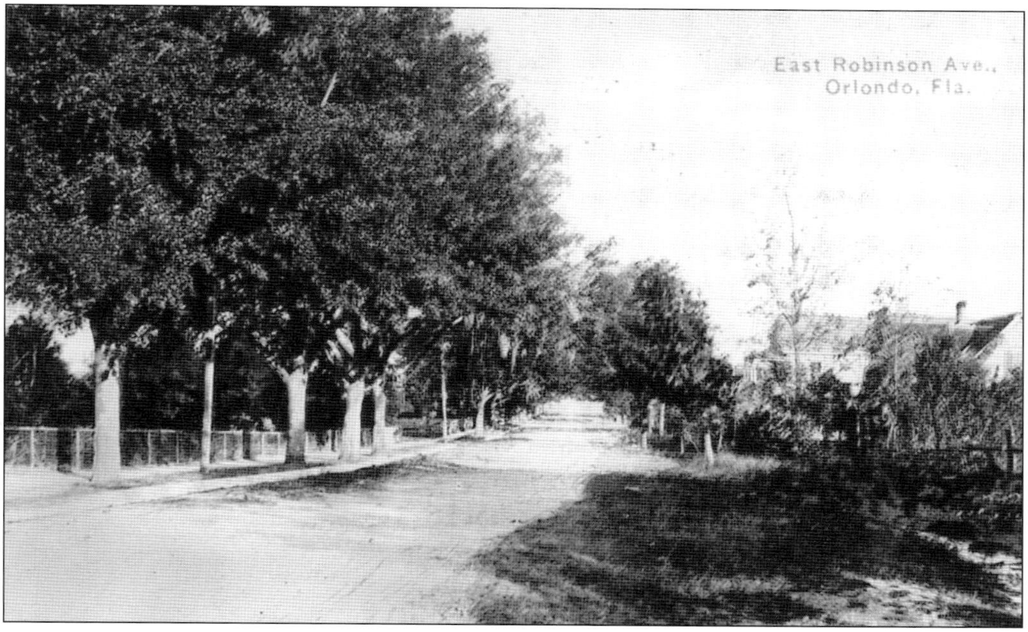

"A city's or neighborhood's history, its origins, its changes through the years, its past and current values, and even its opinion of itself, are reflected in its buildings." According to *Orlando History in Architecture*, written by the Orlando Preservation Board, the major concentrations of homes in the Orlando of the 1880s were to be found along Robinson, Jackson, Church, Pine, and Washington Streets, as well as along the lanes leading from Main Street down toward Lake Eola. By the 1890s, new residential neighborhoods were developing along the shores of Lake Lucerne, on South Orange Avenue, and along Lake Cherokee. Just as the land boom of the 1920s resulted in new commercial development, it also led to a dramatic increase in residential neighborhoods. (University of South Florida Special Collections.)

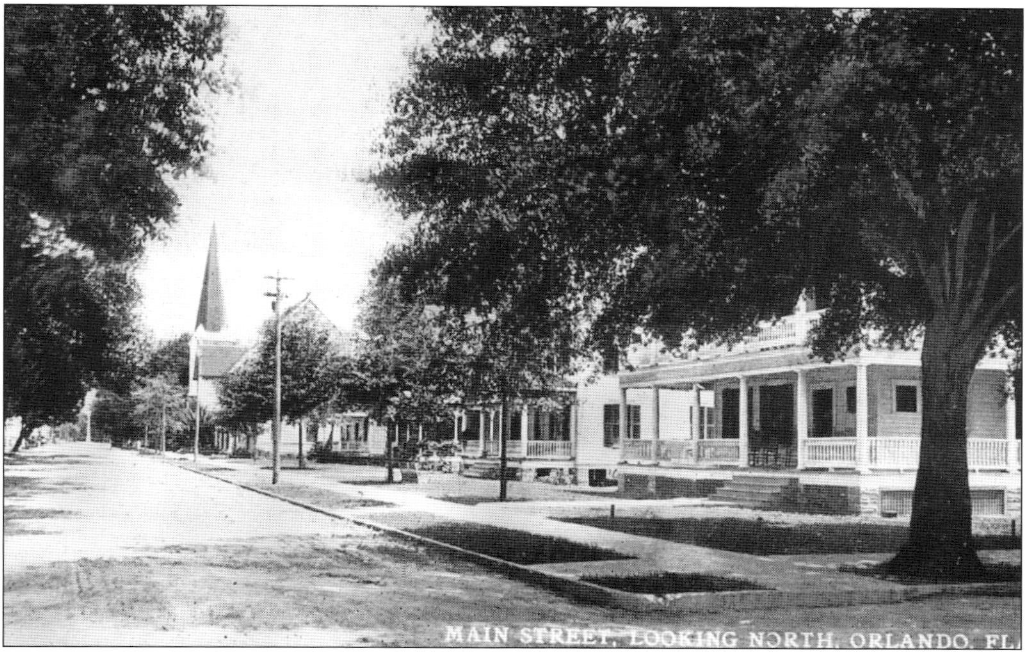

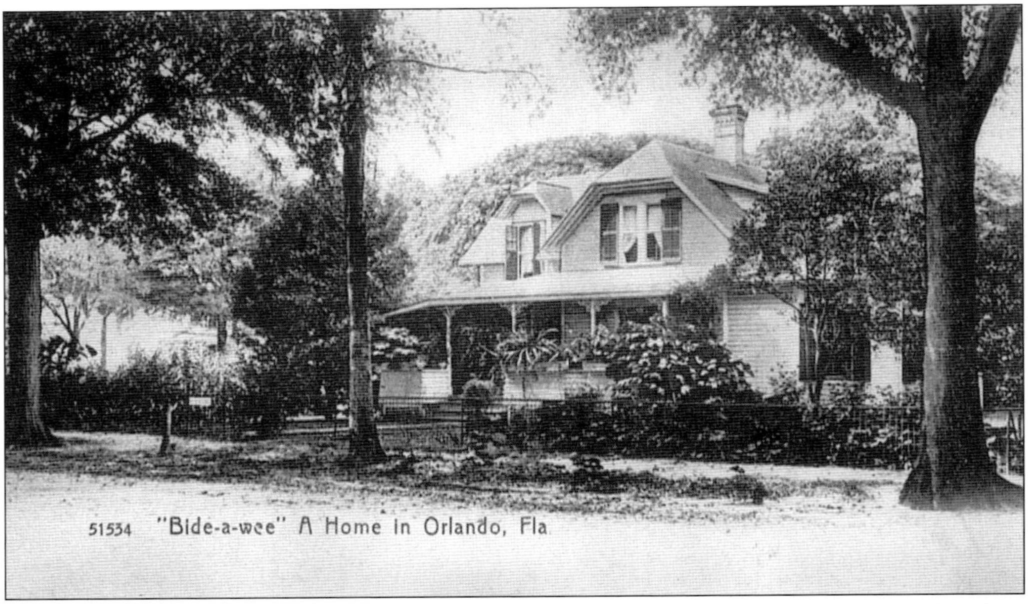

"Bide-a-wee" was the name given to this Orlando residence by its owners. A two-story Victorian-style cottage, the frame dwelling had a large comfortable porch decorated with gingerbread trim, while a yard filled with tropical plants contributed to the "Florida look." Although many dwellings were private homes, others offered winter visitors temporary lodging during the tourist season. (Larry Roberts Antiques.)

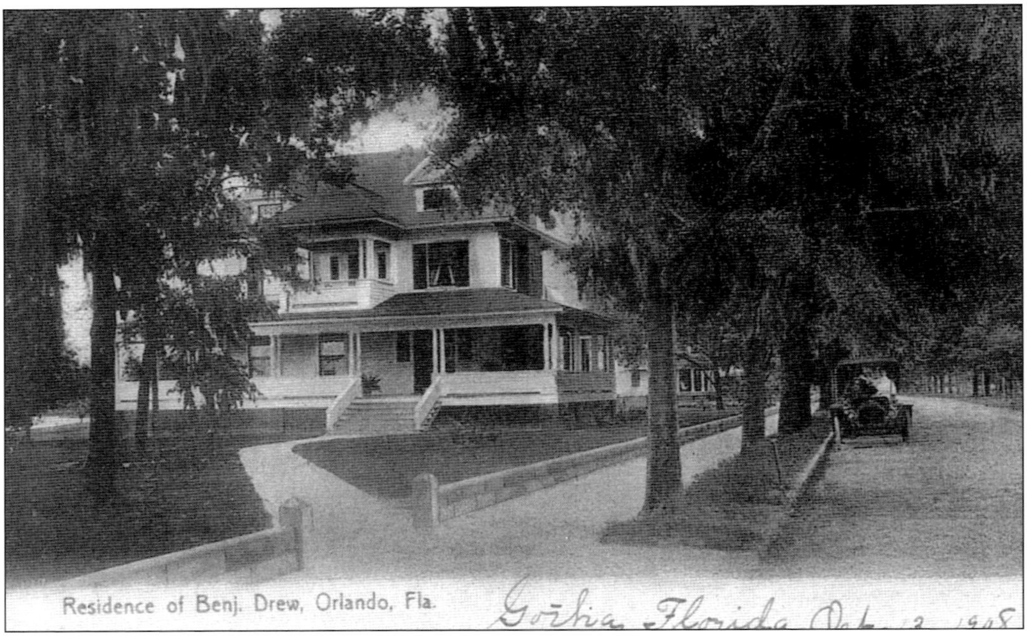

Pictured on a card postmarked 1908, the residence of Benjamin Drew was one of Orlando's most elegant homes. The year was an exciting one for the Orlando businessman who purchased his new home on Lake Eola from S. Waters Howe, who had built the house just five years earlier. Drew was also robbed of $90 when he was the victim of a stagecoach robbery in Yellowstone Park during a tour of the West. The building would later become the Elks Home. (Larry Roberts Antiques.)

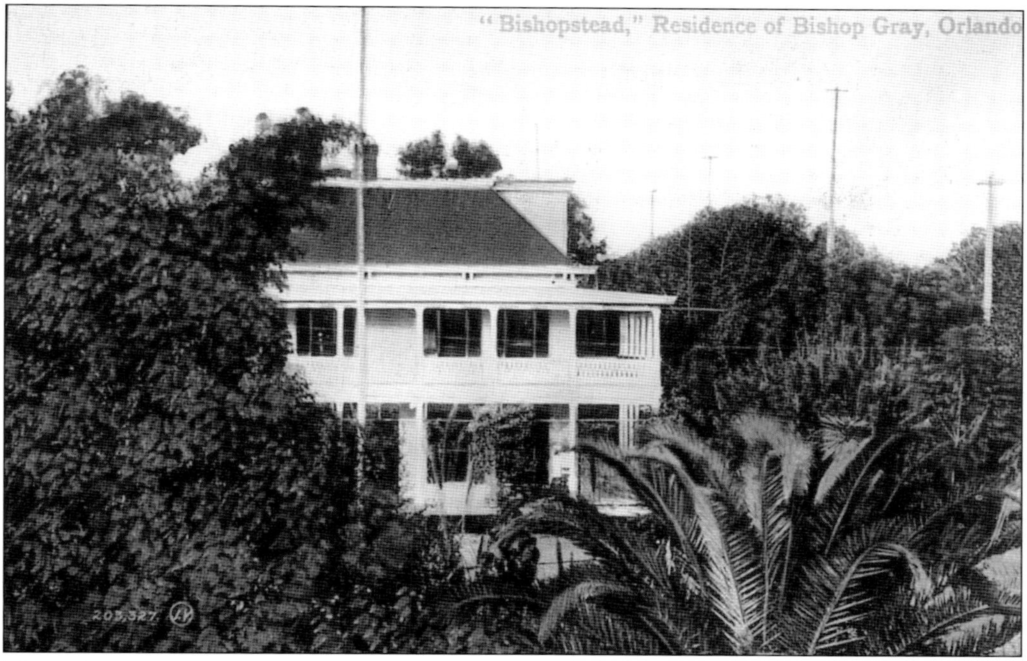

The Bishopstead was originally the residence of L.P. Wescott, a Michigan horticulturist who moved to Orlando in the mid-1870s and created an elaborate tropical garden on the grounds of his new home. The large two-story frame dwelling was reputedly the first house in Orlando to have plastered walls. Several years later, a prominent Orlando resident, Leslie Pell-Clarke, purchased the home from Wescott for $16,000. (University of South Florida Special Collections.)

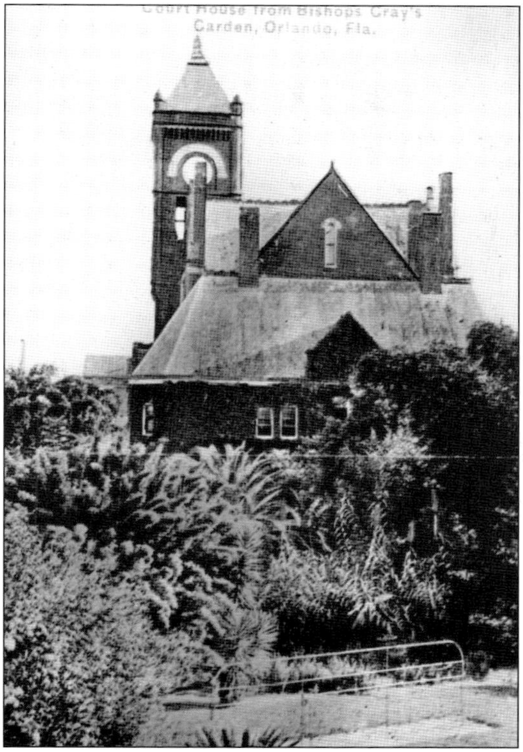

The Pell-Clarkes used the dwelling as their residence until 1900 when they gave the house at the corner of Main and Washington Streets to the Episcopal Church as a home for the bishop. Located across the street from the 1892 courthouse, the Bishopstead was eventually sold to the county as the site for a new courthouse. The selling price in 1924 was $250,000—an appreciable increase in value. (University of South Florida Special Collections.)

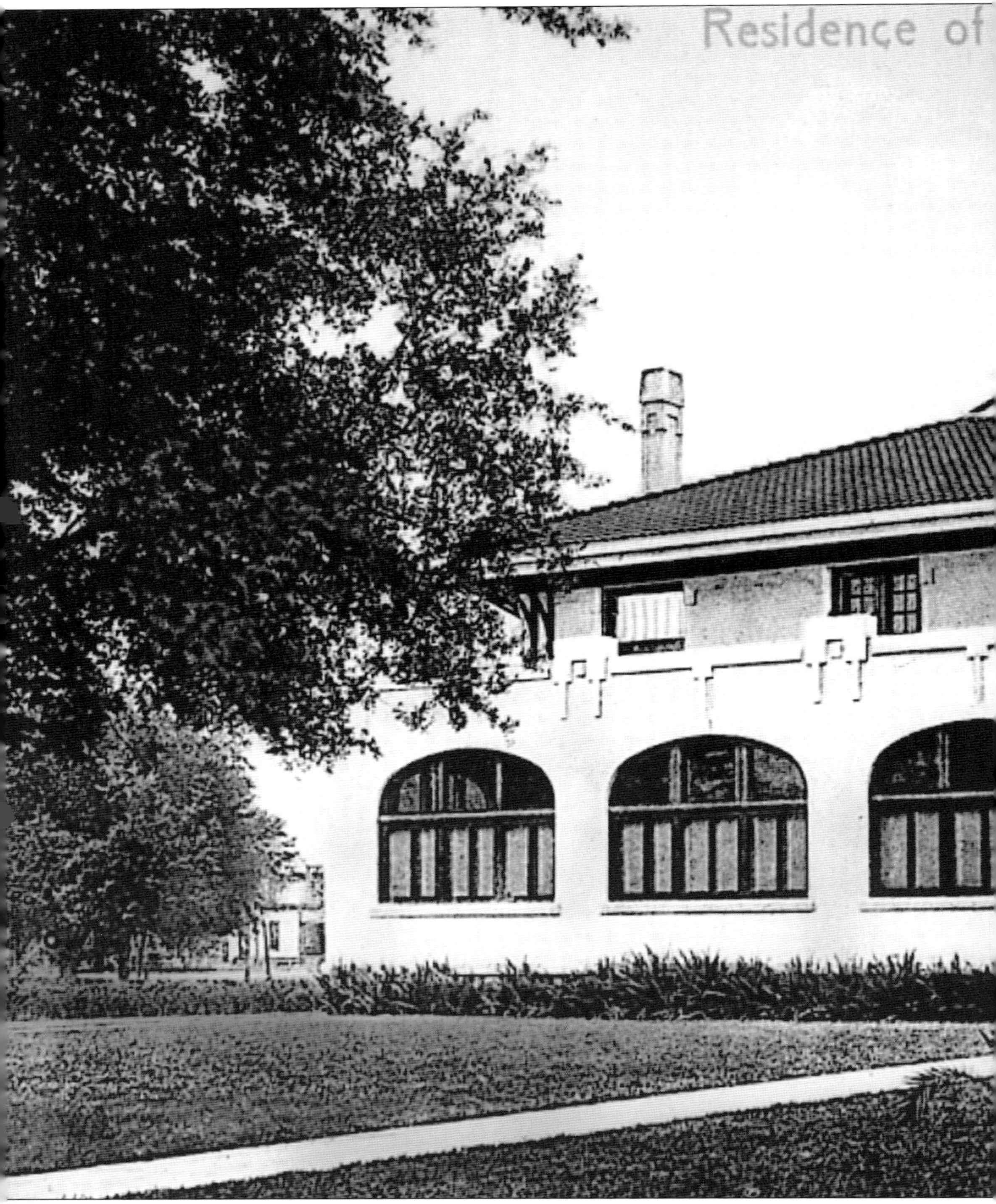

Located on Lucerne Circle East, this Chicago/Prairie-style house was built in 1912 for Florence and C.G. Wescott. A racehorse breeder, C.G. Wescott brought national recognition to Florida the following year when his horses were shipped north to compete in American Trotting Association races. In all probability, Murray S. King, a noted architect in the Orlando area between 1910 and

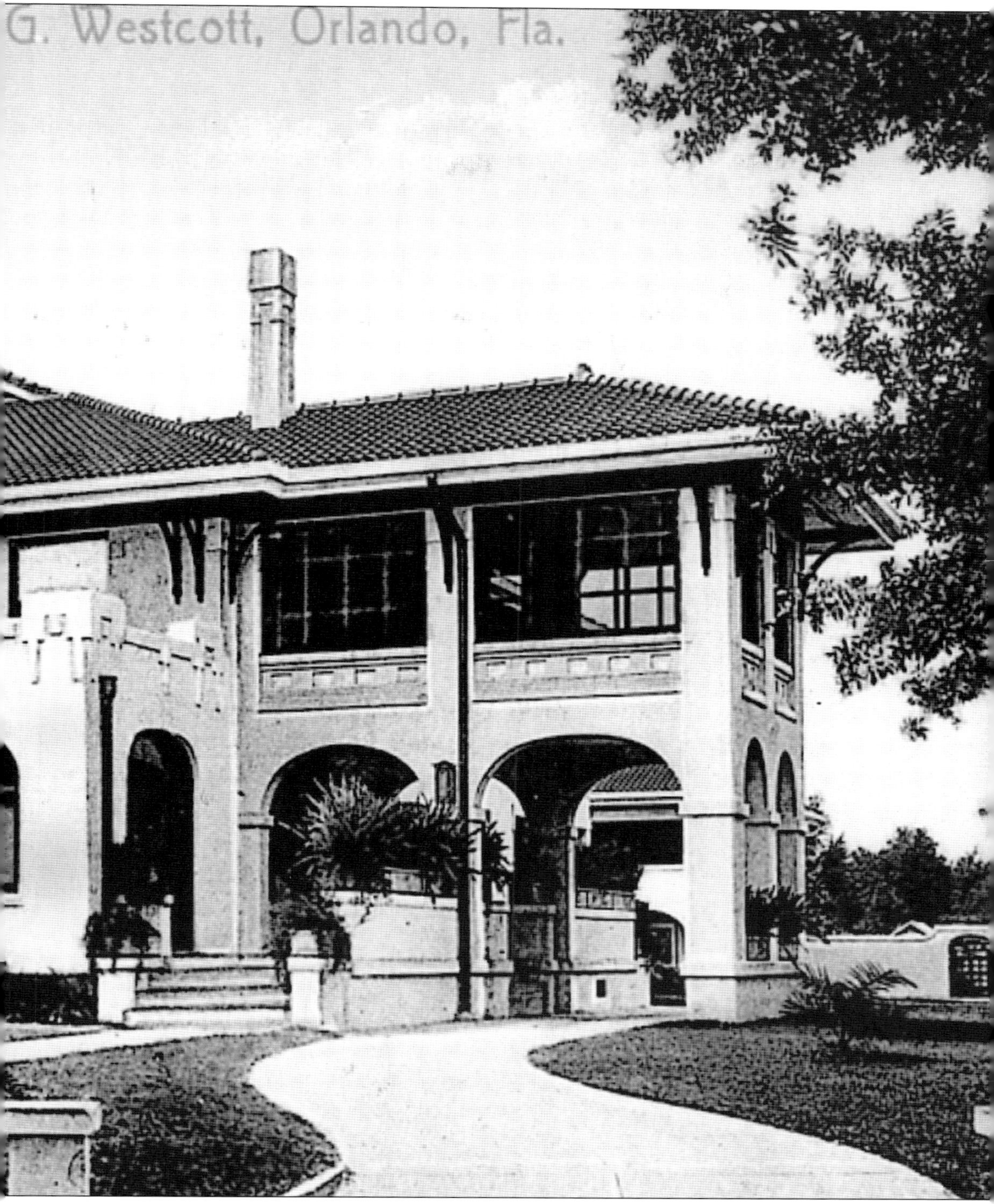

1930, designed the residence. King also designed many of Orlando's commercial buildings during the same time period. William Beardall, Orlando's mayor during the 1940s, and his family later owned the house. (University of South Florida Special Collections.)

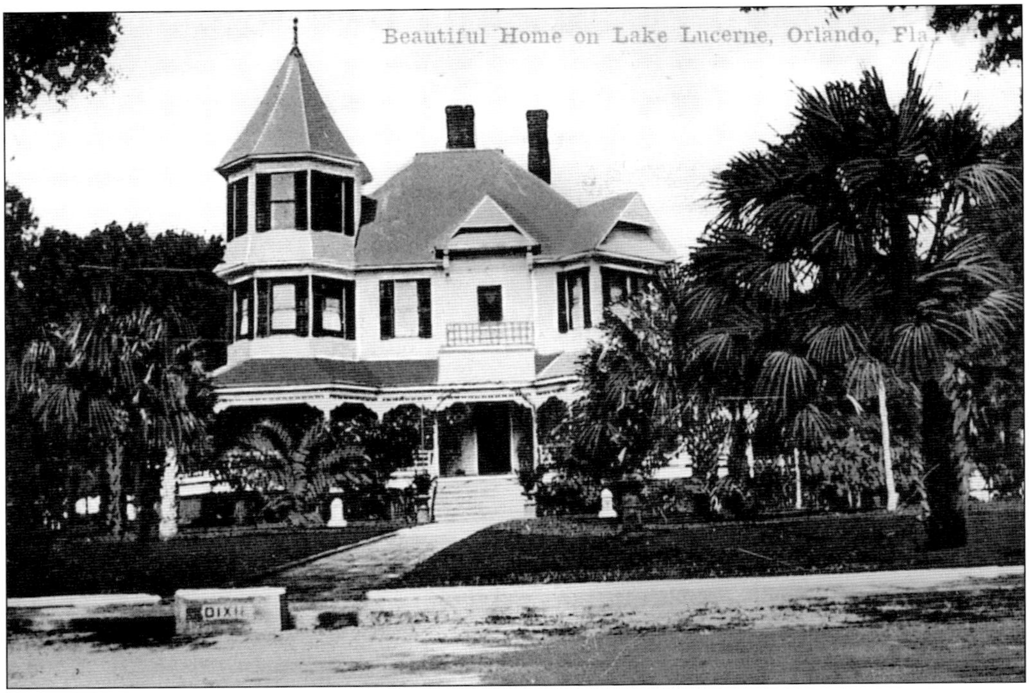

Some of Orlando's most elegant and architecturally significant homes were constructed along the shores of the community's many lakes. Built by affluent merchants, attorneys, citrus growers, realtors, and well-to-do seasonal visitors between the late 1800s and the end of the 1920s real estate boom, these residences were more than just private homes—they were also tourist attractions. Visitors could purchase dozens of postcards that pictured these large elaborate dwellings and their beautifully landscaped grounds as just one more of the many enticements offered by Orlando. (University of South Florida Special Collections.)

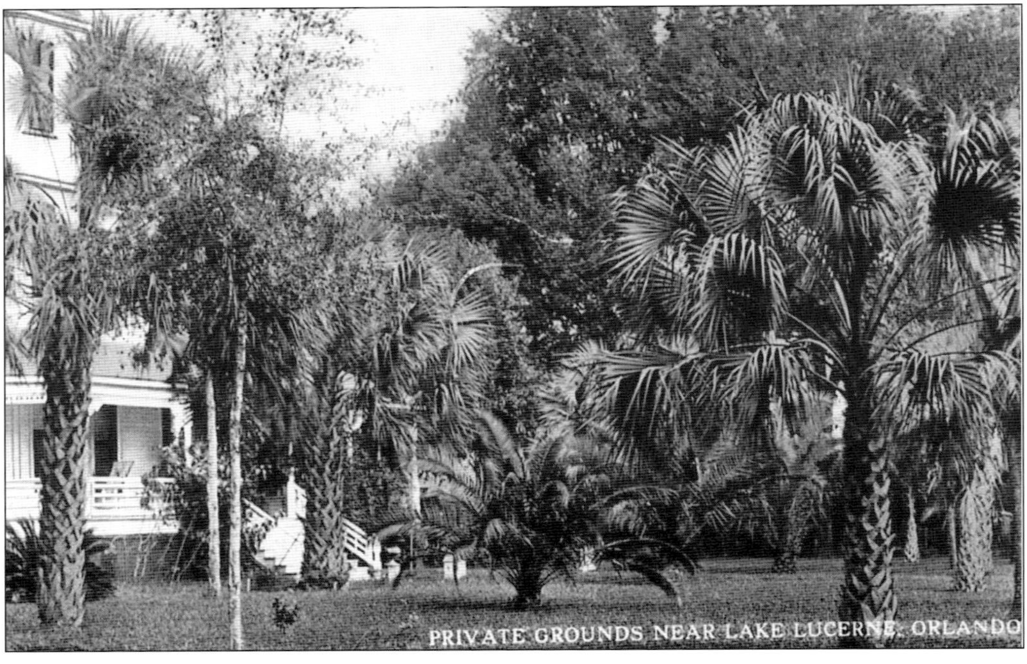

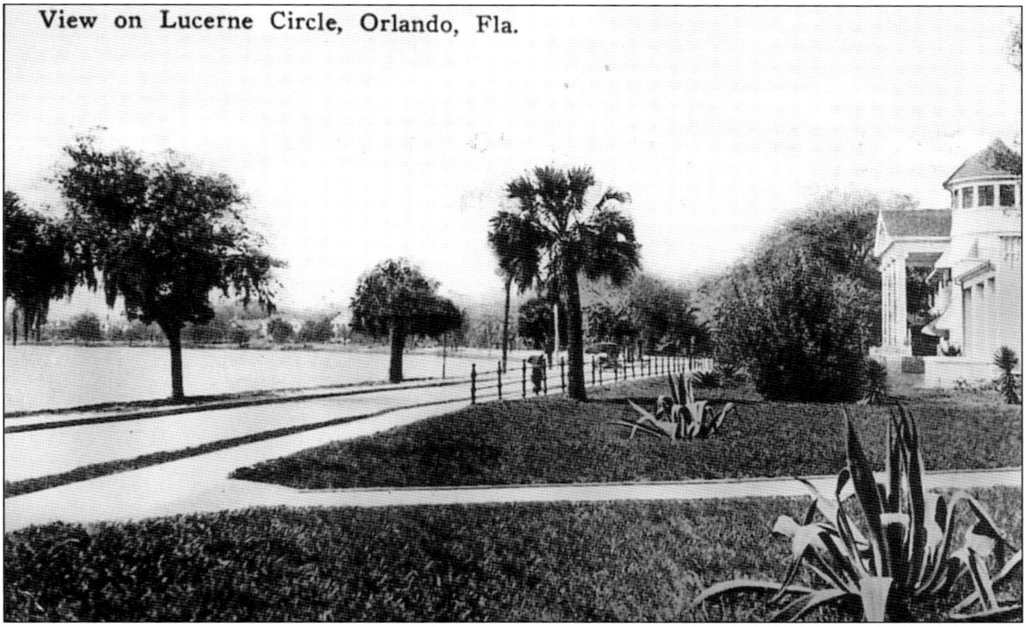

Many of the homes along Lucerne Circle could be counted among Orlando's residential showplaces. Included were all of the popular styles. The large Victorian homes of the late 1800s, Chicago/Prairie-style houses of the early 1900s, Mediterranean and Colonial Revival dwellings of the 1920s, Arts & Crafts-style bungalows, and even a few examples of Art Deco architecture existed along the shores of Lake Lucerne and Lake Cherokee. (University of South Florida Special Collections.)

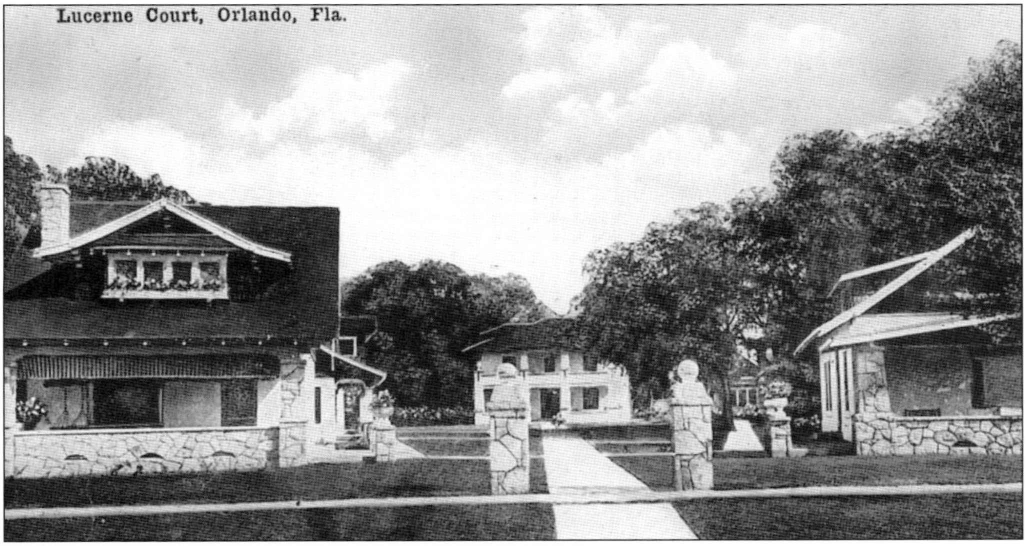

Orlando History in Architecture described Lucerne Court as "a cluster of nine bungalows built around a common courtyard. Unified by the same design approach, each structure is two stories in height, with stuccoed walls below and shingled walls above. The site planning of this group is particularly interesting, as attention is focused down a central axis and across the length of Lake Lucerne, while the interior courtyard is sheltered from the view of outsiders." (University of South Florida Special Collections.)

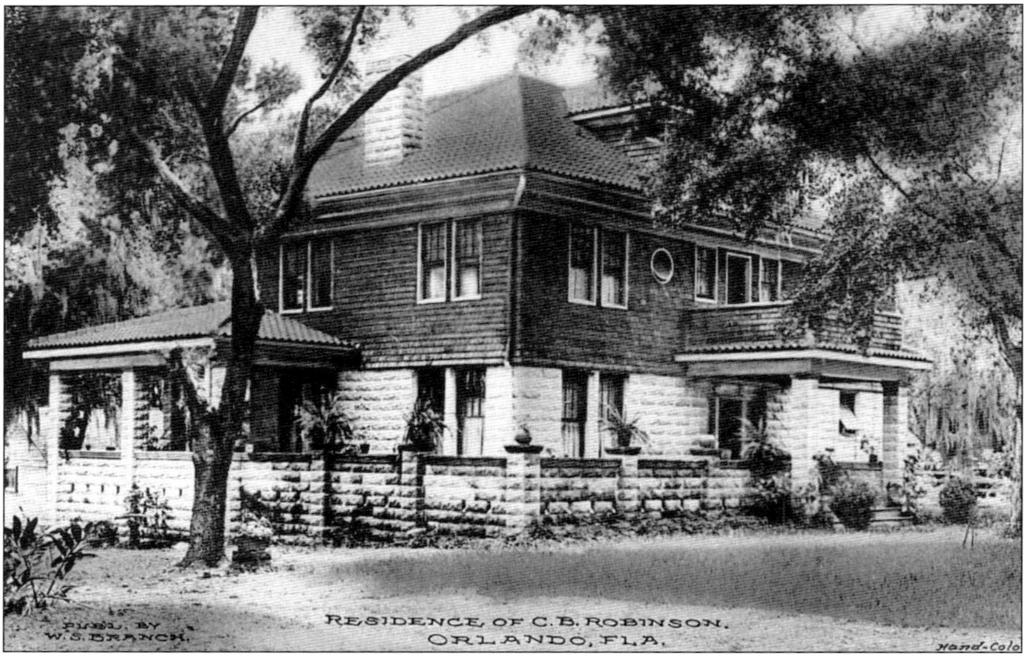

These two postcards provide good examples of the differing styles of architecture in Orlando. The older Robinson house is an eclectic mixture, featuring a tile roof above a shingled upper story and a lower story constructed of rusticated block that has been molded to look like stone. Development of the Lancaster Park neighborhood first began during the land boom of the 1920s, but halted with the financial crash. For that reason, many of the Mediterranean and Colonial Revival homes, although appearing older in style, date from the years immediately following World War II when construction resumed. (University of South Florida Special Collections.)

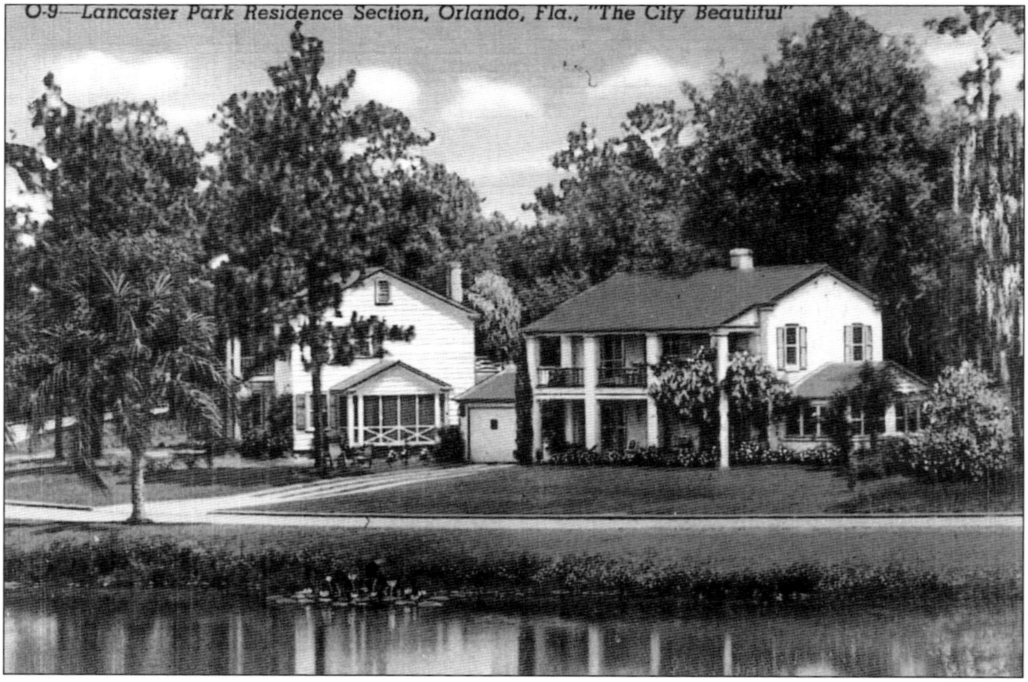

Three

The Civic Scene

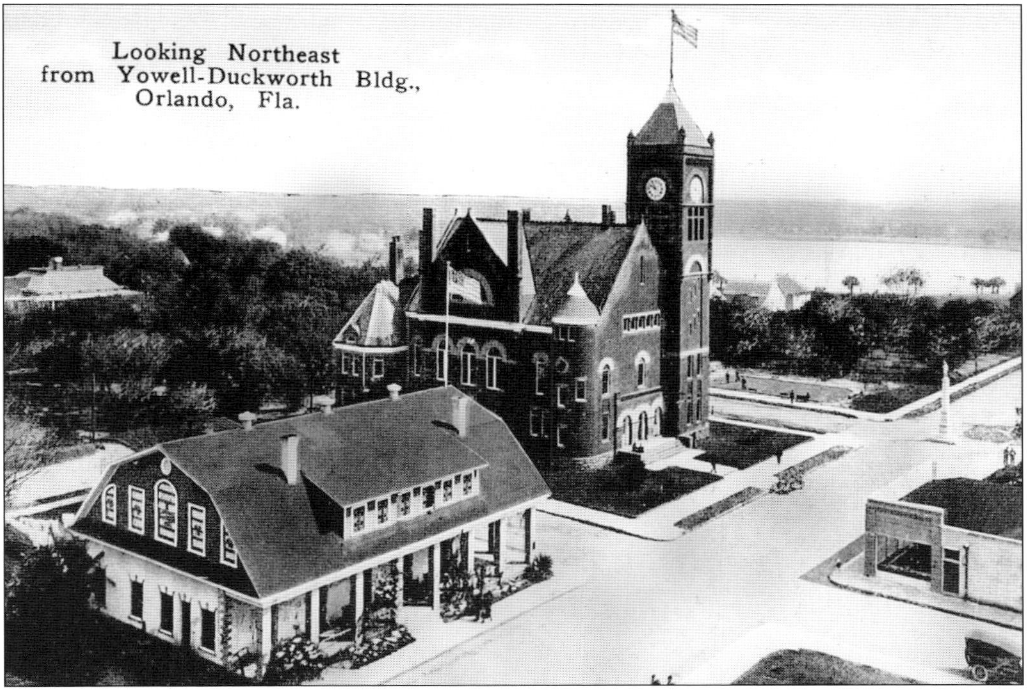

When moving into any new area, obviously a first priority is to find a place to live, a roof overhead, shelter from the elements. Equally important is a way to make a living, a job, a business. For any town, large or small, to be more than just a group of individuals residing in the same general area, however, it quickly becomes necessary to build certain civic institutions. These include the schools, places of worship, governmental entities, and social organizations that contribute to the structure and fabric of a community. Orlando was quick to recognize this. Within 30 years of its founding, an Orlando real estate booklet listed 50 stores, seven churches, a seminary, an opera house, five large hotels, two newspapers, a courthouse, a public school, four drug stores, and several restaurants. (University of South Florida Special Collections.)

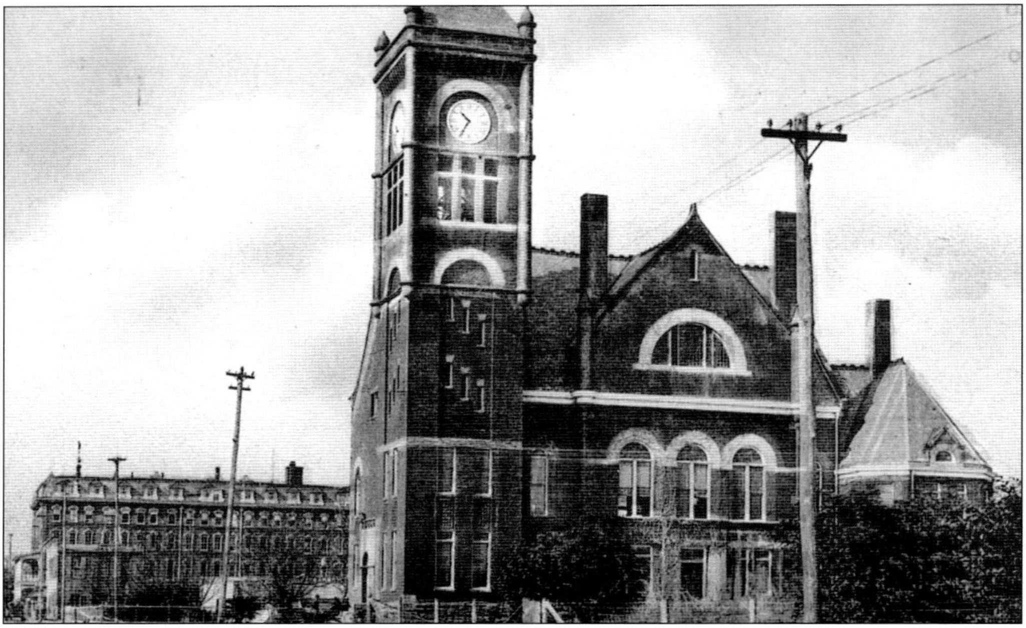

Orlando had a succession of four wood-framed county courthouses, all of which were either destroyed by fire or outgrown. Their replacement, a red brick edifice dedicated on January 15, 1892, epitomized Victorian architectural fashion. A.S. Wagner was the building's architect, while W.C. Green & Company served as the general contractor. A local businessman, W.C. Sherman raised several thousand dollars for the clock and bell that were installed in the 80-foot-high courthouse tower in 1895. (University of South Florida Special Collections.)

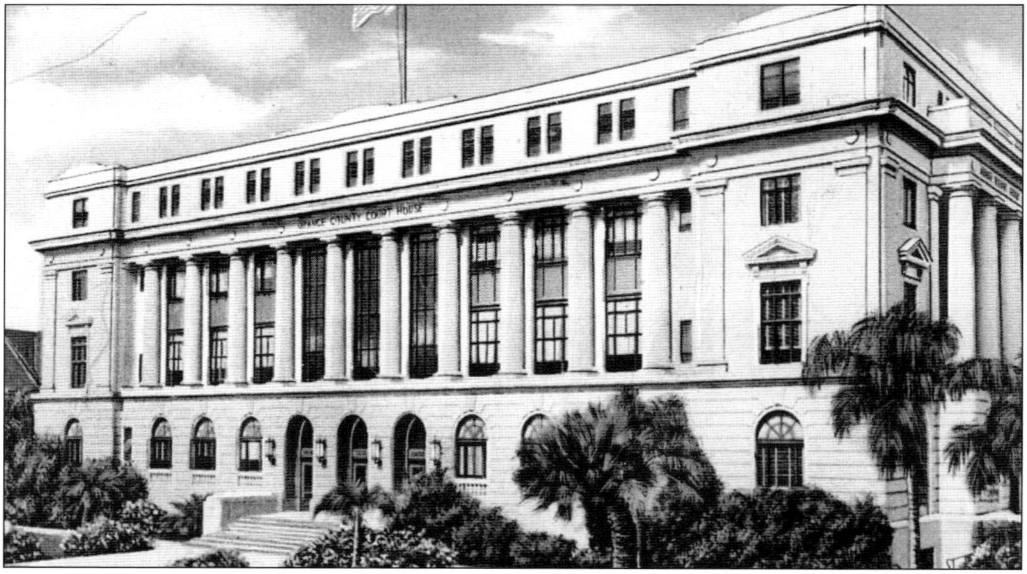

By the 1920s, the brick courthouse had been outgrown and relegated to use as a location for county offices. Reflecting the optimism of the boom era, a new $1-million courthouse designed by local architect Murray King was dedicated on October 12, 1927. Occupying an entire block, the new courthouse was built on the former site of the Bishopstead, purchased from the Episcopal Church by Orange County in February 1924. (University of South Florida Special Collections.)

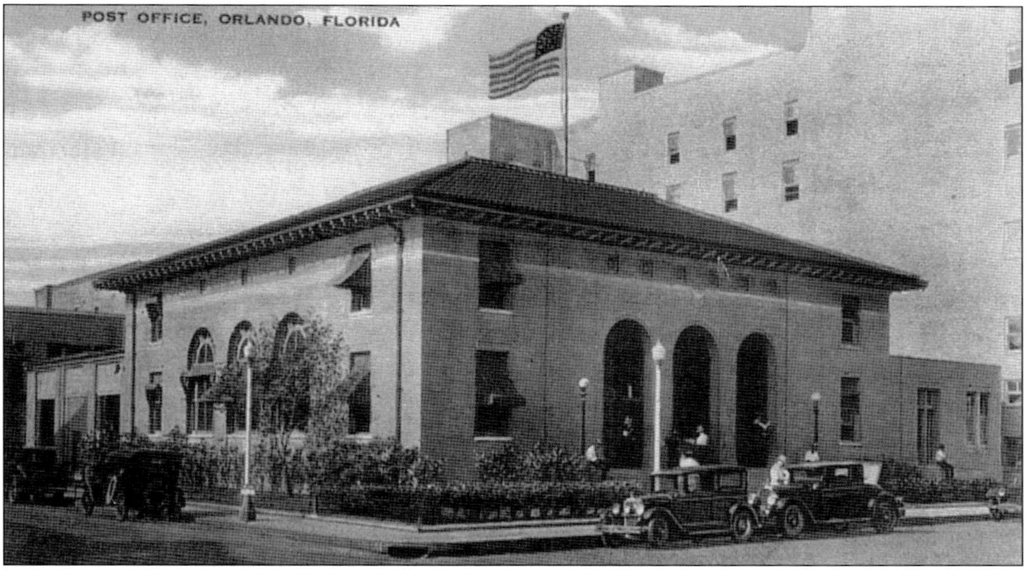

Postal service for a community known as Jernigan was first established in 1850; the designation was changed to Orlando on September 19, 1857, under postmaster John R. Worthington. The post office moved from house to house under different postmasters until 1871 when E.W. Spier erected a permanent one-story building on the corner of Pine and Main Streets. After several additional relocations, the post office was established in 1917 on the southwest corner of East Central Avenue and Court Street. (Larry Roberts Antiques.)

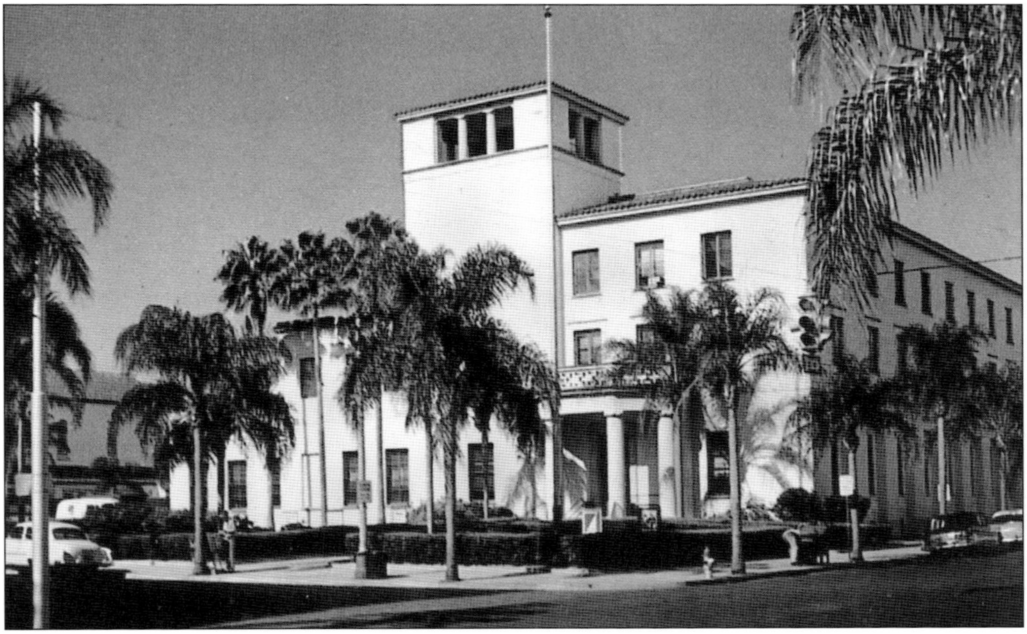

Orlando's first home mail delivery had begun in 1905 following the installation of numbers on houses and businesses. On April 14, 1941, Orlando's new post office and federal courthouse building was officially dedicated. Two weeks later, employees moved out of the old 1917 post office and into the new facility. The city's first airmail service started in March 1929; by 1950, eight airmail flights going north, and seven to the south departed daily. (University of South Florida Special Collections.)

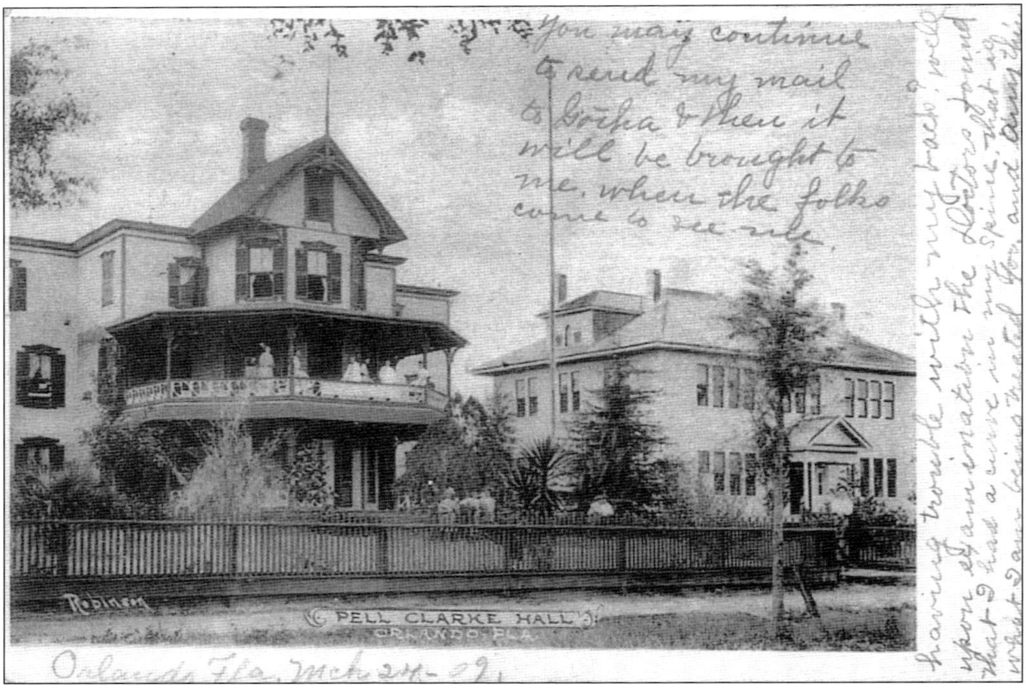

The Cathedral School began in October 1900 in the former home of Bishop William Crane Gray. When Leslie Pell-Clarke contributed his home to the Episcopal Church for use as the Bishopstead, Bishop Gray's former home at Central Avenue and Liberty Street was converted into a school named the Pell-Clarke School for Girls in honor of the donor. Subsequently renamed the Cathedral School, it was later expanded to serve as a boarding school for students from across the nation. The October 1, 1929 edition of the Orlando *Morning Sentinel* advertised the Cathedral School as follows: "A Boarding and Day School for Girls. Kindergarten, Primary, Intermediate and High School. Telephone 3473." The school, which changed its policy to become a day school for both male and female students in 1930, was demolished in 1967 to make way for a parking lot. (Larry Roberts Antiques and University of South Florida Special Collections.)

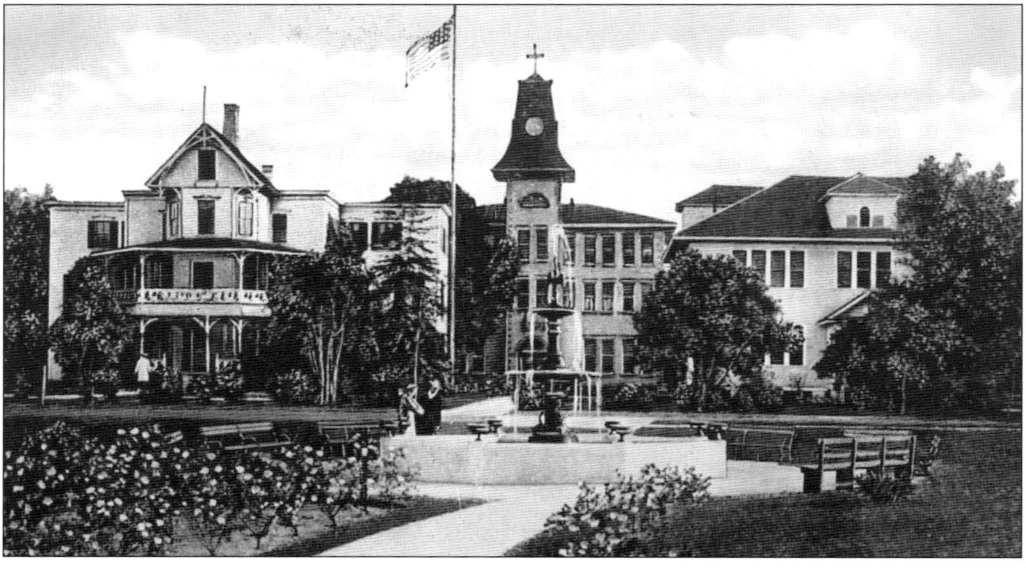

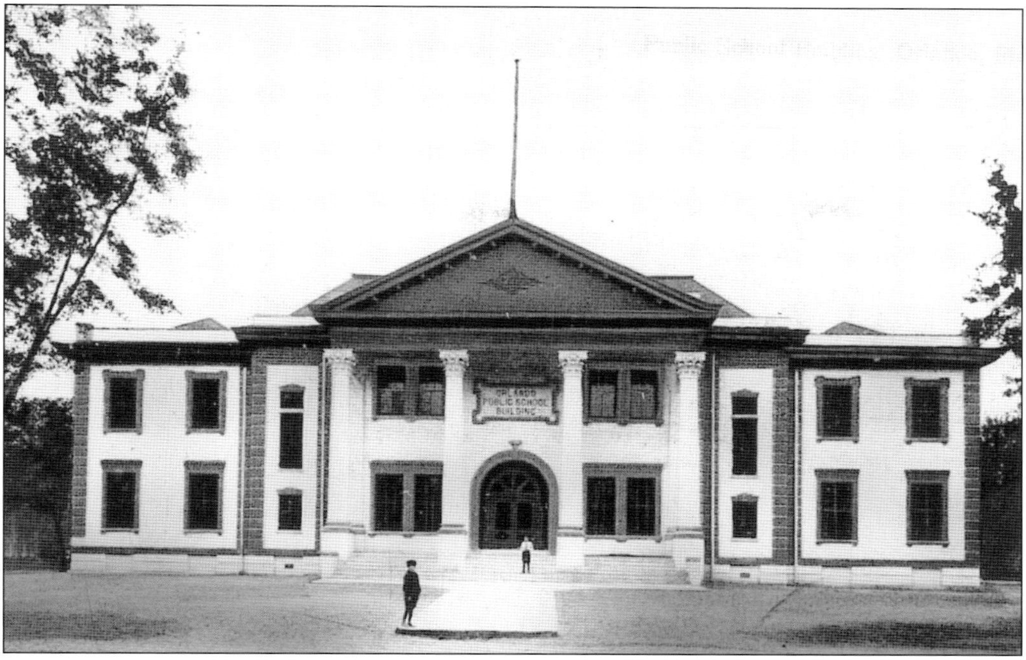

In 1872, the Free Church Building was used for public school classes during the week and for church services on Sunday. The city purchased the former Methodist academy on Orange Avenue for use as a public school in 1886 but in 1906 spent $23,000 to construct this new brick school building on Jackson Street. According to the back of the postcard, "There is no finer public school building in the state, if indeed anywhere." (University of South Florida Special Collections.)

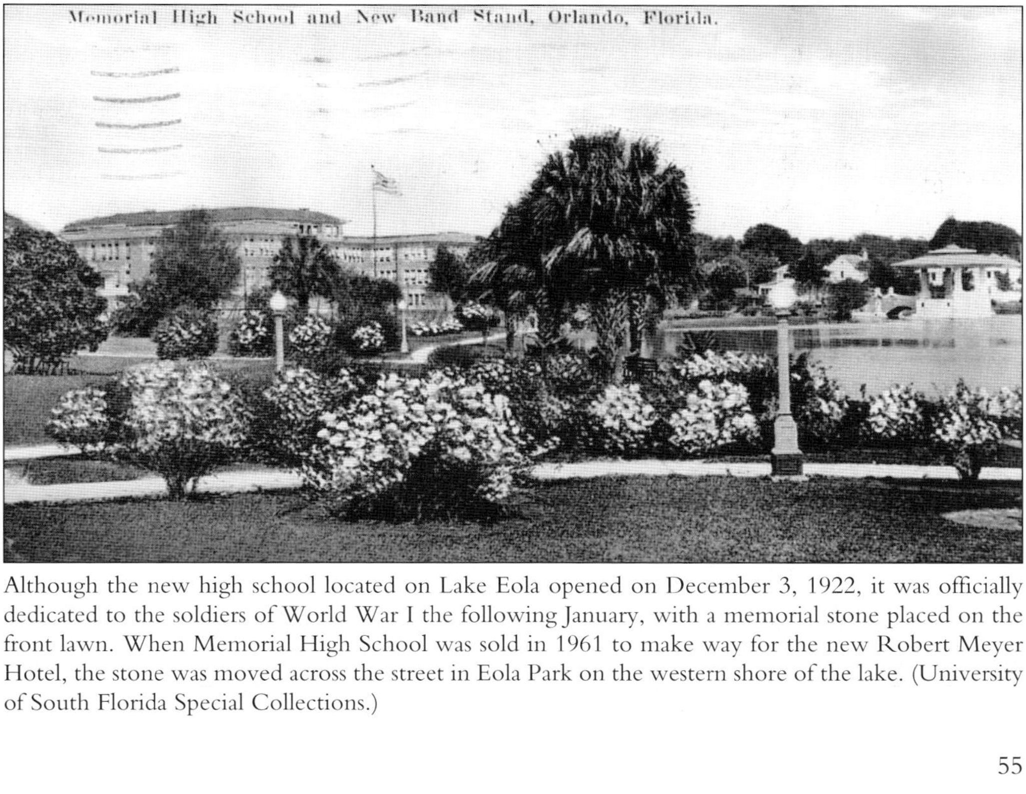

Although the new high school located on Lake Eola opened on December 3, 1922, it was officially dedicated to the soldiers of World War I the following January, with a memorial stone placed on the front lawn. When Memorial High School was sold in 1961 to make way for the new Robert Meyer Hotel, the stone was moved across the street in Eola Park on the western shore of the lake. (University of South Florida Special Collections.)

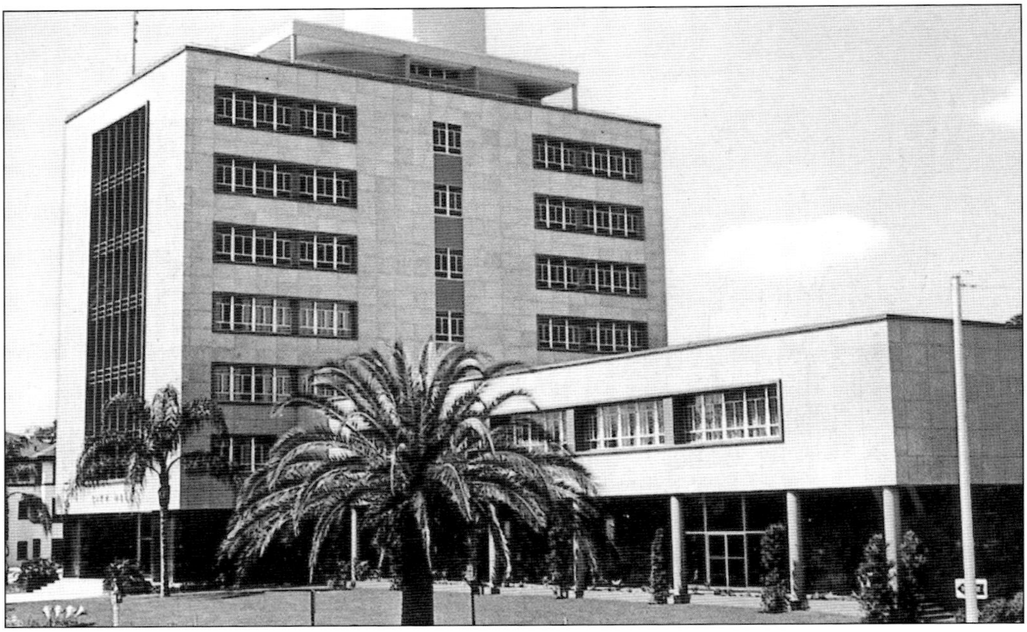

On October 3, 1958, the new $1.6-million Orlando City Hall on the corner of South Orange Avenue and South Street was officially dedicated. It replaced the old 1906 school building pictured on the previous page. Used as city hall since 1924, the former school building was turned over to the police department for use until it would finally be demolished in 1972. (University of South Florida Special Collections.)

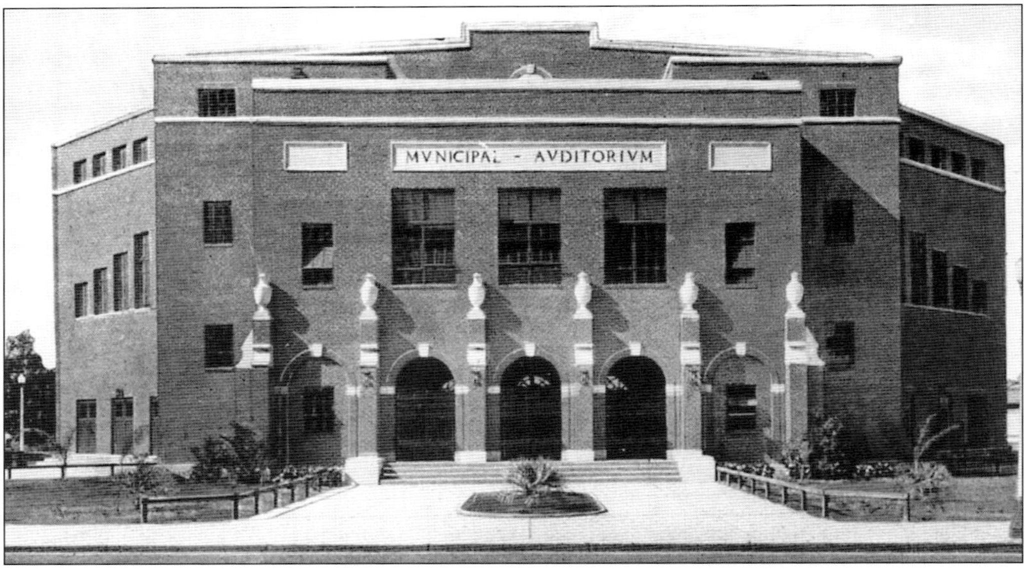

A series of operatic performances by the Philadelphia La Scala Grand Opera Company inaugurated the just-completed Municipal Auditorium on February 21, 1927. An October 26, 1929 advertisement touted less sophisticated entertainment: "Rod La Rocque's most colorful star picture 'Stand and Deliver' with Lupe Velez and a Brilliant Cast. A Story Brimming with Thrills and Laughs. Comedy. Pathé News. Adults—20¢ Family—50¢ Children—10¢. First show 7:00—second show 8:30." (University of South Florida Special Collections.)

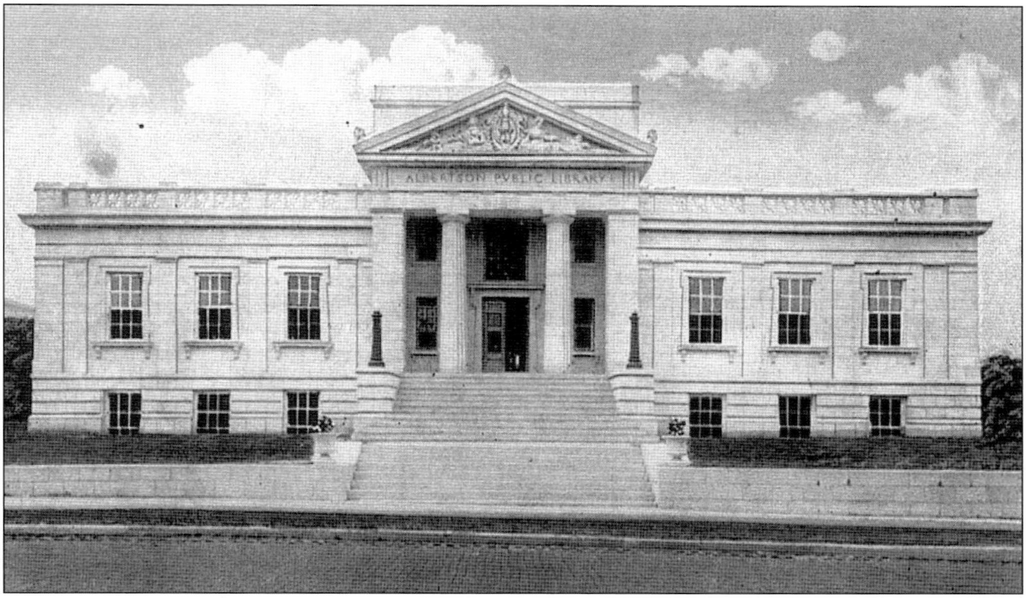

The literary needs of Orlando's citizens were also accommodated, thanks in part to a benefactor's generosity. Late in 1920, when Captain Charles Albertson donated his $75,000 collection of more than 12,000 books, plans were made for construction of a library. On November 8, 1923, the new $110,000 Albertson Public Library, offering patrons a selection of 20,000 books from which to choose, opened for business. According to the local newspaper in late 1929, the newest selections included *Some Famous Sea Fights* by Green and Frost, Chalmer's *A Dozen Dogs or So*, and Boyd's biography of Mad Anthony Wayne. Not until 1966 would a new library replace the Albertson Library. Built of poured concrete imprinted with wood grain designs, the new building was named the Orlando Public Library, while the Albertson Library name was retained for the genealogy and local history department. (Larry Roberts Antiques and University of South Florida Special Collections.)

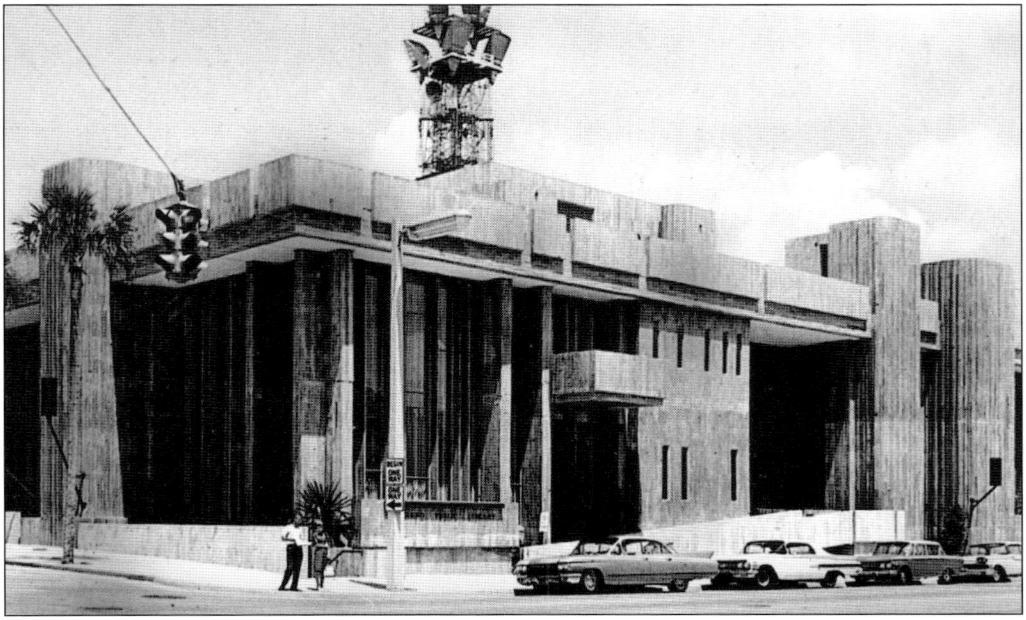

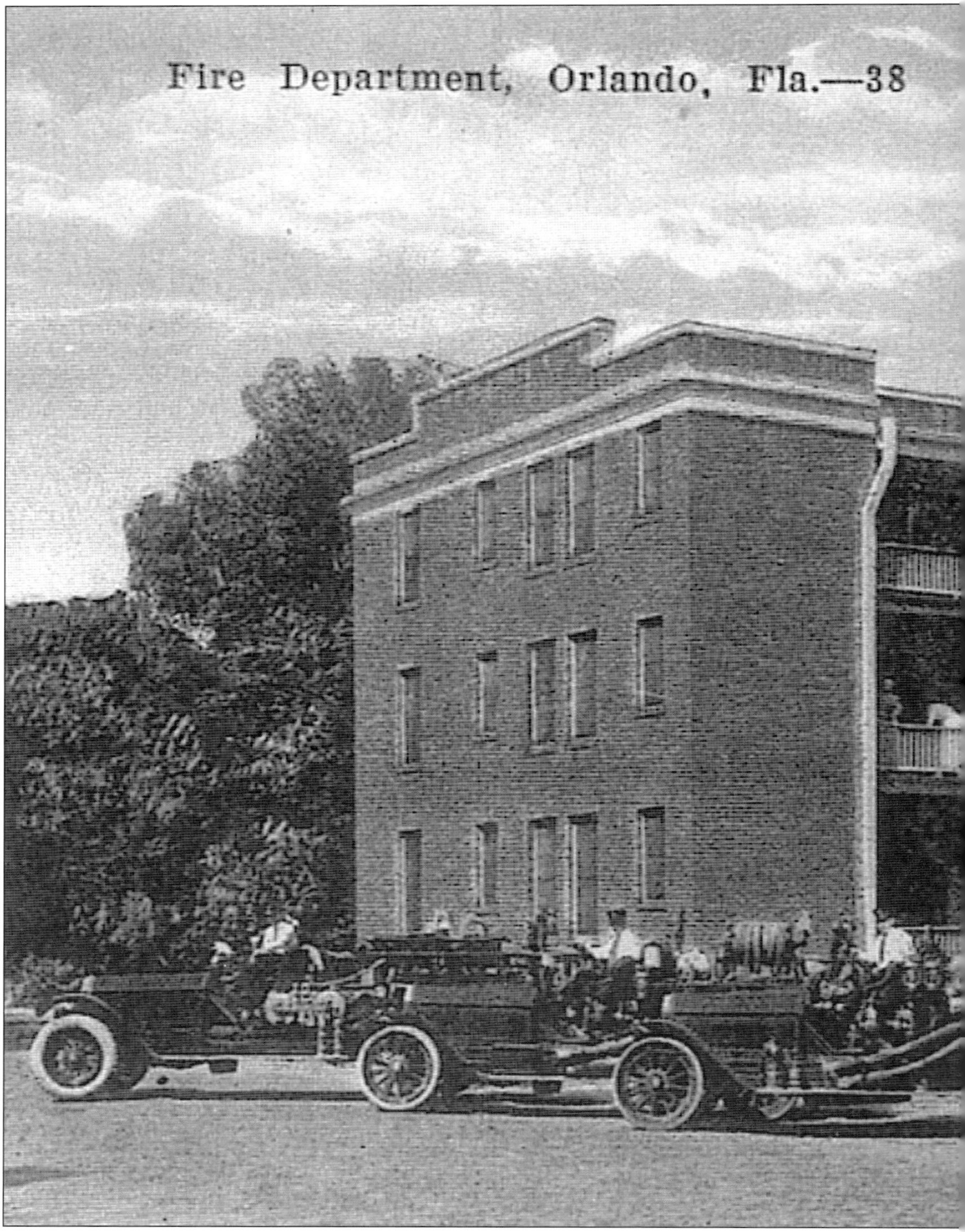

Catastrophic fires hit almost every town in Florida in the late 19th and early 20th centuries. Wooden construction of buildings, the use of kerosene and oil for indoor heating and lighting, inadequate water supplies, untrained firefighting personnel, and poor equipment all contributed to rapidly spreading fires that consumed major portions of turn-of-the-century communities. Orlando was no exception, with two devastating fires in the 1880s that destroyed large sections of the downtown. One positive

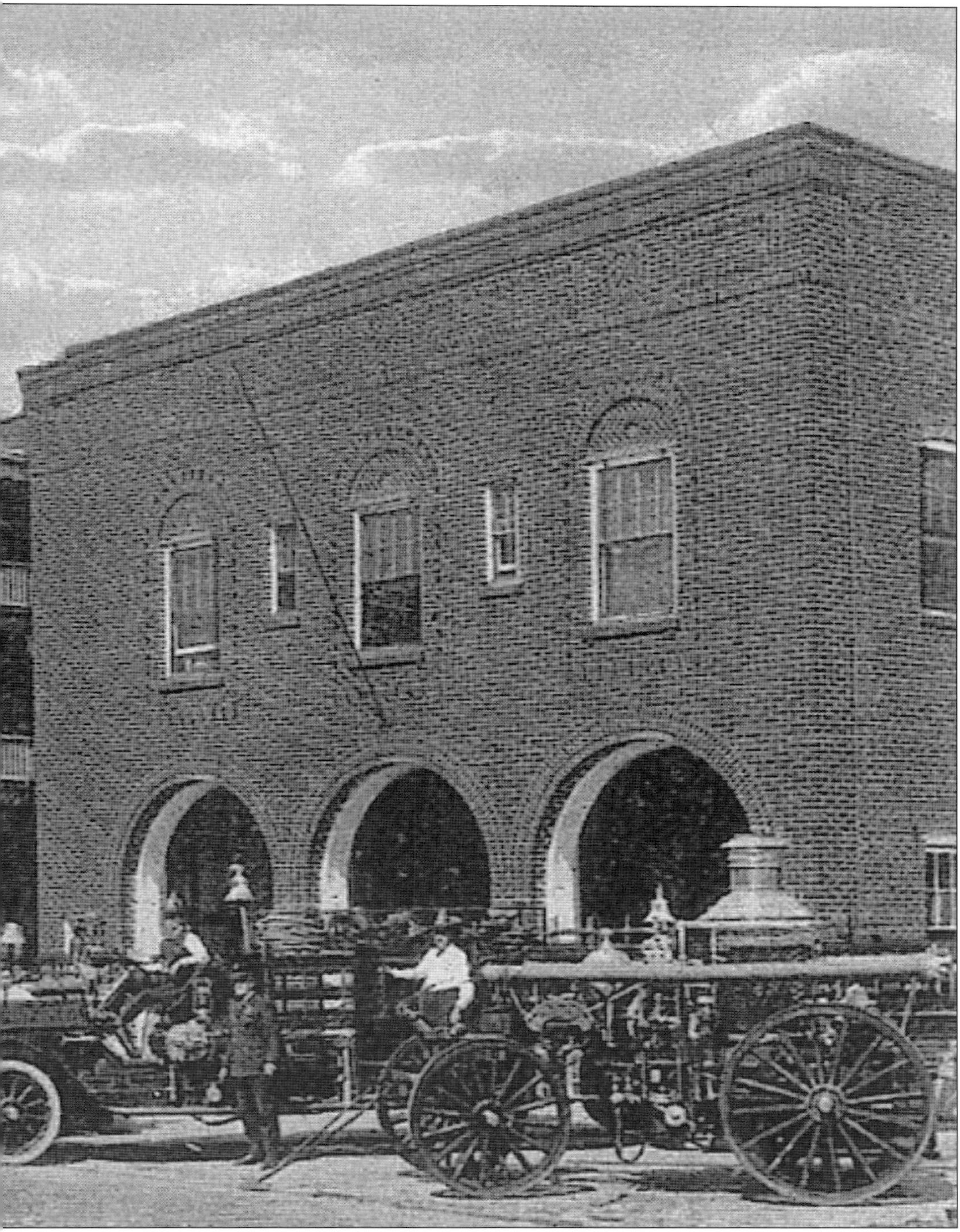

result of the fires, however, was the formation of the Orlando Hook and Ladder Company No. 1 in 1885, followed by consolidation of the volunteer forces into the Orlando Fire Department in 1890. Motorized equipment was first acquired in 1915; the department moved from Oak Street to a new $17,708 firehouse on North Main Street in 1920. Construction of two additional fire stations followed in 1926. (Larry Roberts Antiques.)

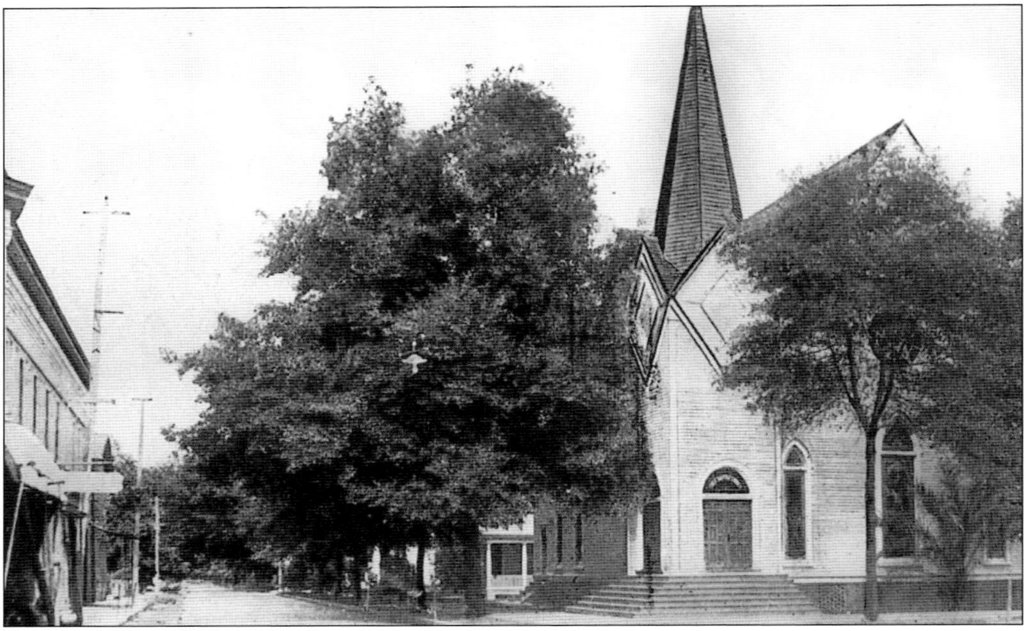

Churches played a major role in the formation of a community. Often congregations met in private homes or shared a common building with members of other denominations until sufficient funds were accumulated to construct a church of their own. Started in 1871 as the Bethel Baptist Church of Orlando, the First Baptist Church spent $6,000 to build this frame church in 1897. Eighteen years later, a much larger new brick church at Main and East Pine Streets replaced the older frame structure. Early in 1918, the Orlando *Morning Sentinel* reported that the congregation was greatly saddened by the departure of their pastor, Dr. E.T. Poulson, after four and one-half years to accept the call of the First Baptist Church in St. Petersburg. The article cited Poulson as having raised more funds during his tenure than any other previous pastor, terming him "not only a strong preacher but a builder as well. Our new church edifice is an example of his efforts along this line." (University of South Florida Special Collections.)

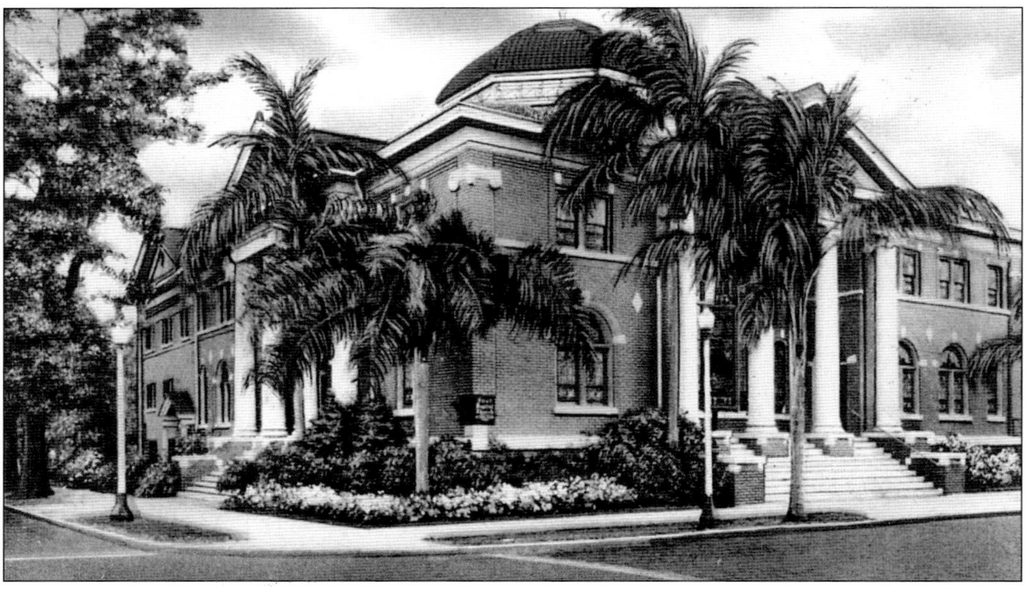

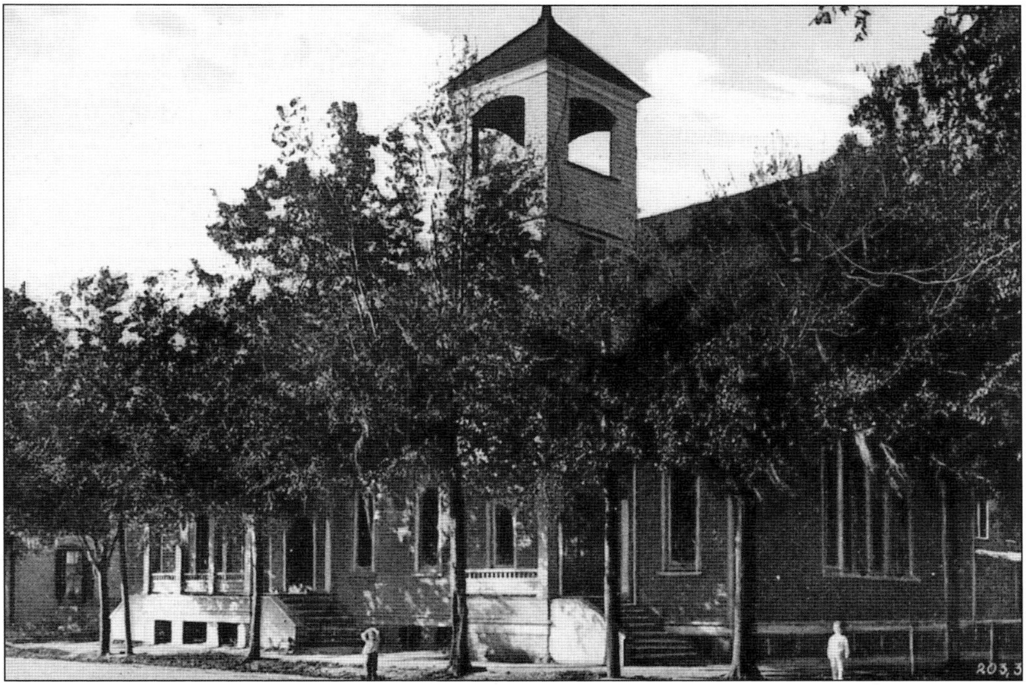

The First Methodist Church, organized in 1881, had as its first church building a $1,000 wooden structure. In 1914, the congregation moved into a new $50,000 brick church at the corner of Main and Jackson Streets and, just eight years later, erected an adjacent $60,000 educational and Bible school building. Advertisements in the October 26, 1929 edition of the *Morning Sentinel* read, "Rev. O.E. Rice, pastor. Rev. P.M. Boyd, associate pastor. Church school at 9:30 a.m., Maxwell W. Wells, general superintendent. The school operates eight different departments, each with its own worship service followed by the separation of classes into their individual rooms. Morning worship at 11 o'clock and evening worship at 7:30 as usual." By 1946, First Methodist, with the largest Sunday school of any Florida church, was planning a $125,000 expansion program. (University of South Florida Special Collections.)

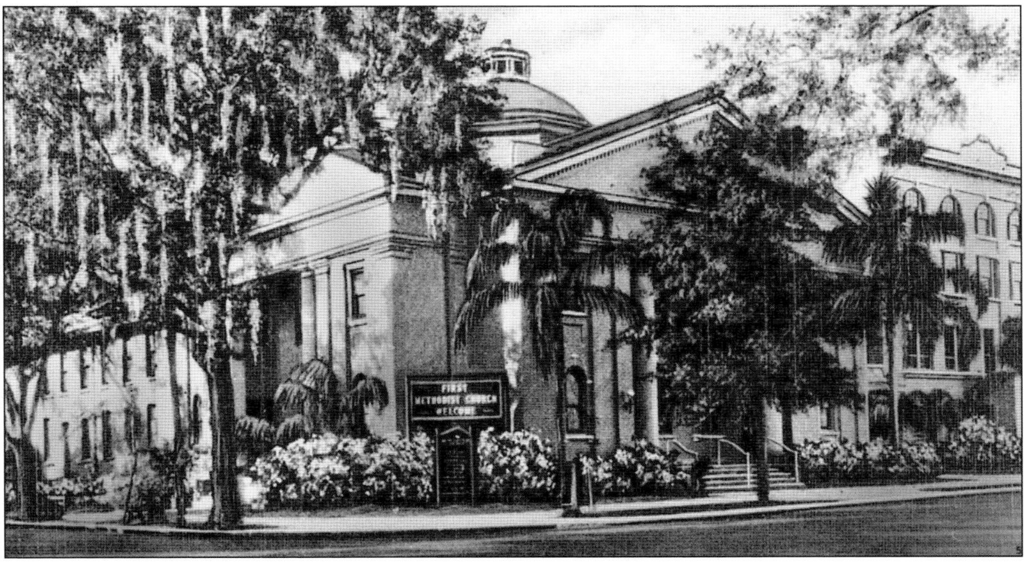

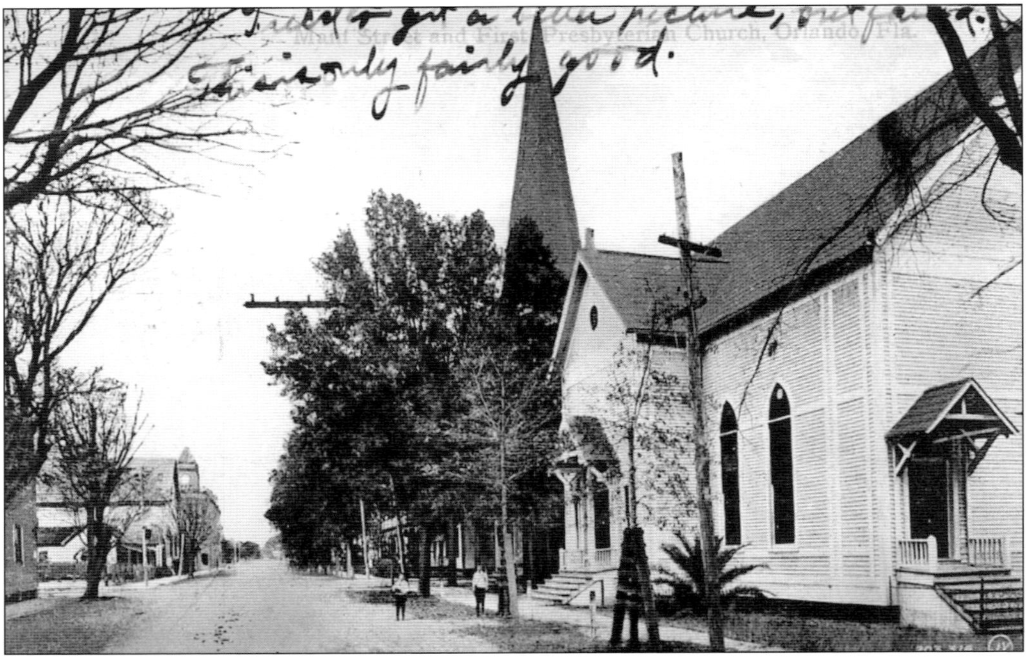

The Presbyterian Church was a popular denomination in Orlando. Organized in 1876, the church occupied a succession of different structures, including a wooden edifice dating from 1888. On December 27, 1914, the congregation moved into their new larger building designed by architect Murray King. Adding to the beauty of the church were stained-glass windows made by the Jacoby Art Glass Company of St. Louis. In an effort to attract more parishioners, the church placed advertisements in local newspapers in January 1918, offering "Evangelistic services every morning at 10:30; every evening at 7:30, January 6th to 20th. The Rev. R.G. McLees of Virginia will be the preacher. A 15-minute song service every night by a large chorus. Comfortable pews. Restful auditorium. Virile Gospel. Visitors and tourists and especially the resident people of Orlando will be warmly welcomed." (University of South Florida Special Collections and Larry Roberts Antiques.)

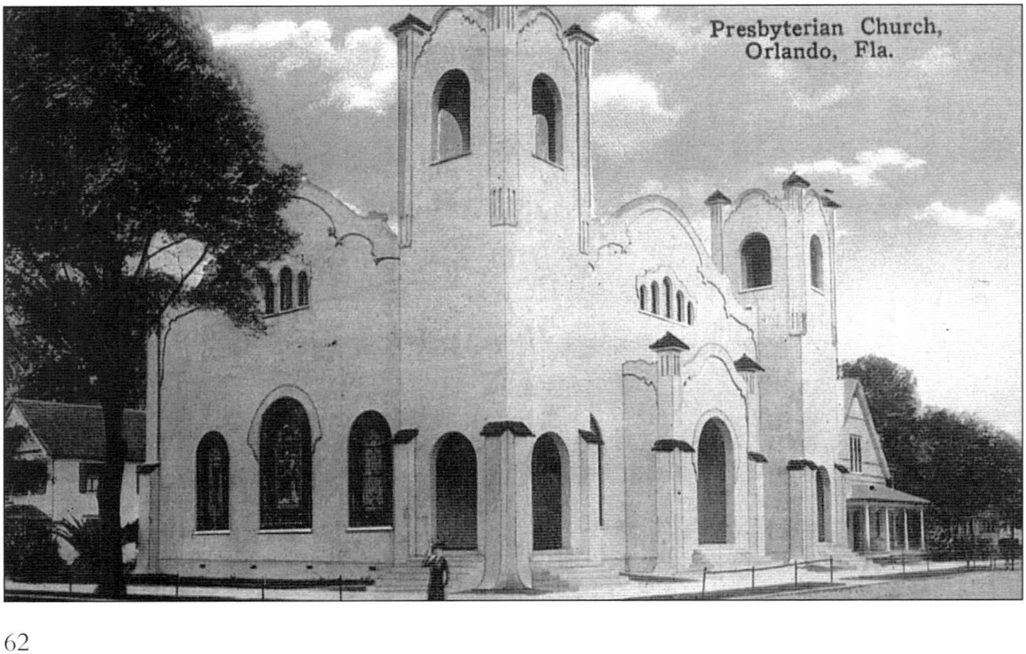

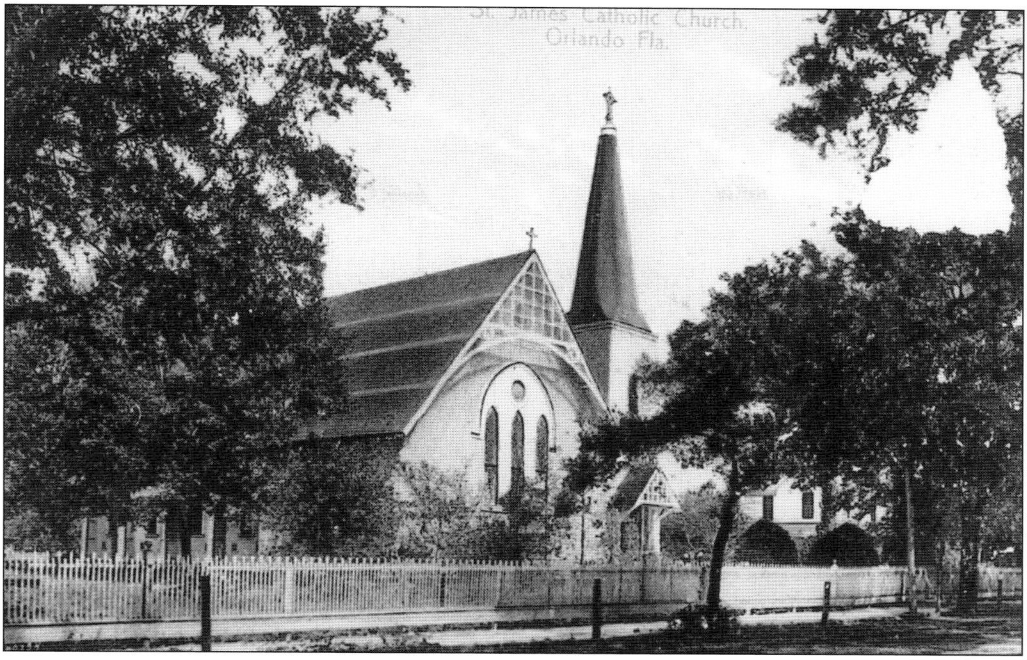

St. James Catholic Church was built on a one-square-block lot bordered by Orange Avenue and Main, Jefferson, and Robinson Streets that was purchased in 1881 by Bishop Moore. Four years later Father Felix P. Swemberg ordered construction of the church itself. From 1889 until 1939, the Sisters of St. Joseph convent and school occupied the half of the lot that faced Main Street. When that portion of the property was sold to the federal government for a new post office building, a new school and convent were built on Ridgewood Avenue. By 1950, plans were underway for construction of a new $300,000 church. (University of South Florida Special Collections.)

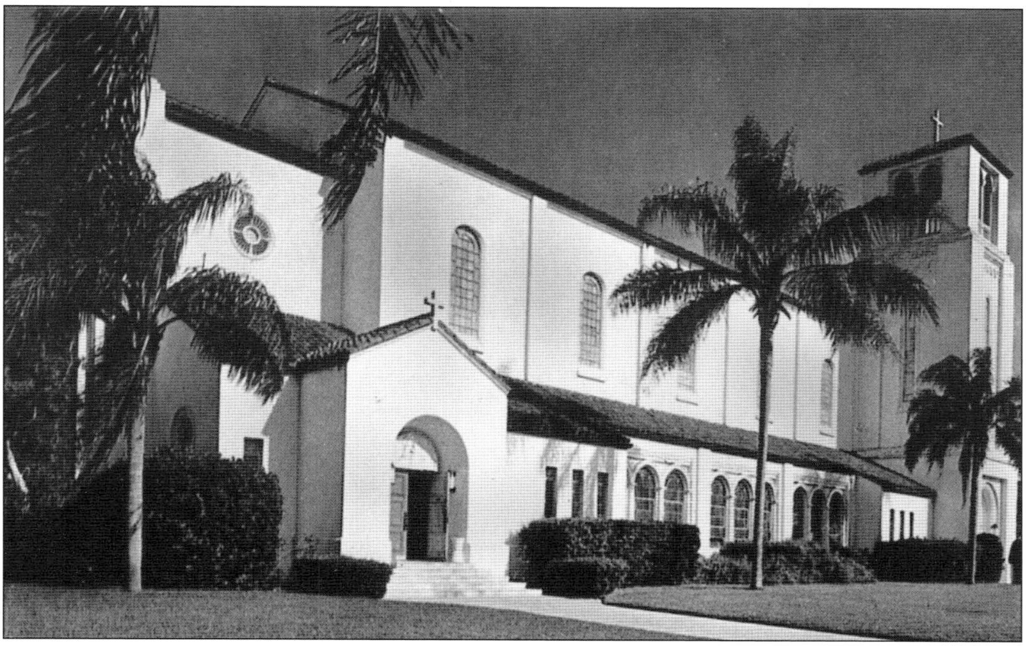

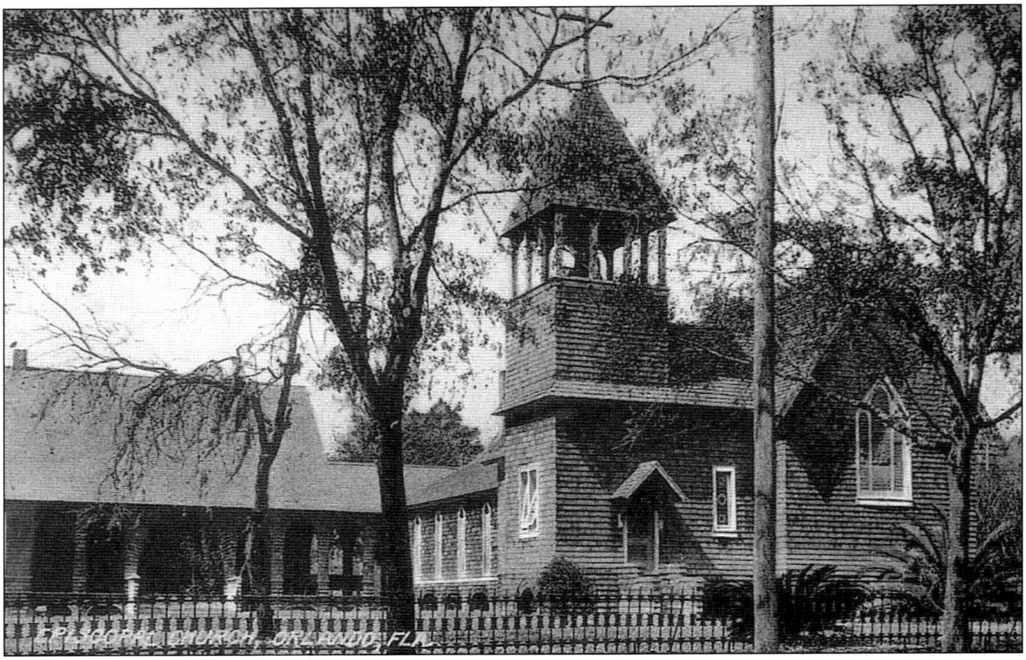

The Episcopal Church in Orlando had humble beginnings, with its first services conducted in private homes by a man who was a grandson of Thomas Jefferson. By 1884, a small church building erected at Main and Jefferson Streets two years earlier had been enlarged and organized into St. Luke's Parish. This structure was further expanded in 1902 and its name was changed to St. Luke's Cathedral. In 1922, the building, eventually to be used as church offices, was moved to the south side of the lot. Plans were underway for construction of a new cathedral that was to be designed in the Gothic Revival style, popular throughout the United States during the 1920s and 1930s. (Larry Roberts Antiques.)

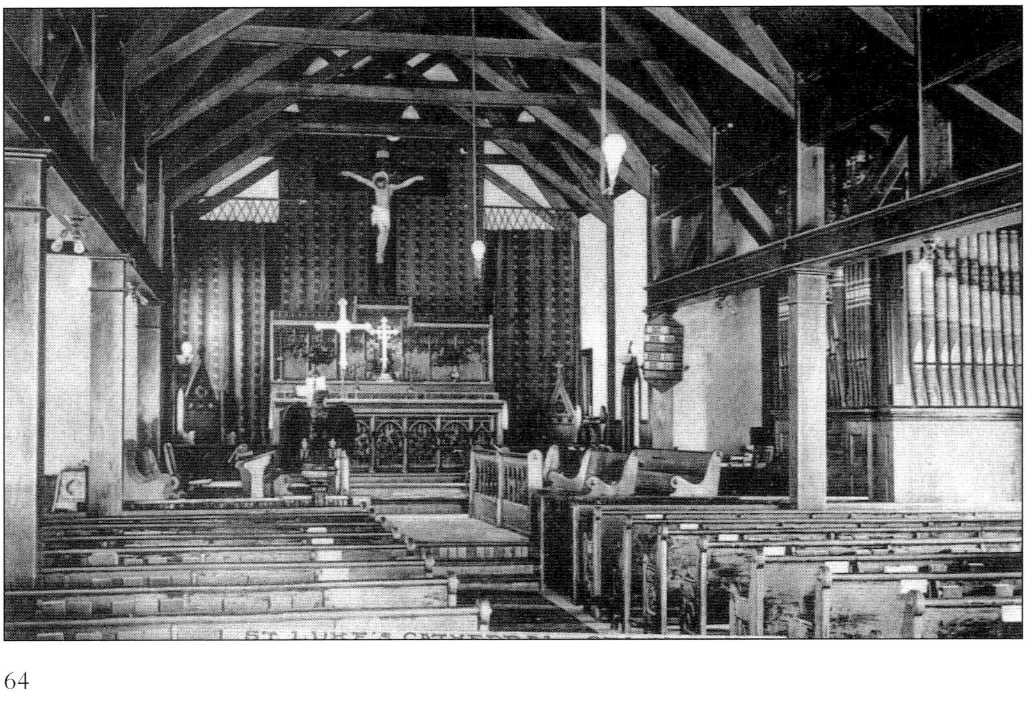

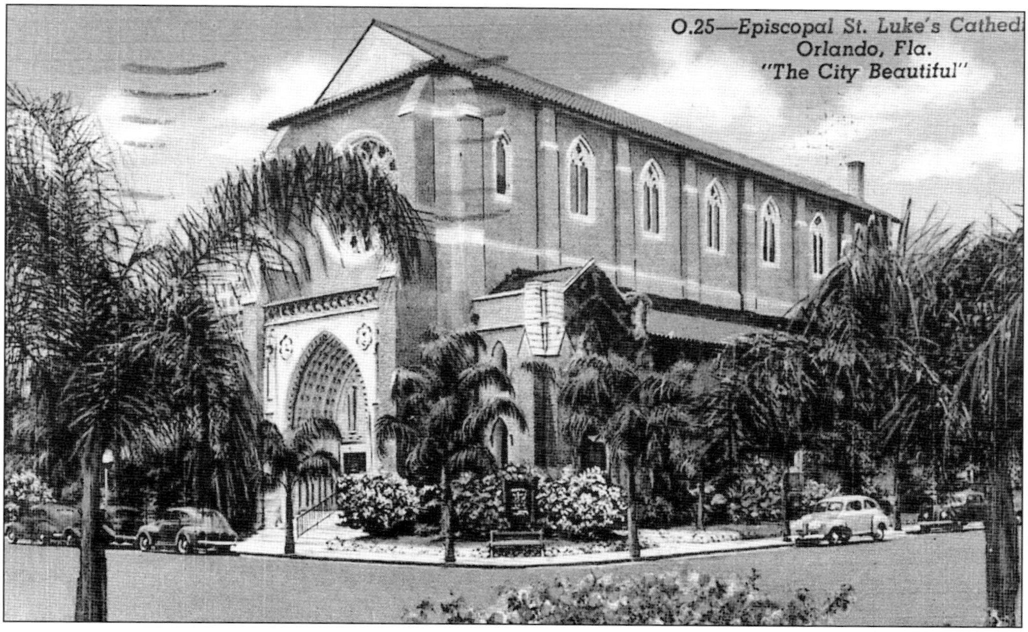

Begun in 1925 and dedicated on Easter Sunday of the following year, the Cathedral of St. Luke cost $130,000 and included an ambulatory (cloister walk), colombarium (wall niches for ashes), a bell tower, a 3,000-pipe organ, and exceptional stained glass. Newspaper articles reported that the church "seats approximately 700 persons. Its interior is noted for its exquisite nave." (University of South Florida Special Collections.)

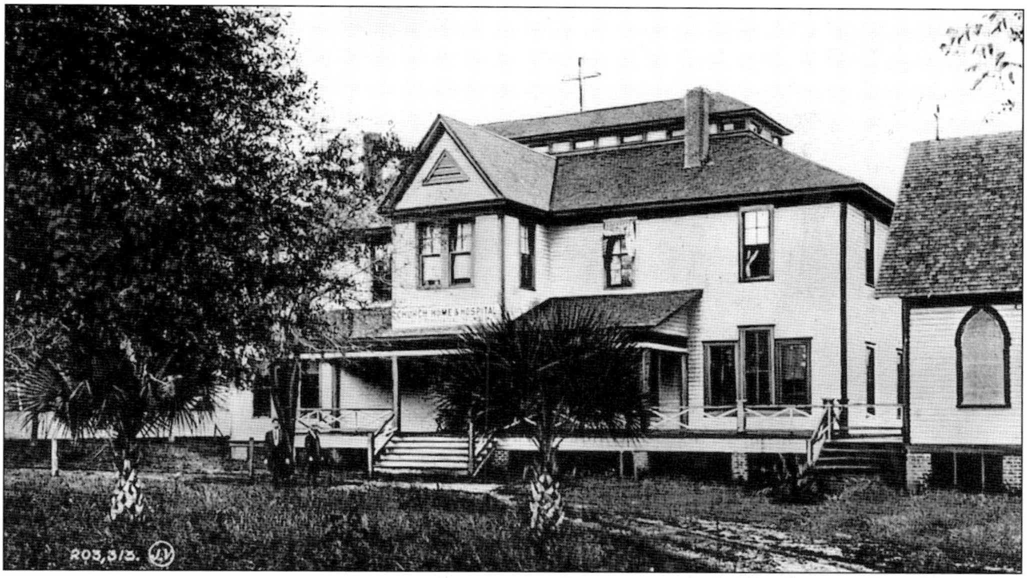

The Church Home and Hospital at the corner of Anderson Street and Delaney Avenue was another enterprise of the Episcopal Church in Orlando. Originally organized by the Cottage Hospital Association in 1892 as a home for dependent women, it consisted of several small buildings or cottages. Bishop Gray and the Episcopal Church took it over in 1895, enlarging it into the city's first hospital, complete with operating rooms, dining facilities, a laundry, chaplain's quarters, wards, and private rooms. (University of South Florida Special Collections.)

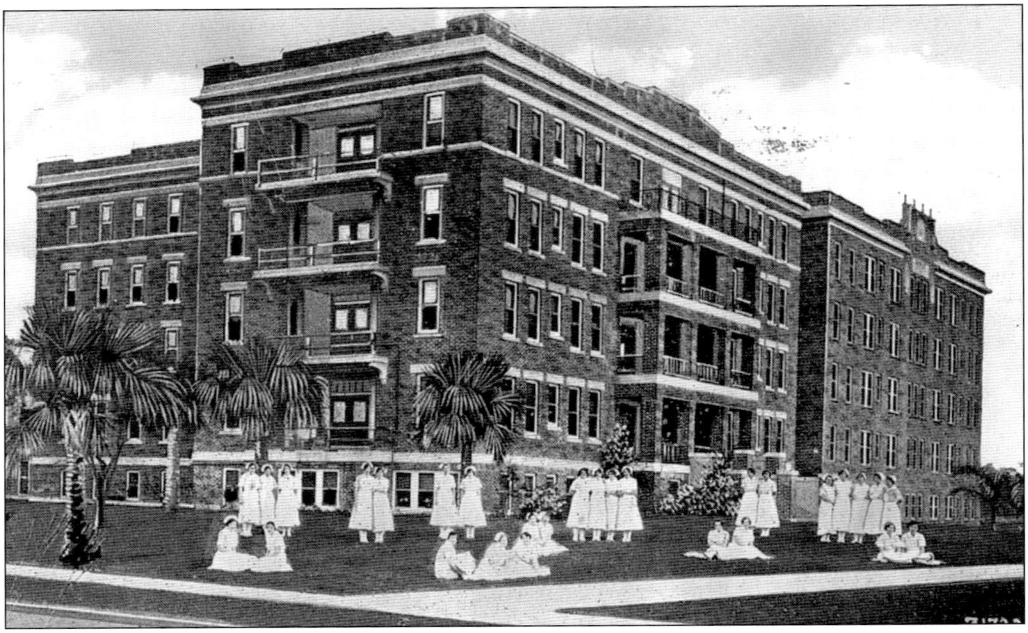

The closing in 1916 of the Church Home and Hospital led to the establishment of Orange General Hospital two years later. With the founding of a new community hospital as their goal, a group of interested businessmen and physicians mounted a campaign to get every person in the county to pay an annual membership fee of $5 in the Orange General Hospital Association. A site on Kuhl Avenue (now South Orange) was selected because of its elevation; more than $200,000 was spent for the land, building, and equipment. Completed in November 1918, the new Orange General Hospital would continue to grow over the years. Always popular as a training site for nurses, the hospital built a $25,000 nurses' home in 1923. Fifty additional rooms were constructed in 1926; further expansions would follow in 1950. As a tribute to World War II veterans from Orange County, the name of the hospital was changed in 1946 to Orange Memorial Hospital. (University of South Florida Special Collections.)

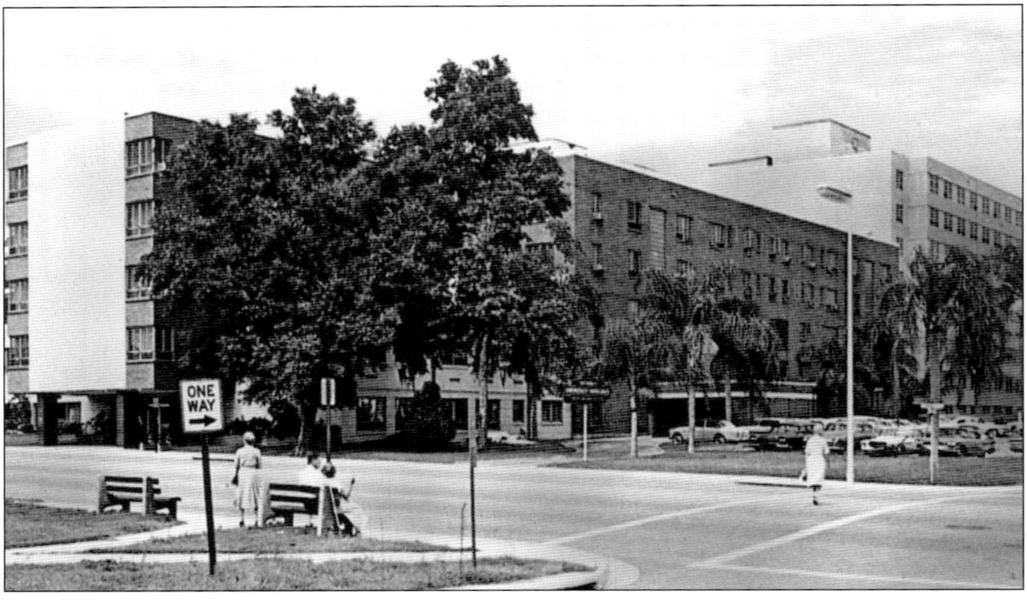

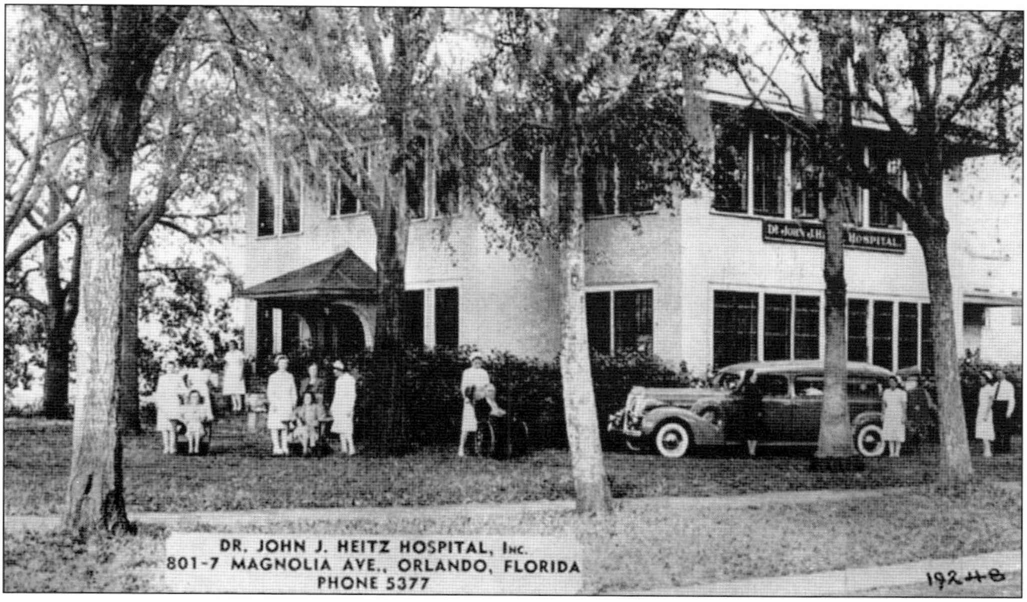

Books such as George M. Barbour's *Florida For Tourists, Invalids, and Settlers* had long touted the state as a healthy place in which to live. For those suffering from diseases of the lungs such as tuberculosis, as well as a variety of other illnesses, Florida's warm sunny winter weather was believed to be conducive to a speedy recovery. A number of physicians, including Dr. John J. Heitz, established private hospitals in Orlando to cater to these patients. (University of South Florida Special Collections.)

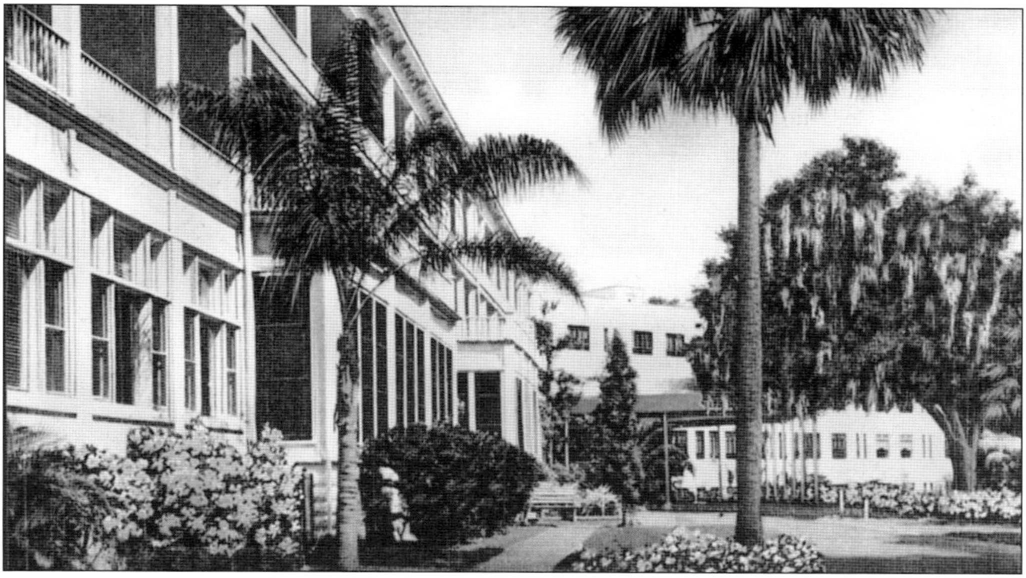

The Florida Sanitarium and Hospital provided a prime example, having been started by Dr. R.L. Harris around the turn of the century when he purchased an old farmhouse and 52 acres of land along Lake Estelle. Dr. Harris converted the house and built several additional small cottages for use as a tuberculosis sanitarium. In 1908, the Southeastern Seventh Day Adventist Conference purchased the hospital, quickly adding a two-story structure near the lake. (University of South Florida Special Collections.)

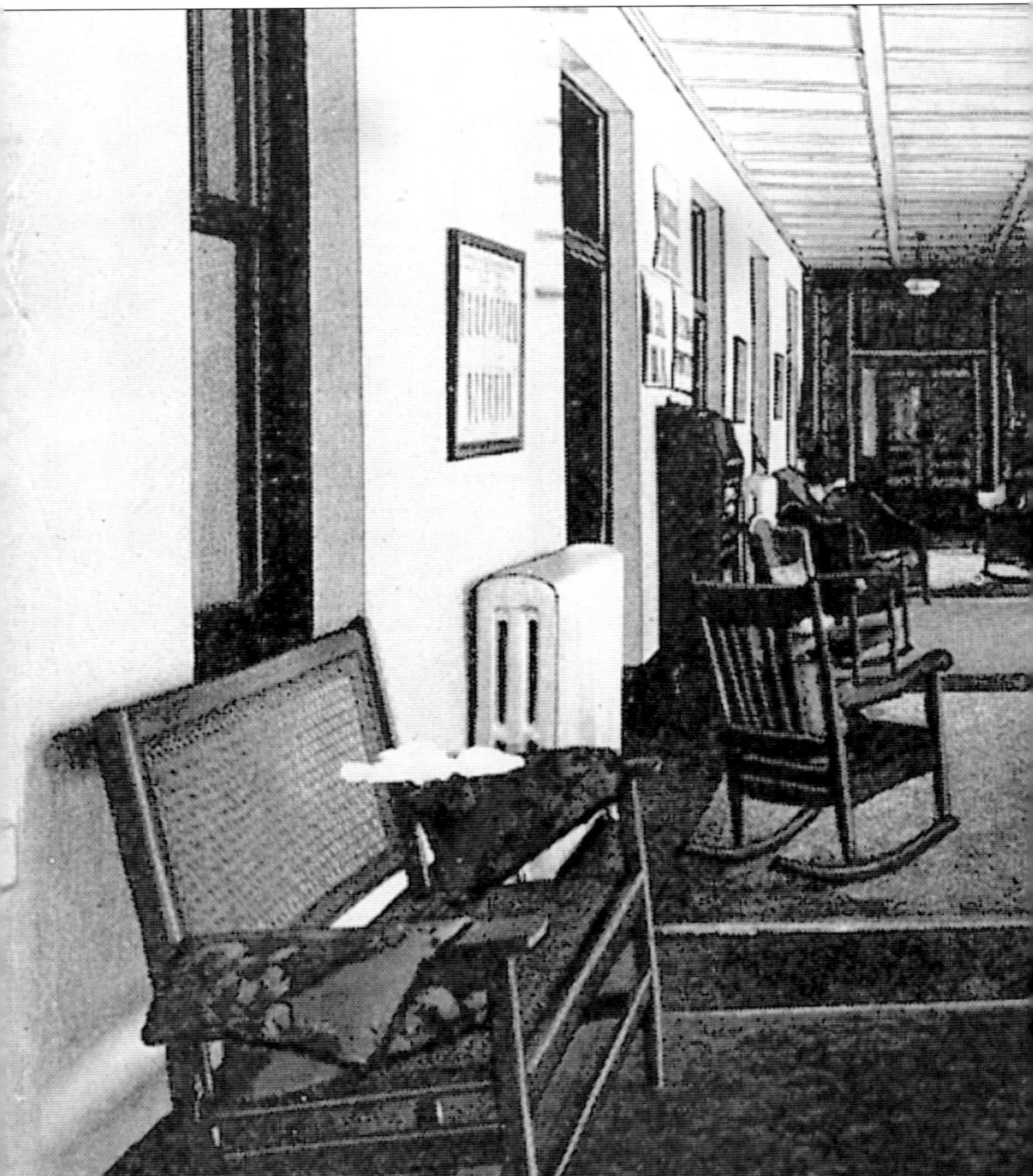

The Florida Sanitarium practiced the Seventh Day Adventist philosophy of "treating patients with combinations of medicine and surgery—and plenty of fresh air, sunshine, moderate exercise, good food, and relaxation." In keeping with that school of thought, the sun parlor of the sanitarium offered the perfect location for patients to relax and recuperate in the warm Florida weather. Further expansion of the facility continued over the years; in 1941 the house was moved to become the

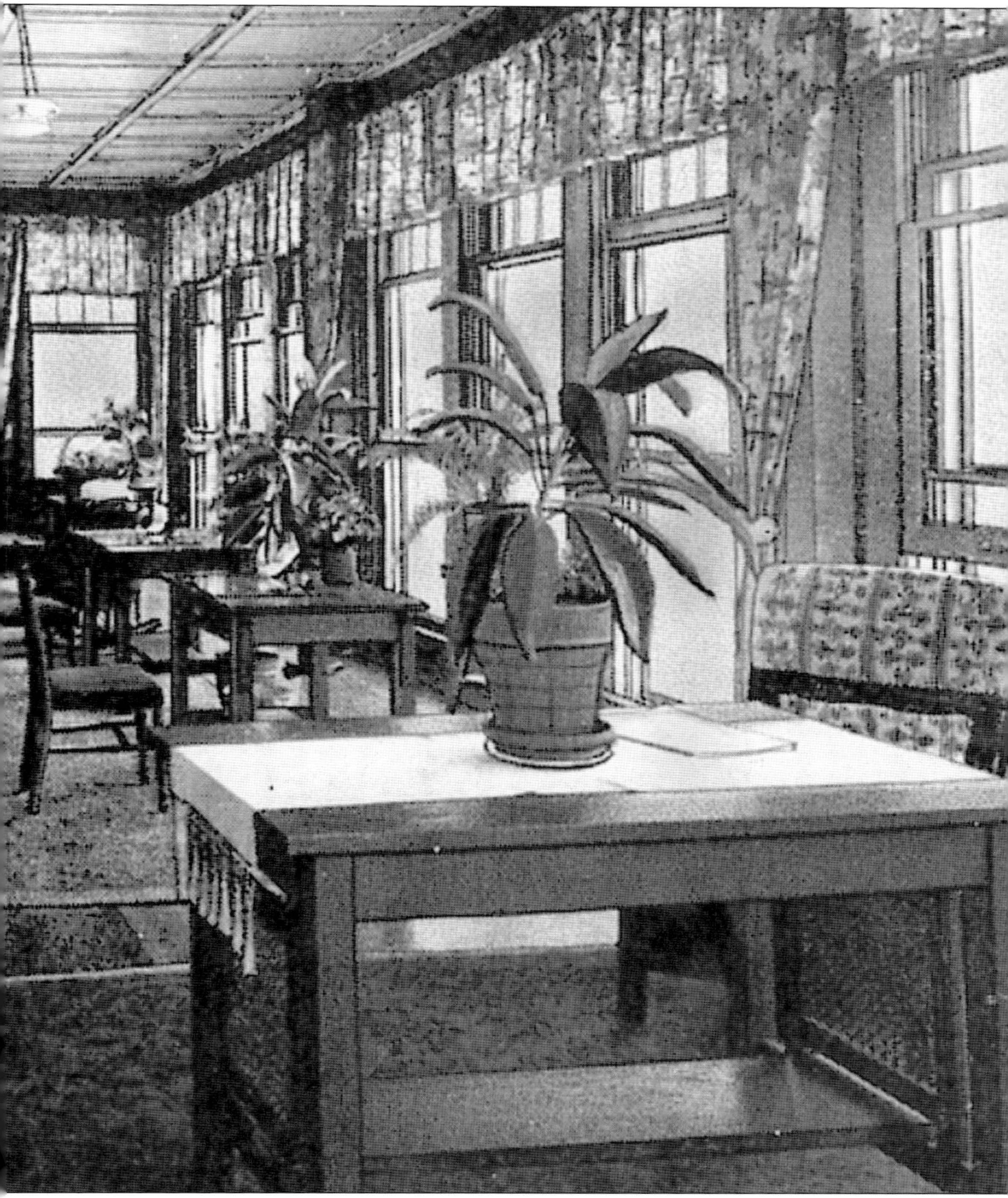

north wing of a new $40,000 hospital. A $350,000 expansion in 1946 added more rooms for a total of 240 beds. Since 1908, the facility has been known by a variety of names, including Adventist Sanitarium, the San, Florida Sanitarium, and The Florida Sanitarium and Hospital. (University of South Florida Special Collections.)

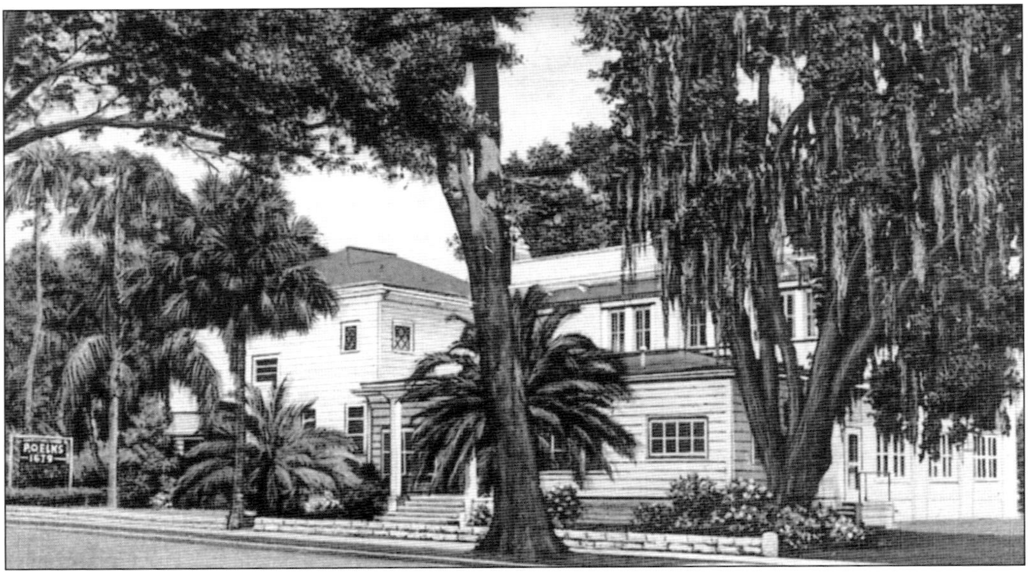

Organized in 1907, Lodge No. 1079, Benevolent and Protective Order of Elks played an active role in Orlando's civic and social life. On January 4, 1918, the *Morning Sentinel* reported, "There will be a dance at the Elks Club tonight. Refreshments will be served and Mr. Umbach has arranged a very nice evening for those who will be present. During the intermission there will be two opera selections." Headquartered in the former residence of Benjamin Drew on Lake Eola, the Elks Home built a $100,000 addition in 1957. (University of South Florida Special Collections.)

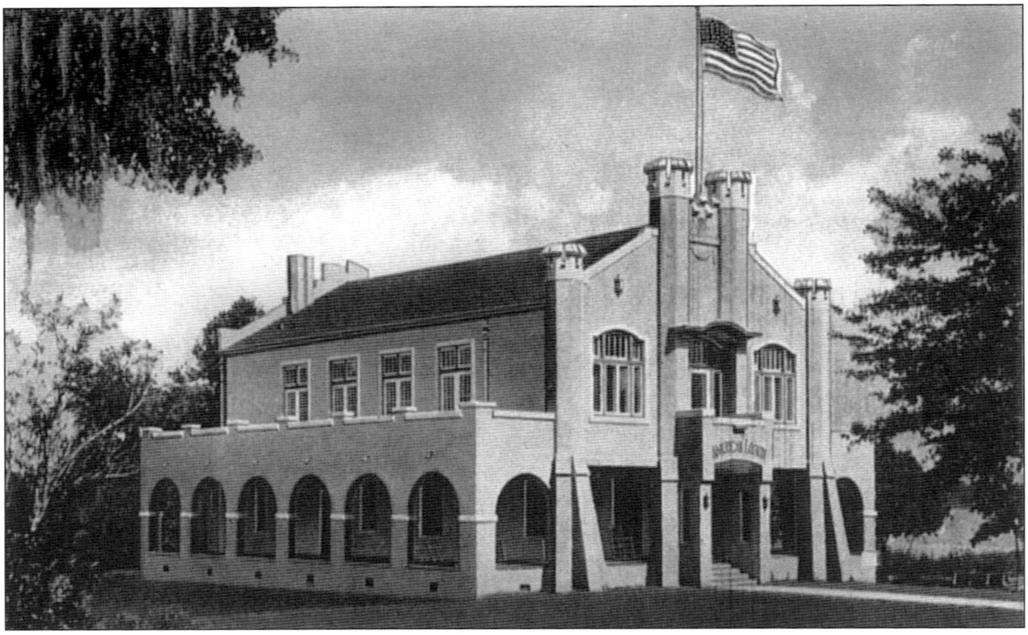

Formed just after World War I, the American Legion was another important fraternal organization in Orlando. In May 1924, the Legion's new home, a $17,500 building on Lake Ivanhoe, was completed, only to be replaced by a new $82,000 structure in 1938. In response to a call for scrap metal donations four years later, the Legion had its World War I German cannon sent to a smelter to be melted into shells to be returned to Hitler piece by piece. (Larry Roberts Antiques.)

Four

Company's Coming

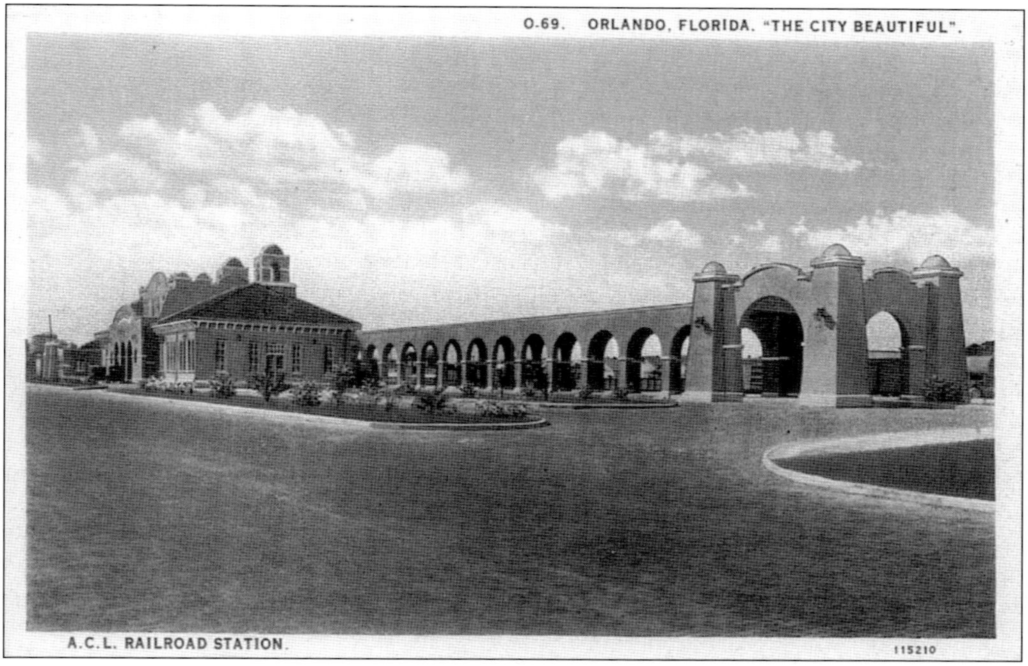

After the railroad came to Orlando in 1880 and further expanded its service in the coming years, large supplies of manufactured goods became more readily available. Opening Florida to newcomers, both permanent and temporary, from all over the country, the railroad was also a major boon to the tourist industry. By 1941, newspaper accounts stated, "Greater Orlando population now totals 50,464 with 40,000 or more visitors coming during the winter months to enjoy its accommodations and climate for one to nine months." Many of those visitors came by rail. From an initial station on West Church and Gertrude Streets for the South Florida Railroad to the beautiful $300,000 Spanish Mission Revival-style Atlantic Coast Line station completed in 1926, the train depot provided newcomers with their first glimpse of Orlando. (Larry Roberts Antiques.)

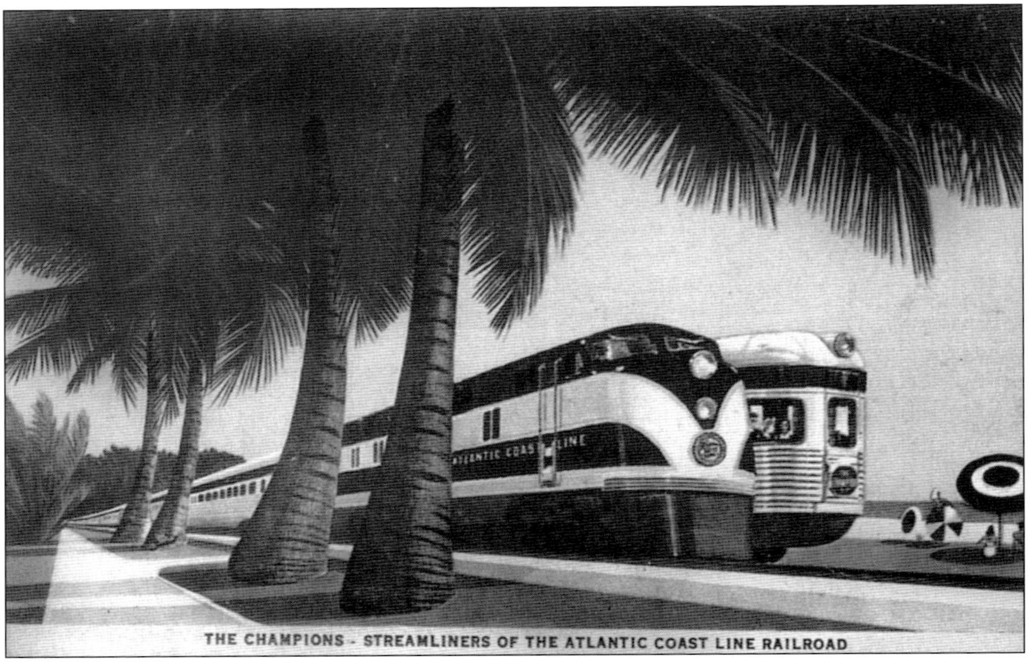

The diesel-powered Streamliners of the Atlantic Coast Line Railroad epitomized the latest in rail travel. Featuring reserved reclining-seat coaches, all-private-room sleeping cars, a tavern-lounge-observation car, and a dining car, the *East Coast Champion* and the *West Coast Champion* offered all of the available amenities, including radio and recorded music. Advertisements promised, "Luxury Coach STREAMLINER (One Night Out) Daily Famous Chicago-Jacksonville Streamliner Leave Chicago 9:40 a.m.; arrive Jacksonville 9:30 a.m.; leave Jacksonville 10:35 a.m.; arrive Orlando 2:55 p.m." (Larry Roberts Antiques.)

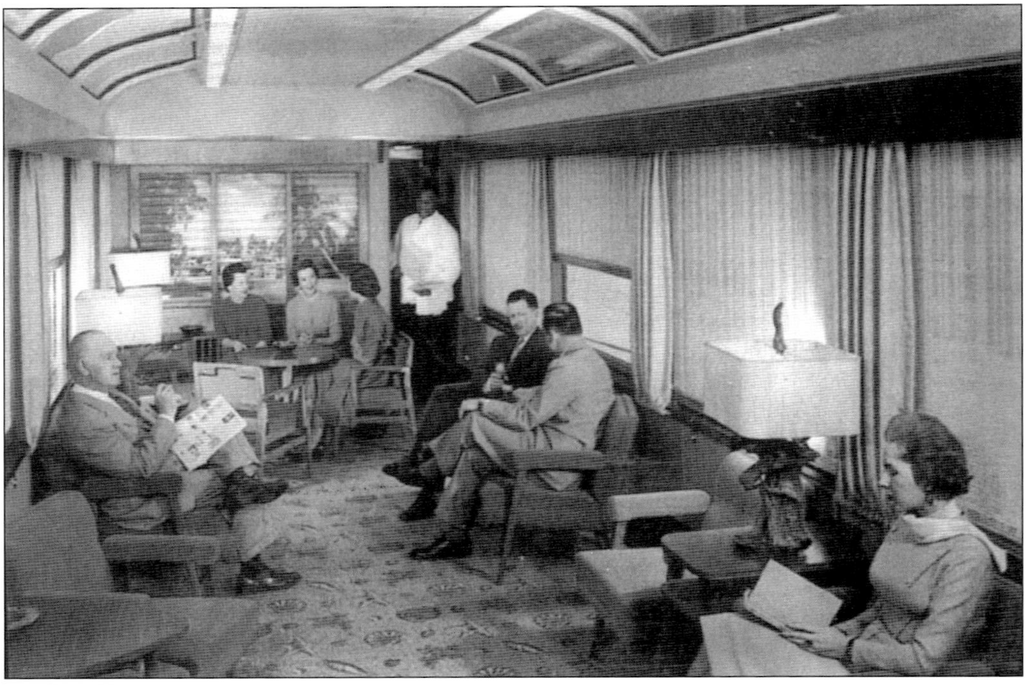

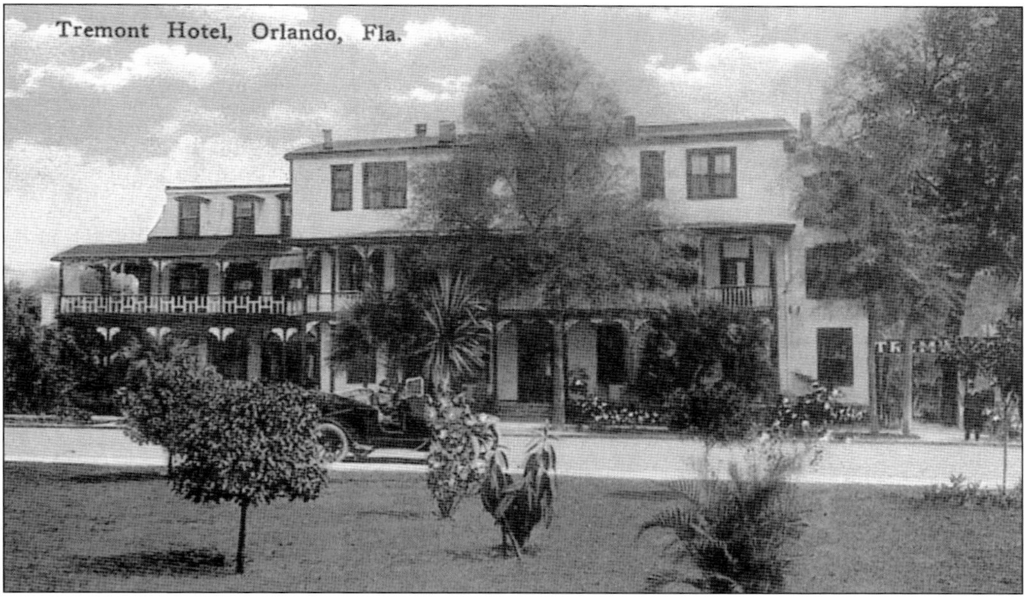

Visitors naturally needed a place to stay—a fact that Captain J.W. Wilmott was quick to recognize in 1895. Combining a portion of the old Charleston House, one of the old Methodist Church buildings, and the old wooden three-story courthouse that had been moved to make way for the new 1892 courthouse, he created the Tremont Hotel on the northeast corner of Church and Main Streets. Sixty years later, the hotel would be razed for a parking lot. (Larry Roberts Antiques.)

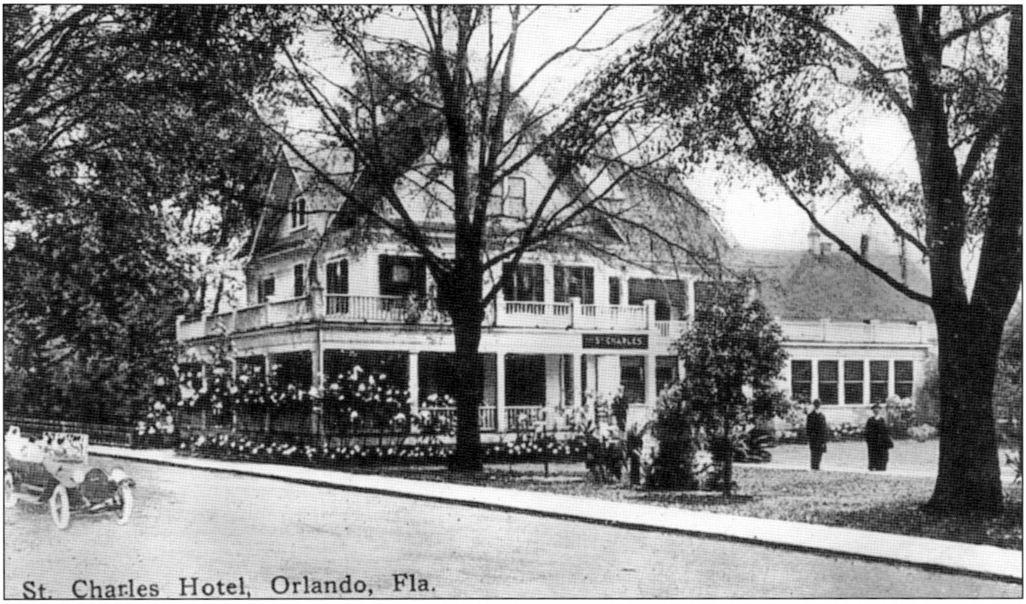

The St. Charles Hotel exemplified the term "adaptive reuse." Originally belonging to Dr. R.L. Harris, the North Orange Avenue property in 1908 was converted into a hotel. In January 1927, the hotel's restaurant offered a special Sunday menu that included a cocktail of Chesapeake Bay oysters or Florida fruit, relish, soup, choice of entrees (broiled bass, roast Southern capon, grilled French lamb chops, grilled Texas ham, prime rib of beef, etc.) vegetables, salad, dessert, and beverage. The cost—$1. (University of South Florida Special Collections.)

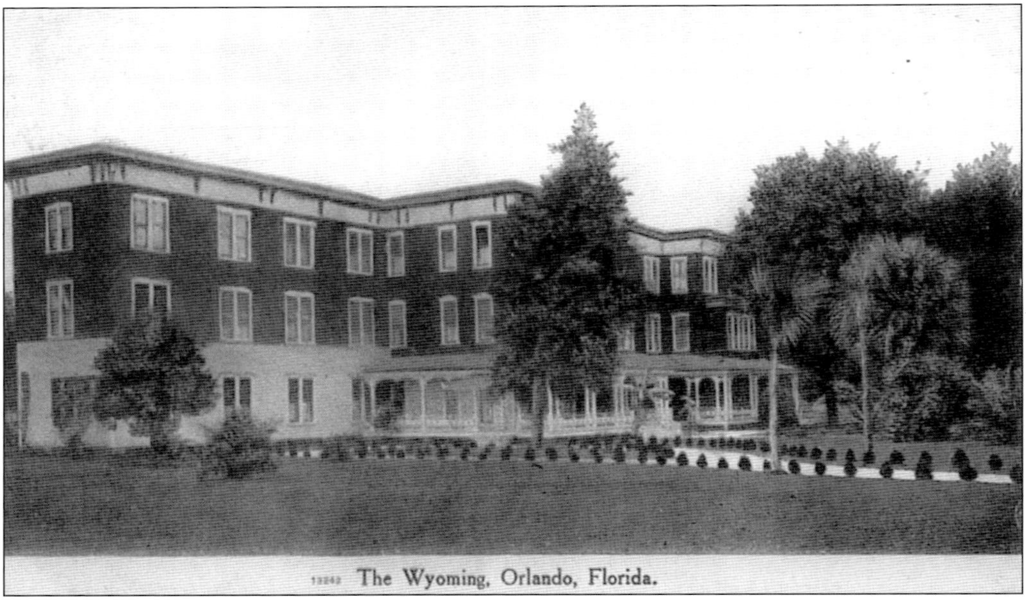

In 1900, the former residence of Nat Poyntz at 424 Magnolia Avenue was converted into a 15-room hotel. Four years later, A.P. Miller expanded the property into the Hotel Wyoming, named for the Wyoming Valley in Pennsylvania. With Murray King as the project architect, Miller's son DeWitt built a $40,000 three-story addition in 1923 for a total of 110 rooms. The wicker chairs on the front porch served as one of the trademarks of a hotel that catered to "many of the important figures of the financial and social world." By 1941, advertisements read: "American Plan Exclusively—November to May. Located in a tropical park, Hotel Wyoming offers quiet and rest within walking distance of shops and entertainment. Bedrooms attractively furnished, steam heated, all with private bath, elevator service. Table and service of unusual excellence. Well-rounded entertainment program." (Larry Roberts Antiques.)

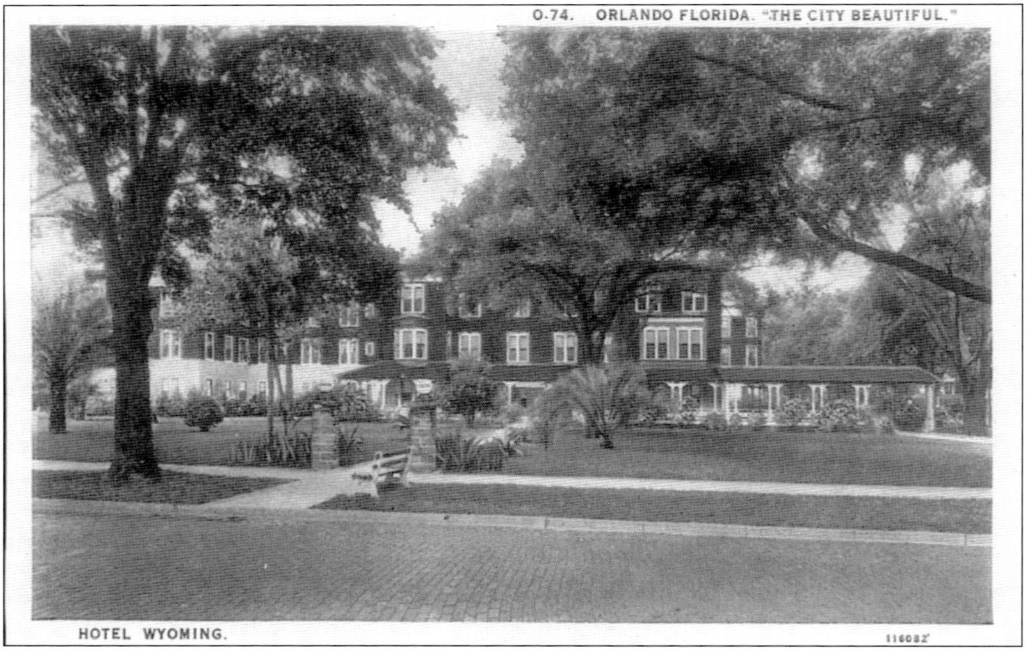

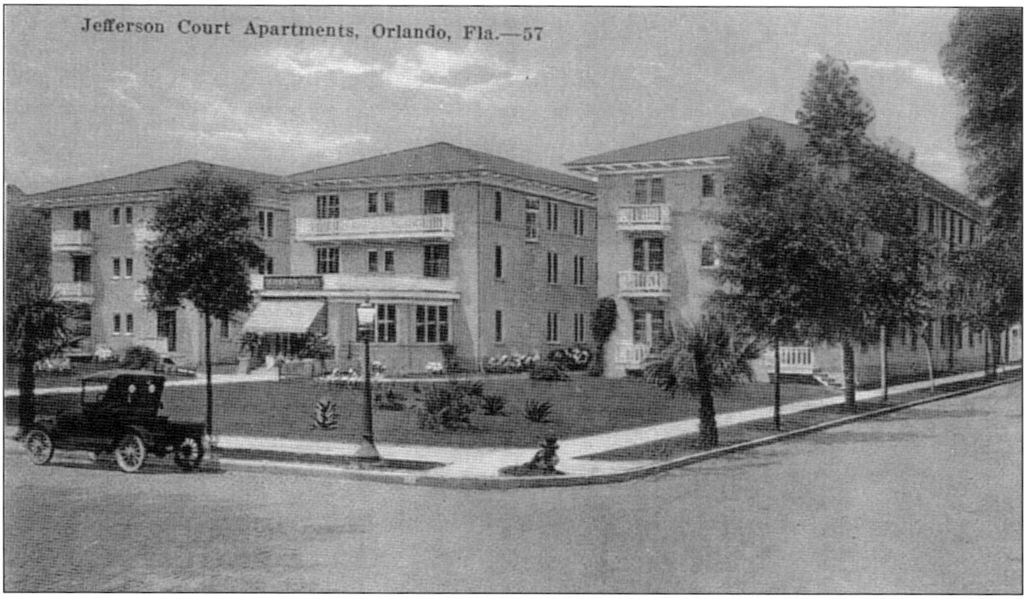

For visitors who desired larger accommodations, the Jefferson Court Hotel and Apartments offered a solution. Completed in 1918, the $125,000 project was funded by a group of local businessmen. According to advertisements, "Jefferson Court Hotel provides the utmost in service and hospitality. Conveniently situated on Orange Avenue in downtown Orlando, yet secluded within its own beautiful and restful gardens away from all noise and traffic. Citrus fruits of all kinds are grown in the Jefferson Court gardens. Jefferson Court is of modern fireproof construction. Rooms and apartments are beautifully furnished, complete in every detail. A large number of apartments are equipped with modern refrigeration and complete kitchenette with four-burner gas range, bake oven, and everything necessary for housekeeping. Bedrooms are provided with double or twin beds with box springs and innerspring mattresses." (Larry Roberts Antiques.)

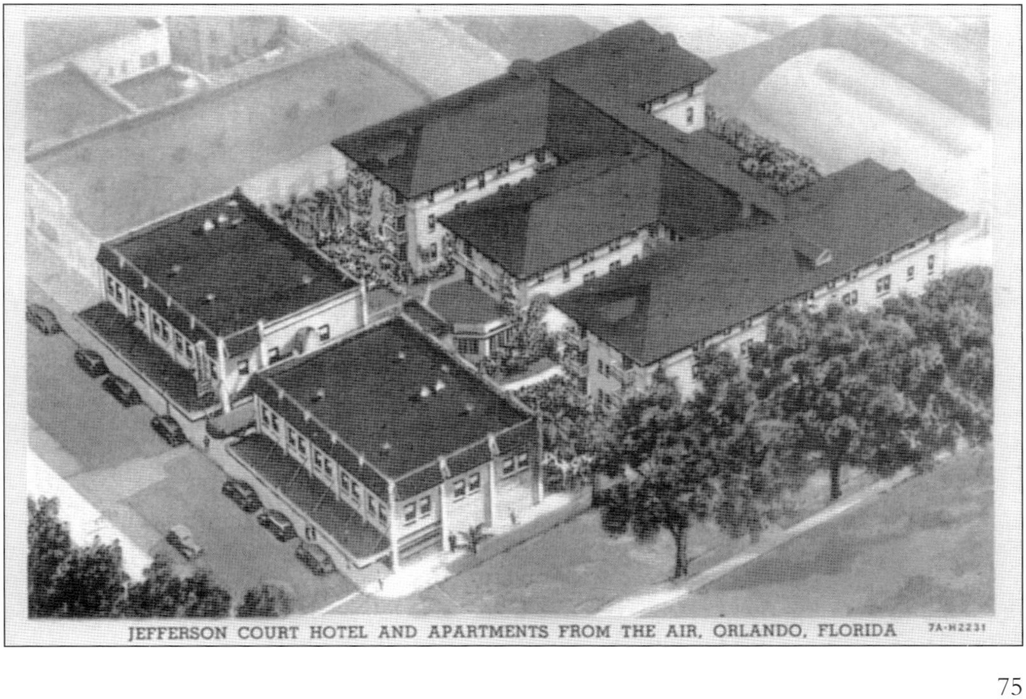

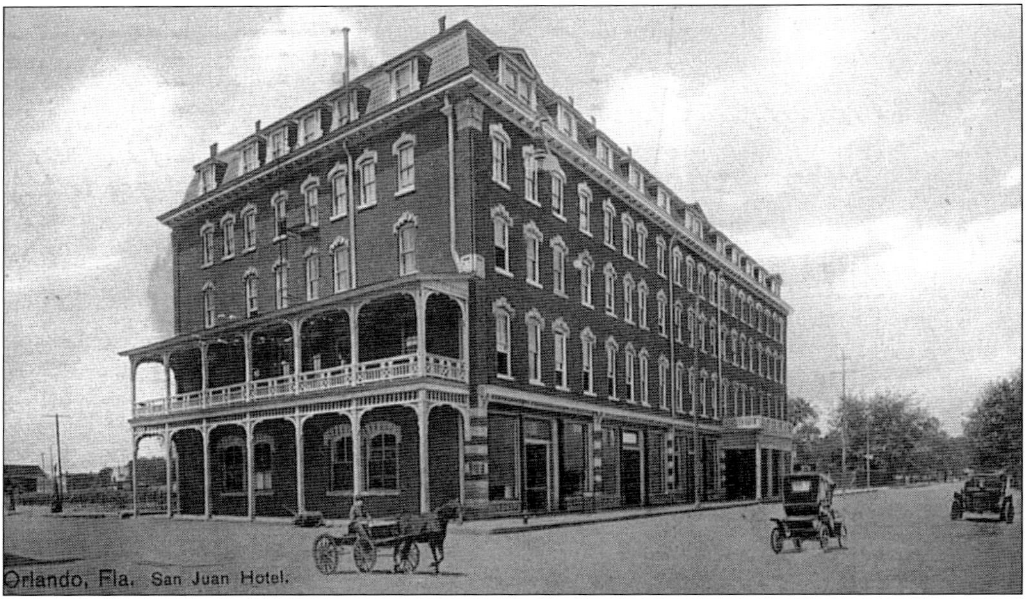

In 1885, Henry Kedney built one of the largest hotels in the state, the three-story San Juan de Ulloa Hotel. Eight years later, Harry Beeman, heir to the chewing gum fortune, purchased the San Juan and immediately added two stories to the hotel in the first of an ongoing series of improvements. A veranda added to the north side in 1903 quickly became a favorite gathering place for local businessmen. Improvements in 1914 included the addition of sample rooms for salesmen, a laundry, 20 private baths, and conversion of the corner barbershop into a cafe. Newspaper accounts routinely mentioned guests at the hotel, saying, "Mr. and Mrs. Paul W. Orchard arrived from the North yesterday and stopped at the San Juan Hotel." On other occasions, the paper reported stays by various notables, such as, "A prominent Floridian arriving yesterday was Mr. J.E. Ingraham, general superintendent of the Florida East Coast Railway. He stopped overnight at the San Juan Hotel." (Larry Roberts Antiques.)

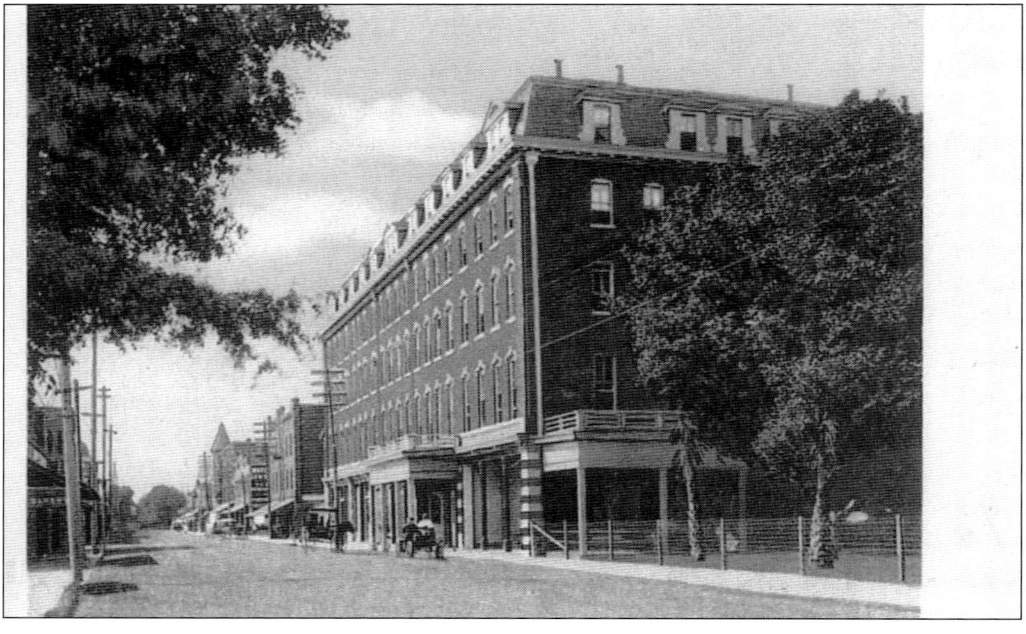

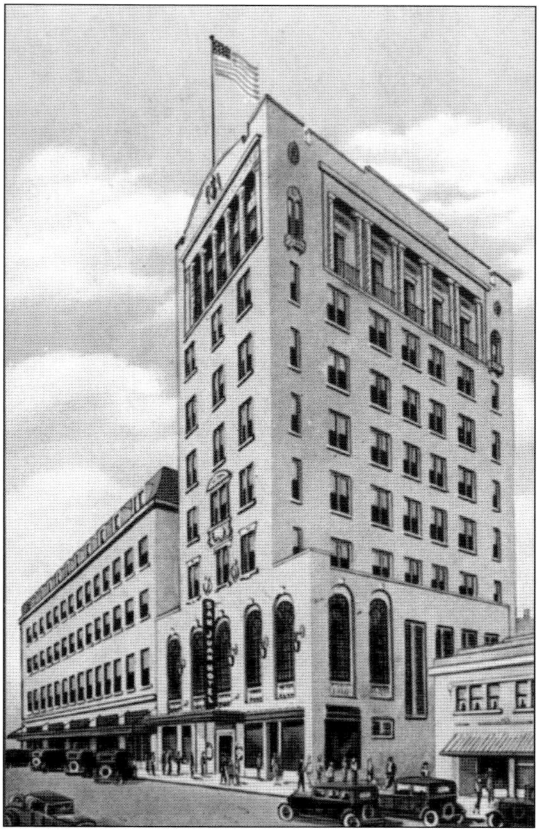

Awarded in 1922, a $357,000 contract for an eight-story addition further enhanced the San Juan's position as the preeminent hotel in Orlando. A new drugstore, the San Juan Pharmacy, also began operation in the hotel. The following year, the Violet Dell florist shop and a men's store opened in the San Juan; S.Y. Way and I.N. Burman signed a 99-year lease for operation of the hotel. In October 1932, Morrison's Cafeteria took over operation of the hotel's dining room. (University of South Florida Special Collections.)

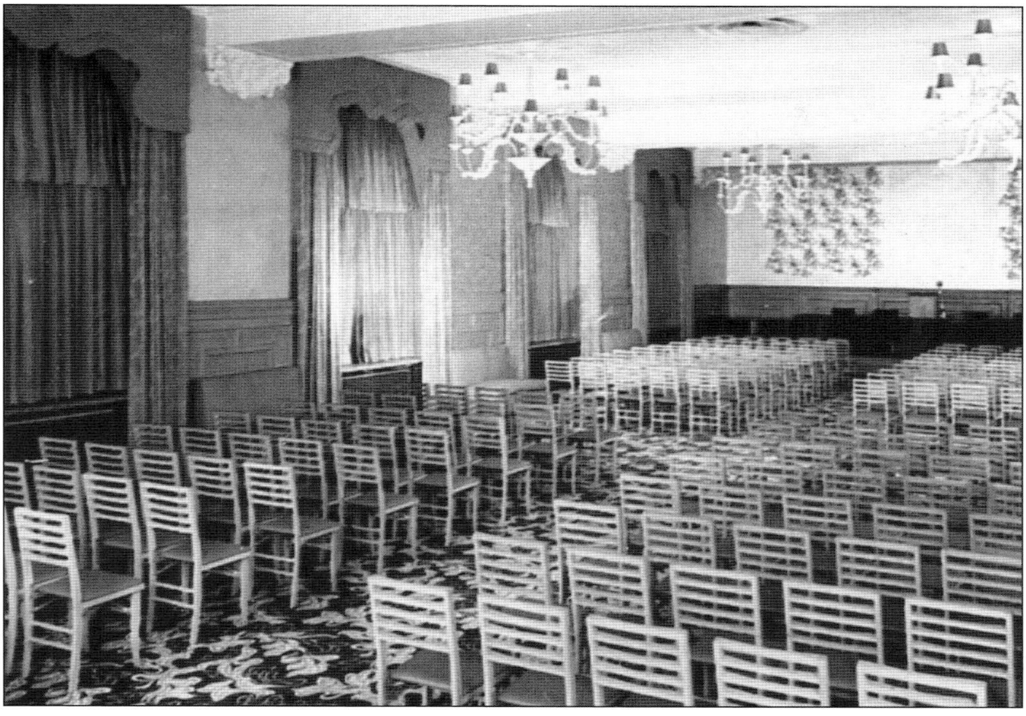

Before that 99-year lease would expire, hard times would force the closing of the hotel. Prior to that sad occasion, however, the San Juan's Grand Ballroom was the scene of hundreds of social functions, banquets, and business meetings. Seating up to 400 people in an auditorium setting, the ballroom could accommodate as many as 325 guests at a banquet. (University of South Florida Special Collections.)

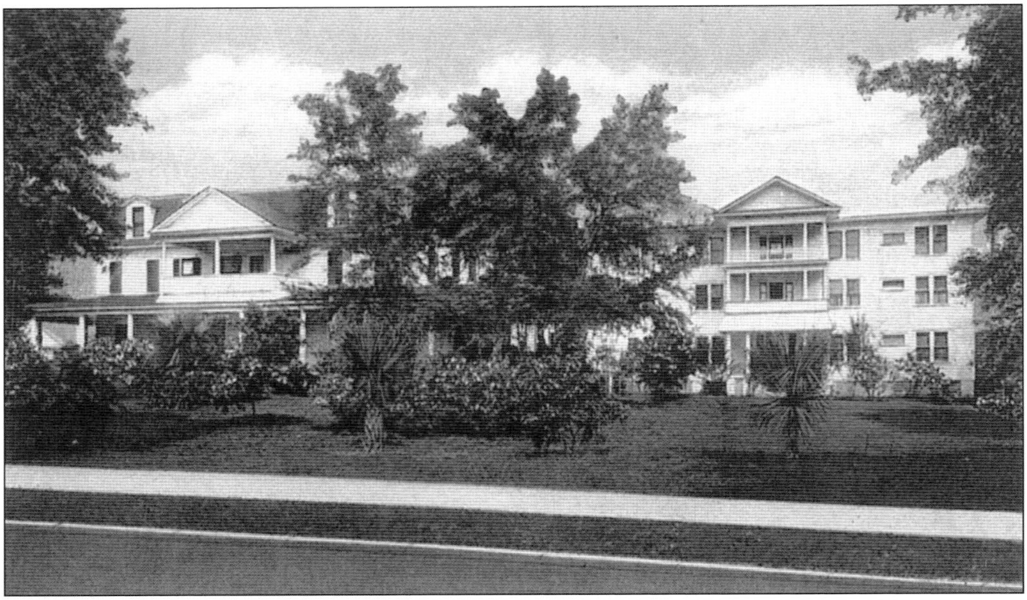

The Lucerne Hotel was another of Orlando's early hotels. After a fire in 1886 destroyed the original hotel on the north side of Lake Lucerne, the new Lucerne Hotel was built on the corner of South and Main Streets. John Rowland, the builder, added 30 more rooms in 1910, enlarging the hotel to the size pictured on this postcard. (Larry Roberts Antiques.)

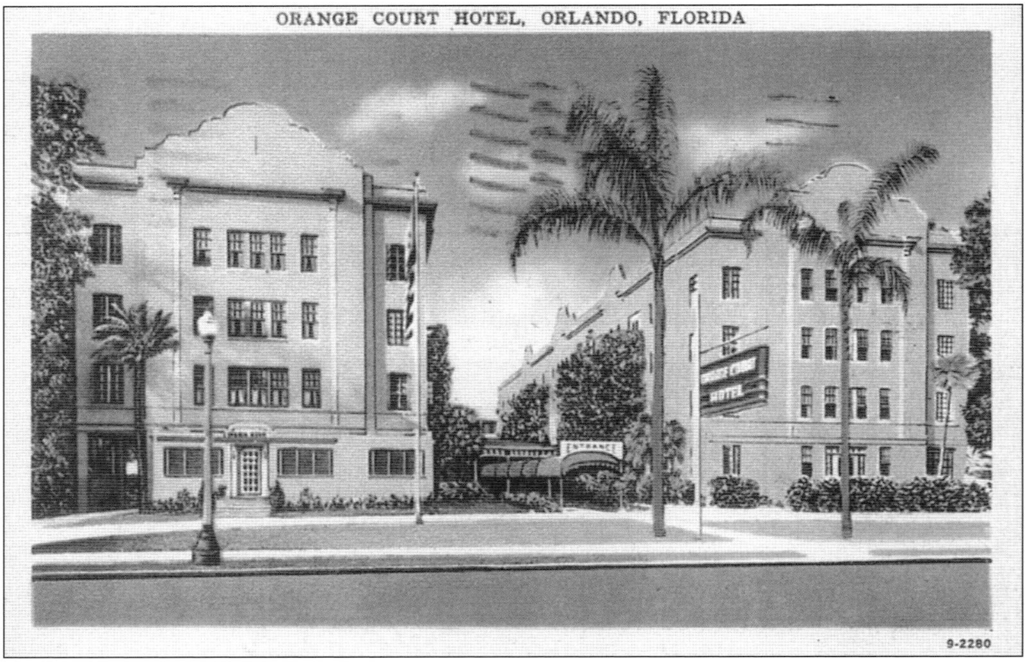

Officially opening on March 4, 1924, the Spanish Revival–style Orange Court Hotel was begun a year earlier by R.E. Grabel and J.N. Wigfall. In 1927 the Orlando *Morning Sentinel* carried ads that promised, "Apartments ranging in price from $100 per month upwards according to size and location, with full hotel service. It really is not expensive to live at the Orange Court." (Larry Roberts Antiques.)

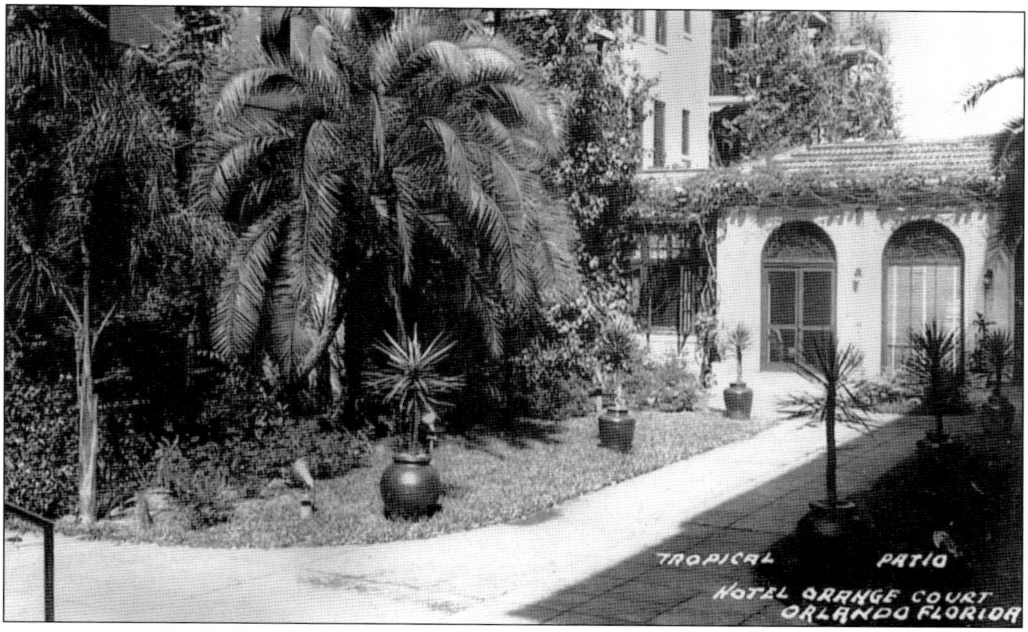

Located on North Orange Avenue between Colonial Drive and Concord Avenue, the Orange Court promoted itself by saying, "The Orange Court, scenic Central Florida's finest hotel, is a modern, fireproof, soundproof building of 175 rooms, served by four elevators, every accommodation with private bath. It is located within walking distance of Orlando's splendid shopping and theatre district and the city recreational centers. Both hotel units and completely equipped housekeeping apartments are available. Other Orange Court attractions include a spacious sun parlor, a game room, a ballroom, a grand indoor swimming pool, free parking space, and beautiful grounds complete with tropical gardens. Dining facilities include an attractive main dining room, private dining rooms for parties, and a banquet room. A uniform standard of quality and service is maintained the year around." (Larry Roberts Antiques and University of South Florida Special Collections.)

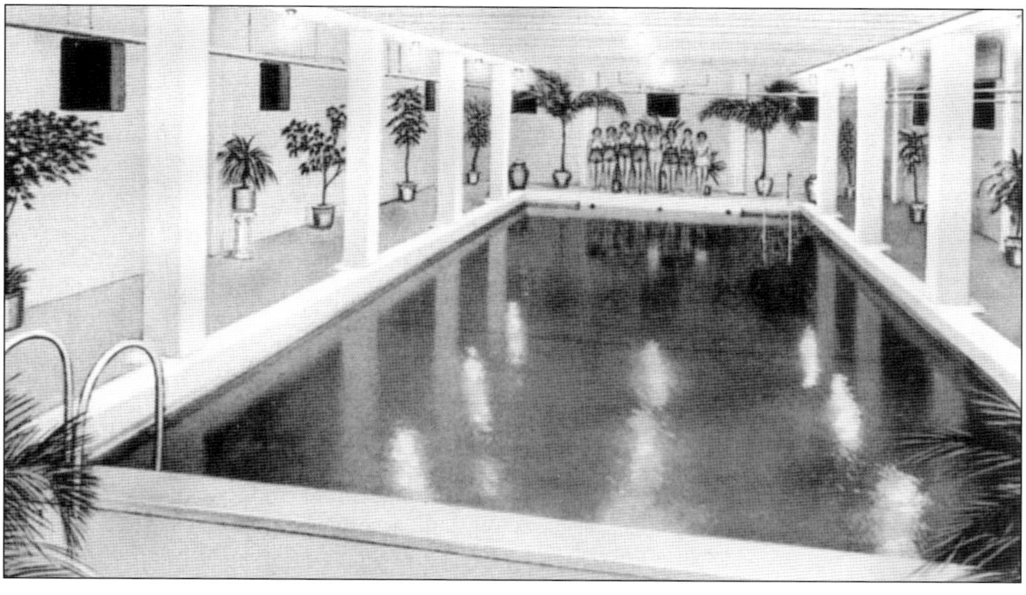

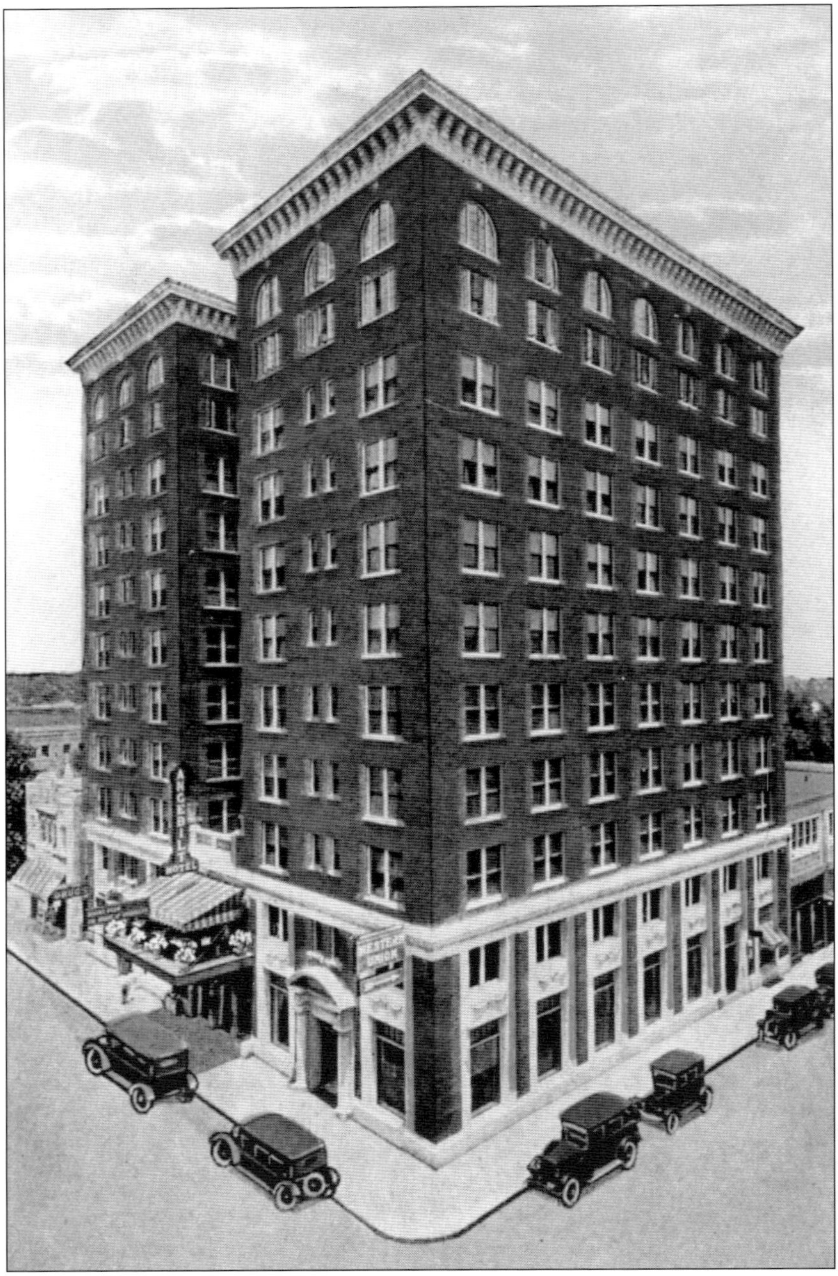

Most of Orlando's elite society attended the formal opening, on March 14, 1923, of the Angebilt Hotel. The Orange Bank & Trust Company announced plans to move in just weeks later. Designed by architect Murray S. King, the 11-story, 240-room skyscraper, with its heavy, bracketed cornice and cut stone trim at the ground and mezzanine levels, quickly became Orlando's leading commercial hotel. Nevertheless, two months after the opening, J.F. Ange sold his interest in the hotel and severed all connections with the project bearing his name. A syndicate of Orlando businessmen eventually purchased the hotel for $1,250,000 in November 1924. By January 1927, Tom Moore, the hotel's manager, was offering "New Year's Dinner at The Angebilt—$2.00; dining room open all day." (University of South Florida Special Collections.)

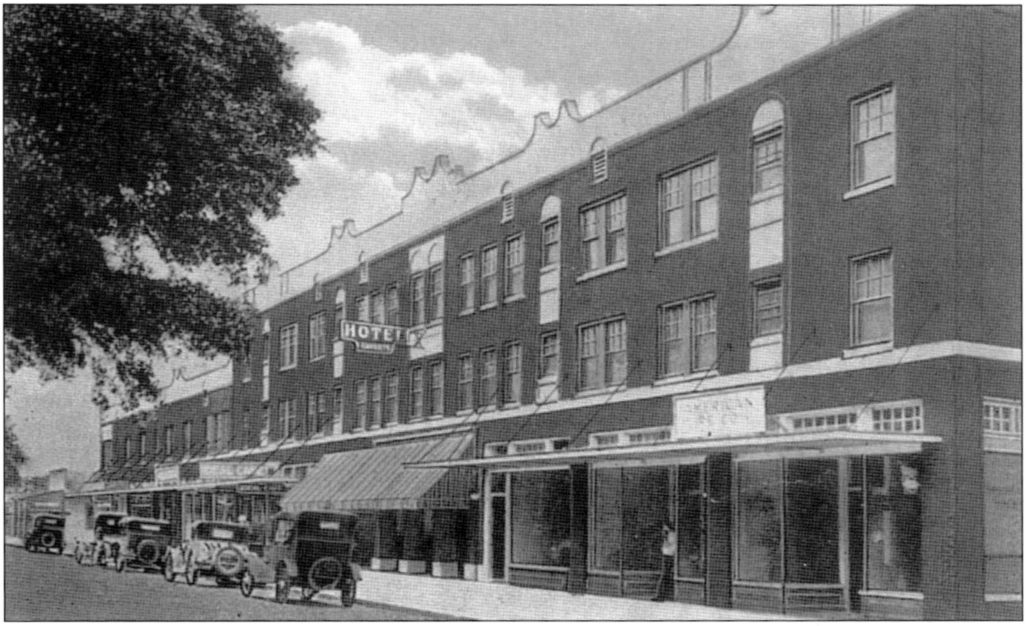

As the Florida land boom of the 1920s brought an increasing number of visitors to Orlando, entrepreneurs saw a need for additional hotel space. The Hotel Roberts opened in November 1924 on West Central Avenue. Unfortunately, the crash and resulting depression were soon to follow. When the economy finally began to show improvement, the hotel sold for $60,000 in 1938 amid plans for remodeling and expansion. (Larry Roberts Antiques.)

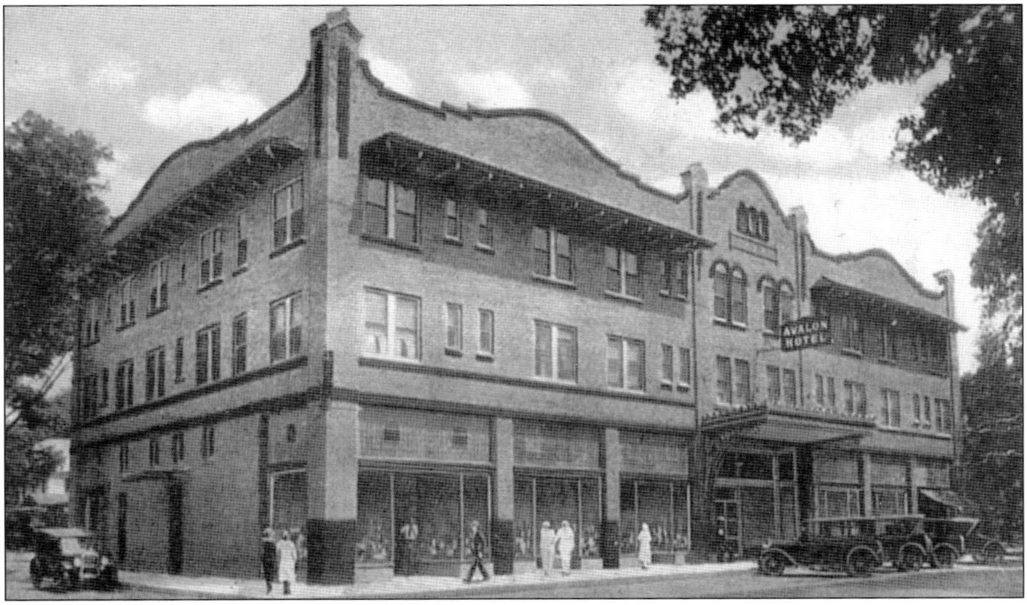

The Avalon Hotel, with 60 rooms plus 7 stores on the ground floor, was a similar situation. Opening in April 1925 at the corner of North Orange and Amelia Avenues, the three-story $225,000 hotel was owned by the U.G. Staton Company. In 1955, a fire caused by overloaded electrical circuits destroyed the hotel, which was insured at that point for only $90,000, a fraction of its original cost 30 years earlier. (Larry Roberts Antiques.)

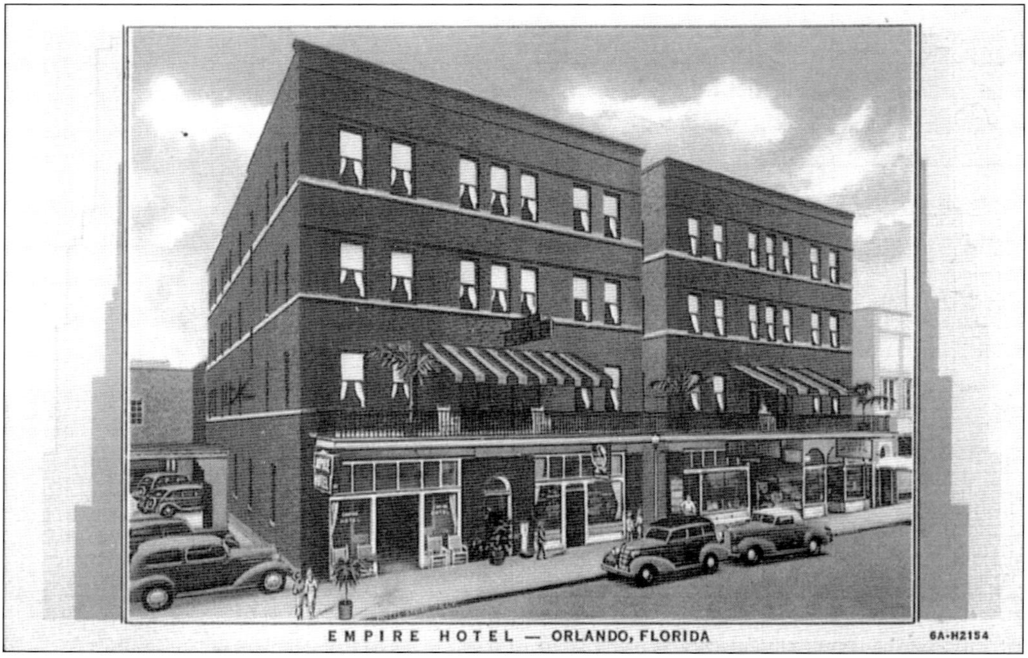

The Empire Hotel was just one of the many enterprises of James B. Magruder, owner of the Magruder Arcade, Lucerne Theatre, and other properties. Billing itself as "Orlando's Most Popular Medium Priced Hotel," the Empire was located at 28 West Central Avenue. In 1922, the hotel was the site of a reception for the stars of *Broad Road*, the first motion picture filmed by the Associated Authors Production Company. Coincidentally, the Empire Hotel's manager, R.E. Grabel, had just been elected president of the film group. (Larry Roberts Antiques.)

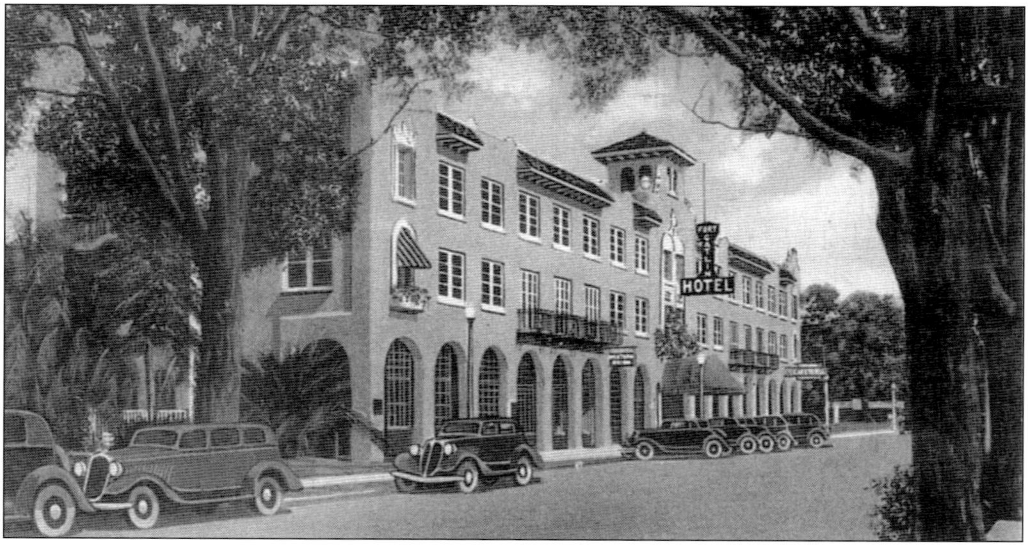

Advertising "150 Rooms, Elegantly Furnished—with Bath," the Hotel Fort Gatlin at 545 North Orange Avenue was built in 1925 at a cost of $600,000. The hotel served as the location of radio station WDBO studios; in 1949, it also became the home of WHOO studios. For many years, the Hotel Fort Gatlin claimed to be "Orlando's Favorite for Breakfast, Lunch, and Dinner." It was demolished in 1965 to make way for offices. (Larry Roberts Antiques.)

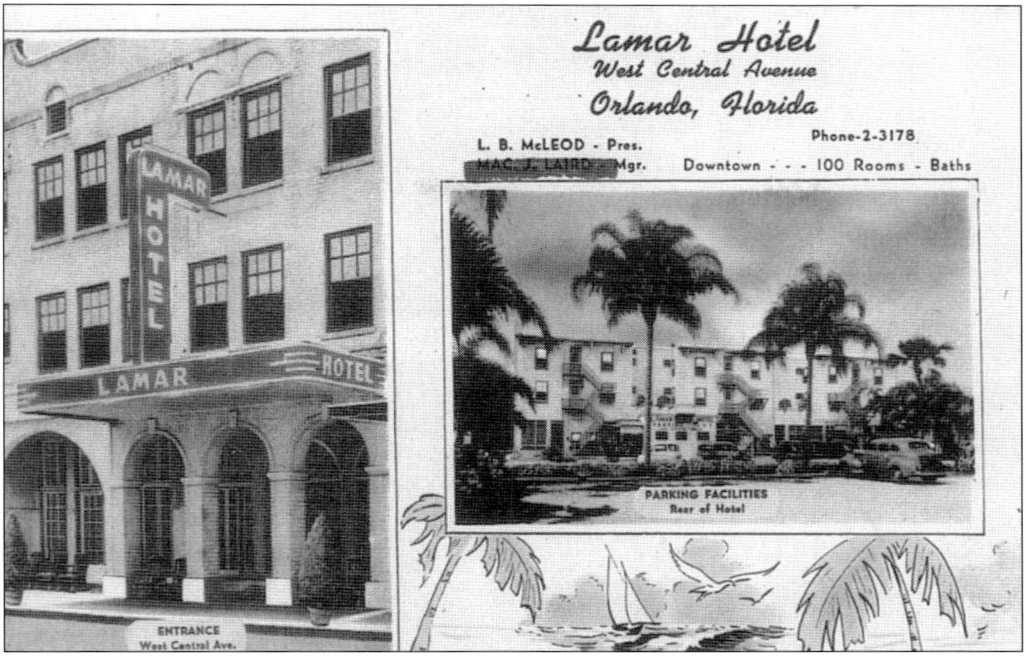

"In the 'Heart' of Orlando's Business and Tourist Center. A very good Hotel with a Year Round Rate! The Lamar Hotel in the HEART of the Business, Tourist and Church Center of 'The City Beautiful,' Orlando, Fla. invites you and your friends to headquarter here, to direct others to the Lamar Hotel. 'Once a guest, Always a booster.' Sample rooms, conventions, meetings, banquets up to one hundred people. Coffee Shoppe and Restaurant in the building." (Larry Roberts Antiques.)

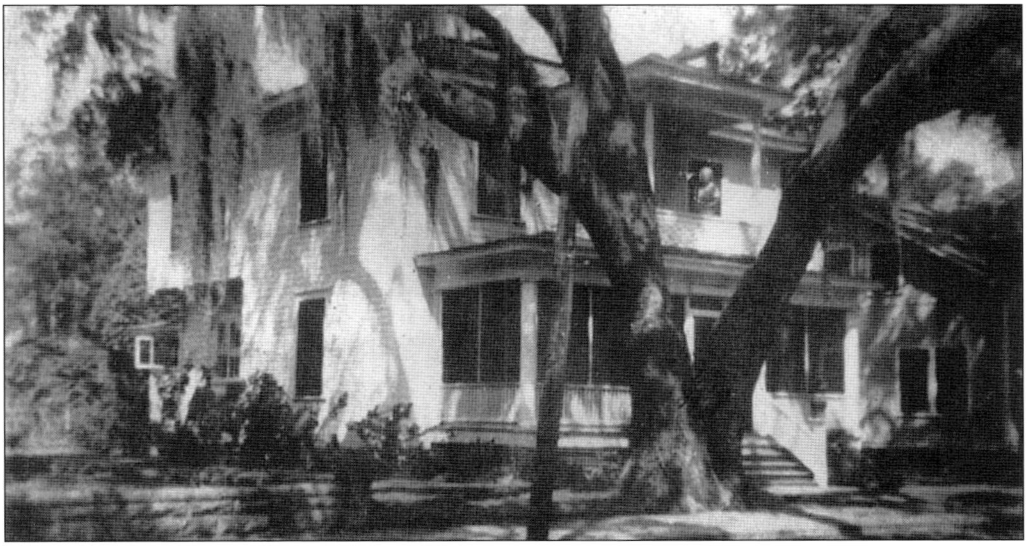

Terming itself "A Tourist Home for Christian Scientists," Twin Oaks provided guests with accommodations at the rate of $18 single, $20 double, including breakfast. Under the management of Minnie Wilson Cutler, Twin Oaks also offered all-day auto trips to nearby communities. No smoking was permitted, either on the porch or in the house! Under a unique ordinance that lasted until 1932, Orlando required that all Christian Science practitioners be licensed by the city. (Larry Roberts Antiques.)

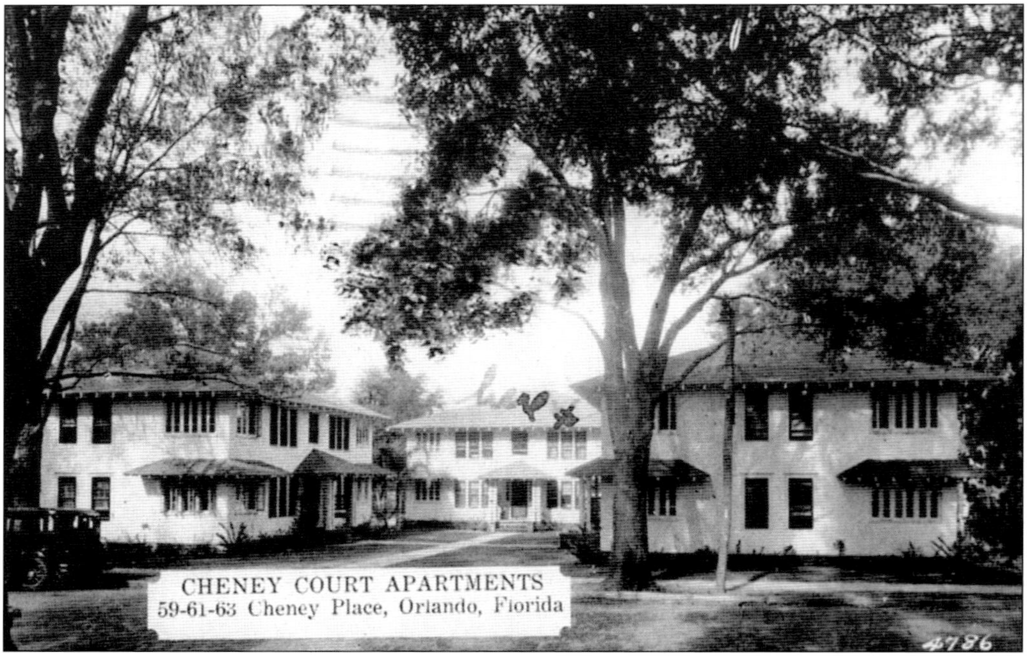

Arriving around Thanksgiving and staying until after the Easter holidays, many winter visitors were really part-year residents. Orlando not only welcomed the "snowbirds," but actually took special steps to attract them. For example, no charge was made for the children of winter visitors entered in Orlando public schools. For tourists planning to spend the entire "season" in Orlando, accommodations such as the Cheney Court Apartments could prove to be more affordable, as well as more spacious, than a hotel room. Likewise, the Allardice Arms Apartment Hotel offered "New DeLuxe Housekeeping Apartments, close to Recreation Facilities and Shopping District" and billed itself as the ideal place to stay while visiting "The City Beautiful." (University of South Florida Special Collections and Larry Roberts Antiques.)

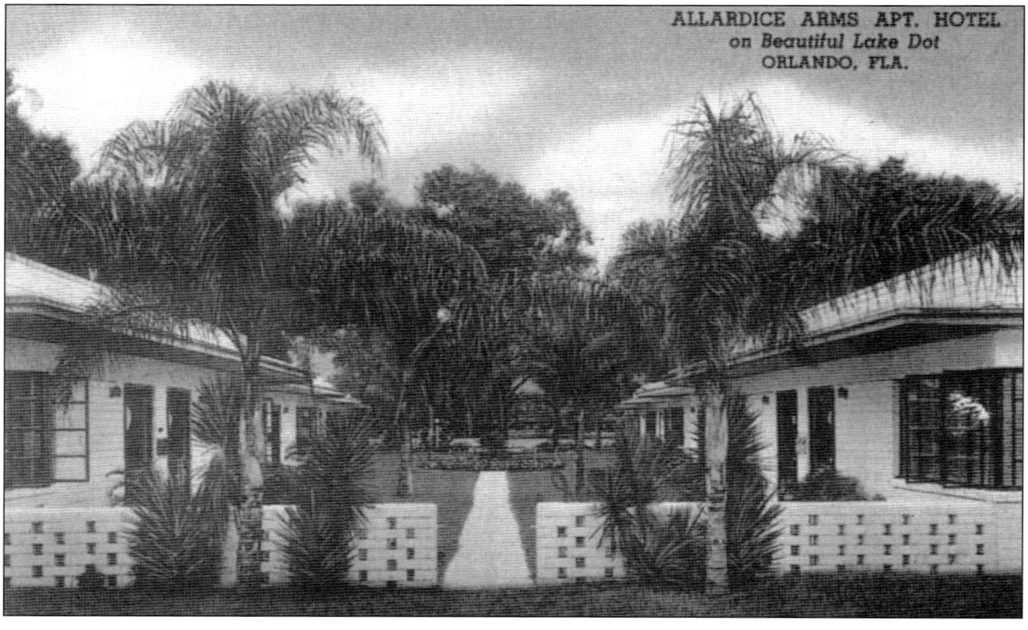

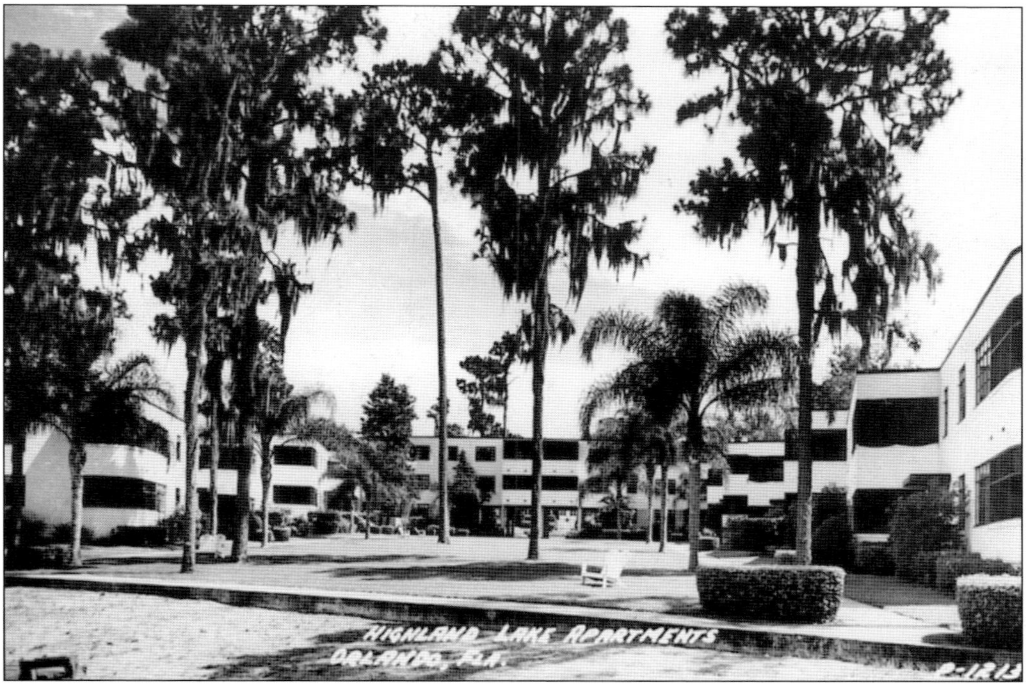

Located on beautiful Lake Highland at 605 Marks Street, the Highland Lake Apartments offered "special attractive rates for the winter season now." Costing $300,000 to build in 1939, the Art Deco–style apartments were advertised as being "New, modern, fireproof, lake front, steam heated, and convenient." On the corner of Marks Street and Highland Avenue, the Bayonet Apartments bragged about "A Distinguished Address" and a location in a quiet residential section close to the heart of town. "All apartments in this new and beautiful building are air conditioned. Each unit has a living room, one or two bedrooms, and a complete kitchen. Garages and laundry room are attached." (University of South Florida Special Collections and Larry Roberts Antiques.)

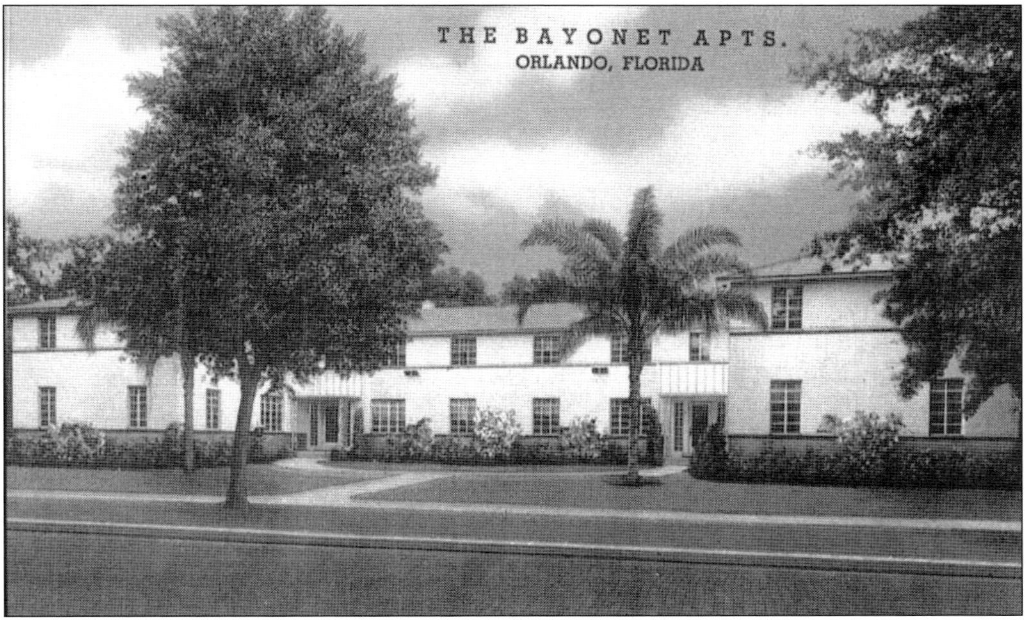

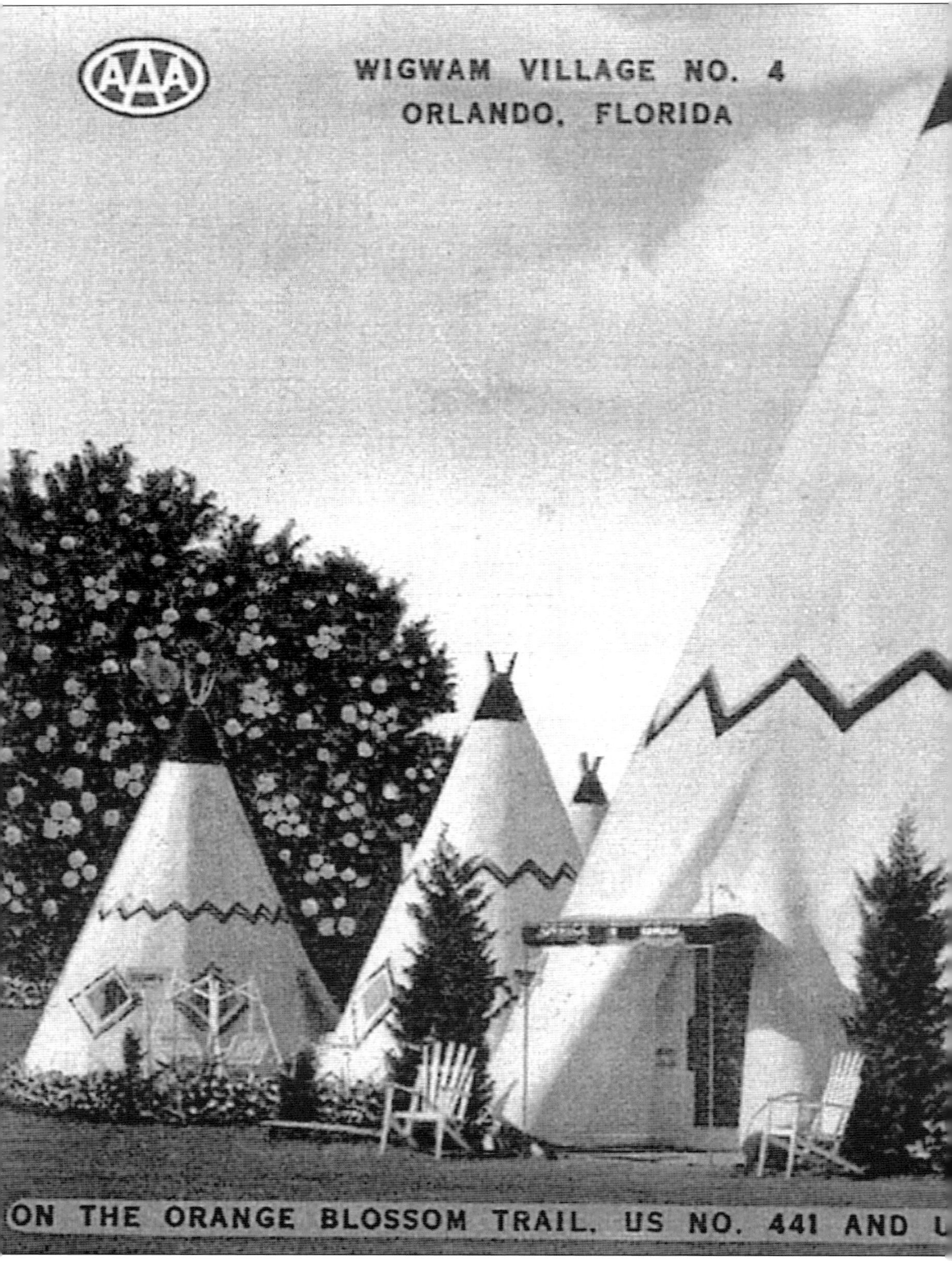
AAA
WIGWAM VILLAGE NO. 4
ORLANDO, FLORIDA
ON THE ORANGE BLOSSOM TRAIL, US NO. 441 AND

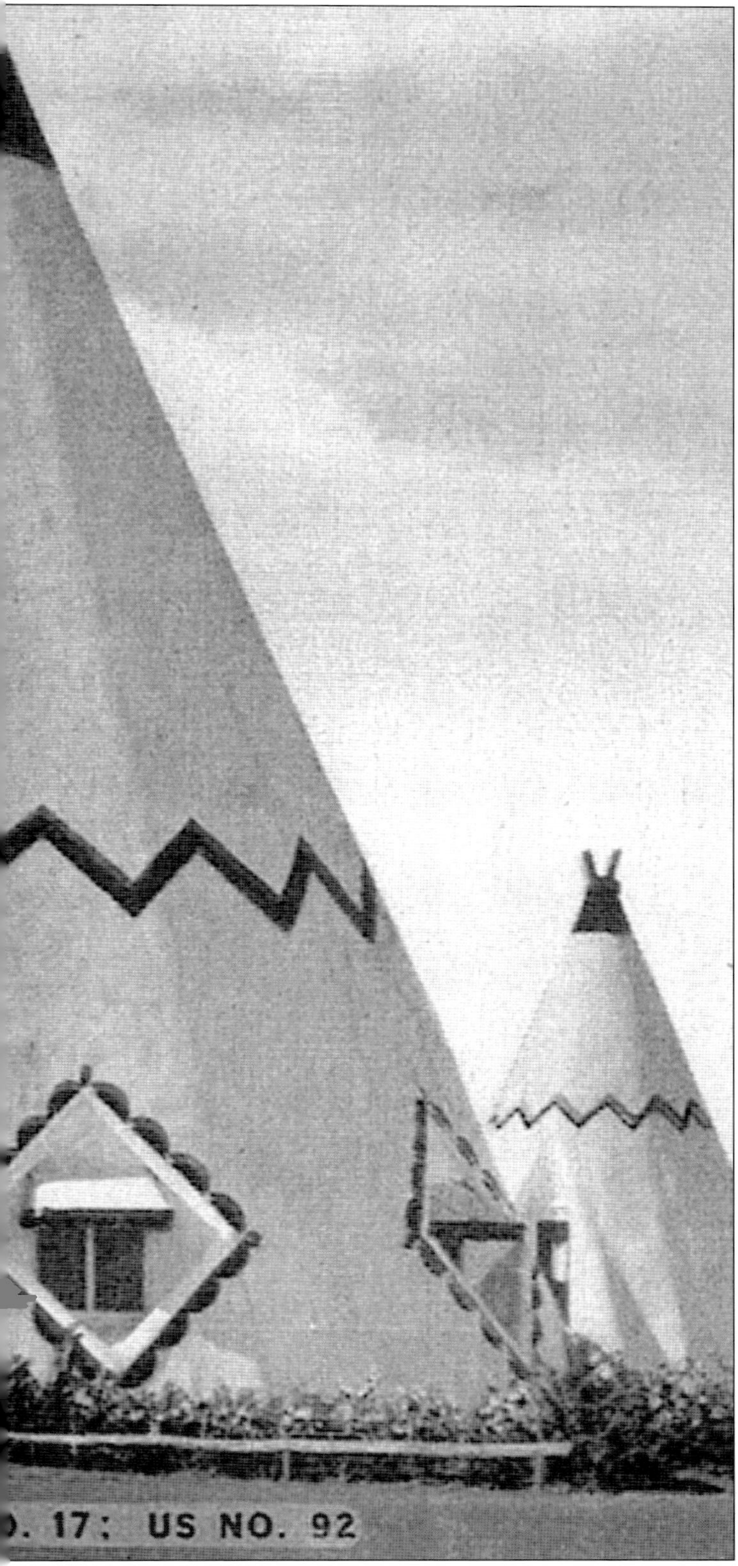

For those with an adventurous spirit or a longing for the Wild West, one enterprising businessman in Orlando had the solution—the Wigwam Village. Mom and Pop Hutton operated a complex that included a grille, gift shop, and auto service, as well as "31 modern teepees with accommodations for parties of 1, 2, 3, or 4 people." Constructed in the late 1930s, Wigwam Village would be removed in 1973 to make way for a Days Inn at the corner of Orange Blossom Trail and I-4. Until then, however, billing itself as "Orlando's largest and finest motel," it was certainly one of the city's most distinctive places to stay. In the words of the sender of this postcard, "Where I was put up last night. Very interesting." (Larry Roberts Antiques.)

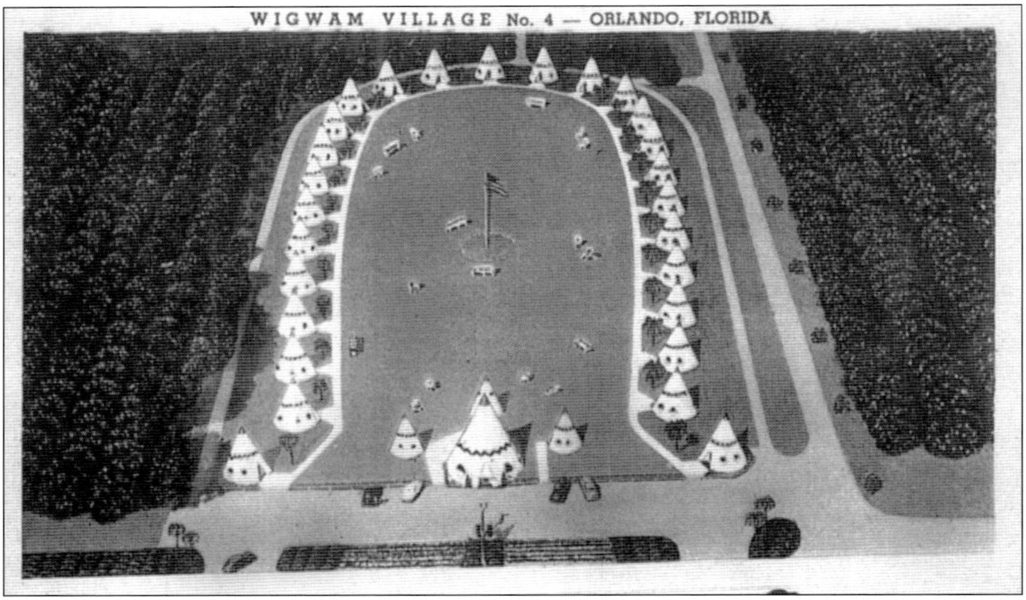

For a vacation experience with a difference, one had to travel no further than the Orange Blossom Trail. "WIGWAM VILLAGES offer you unique tourist accommodations with modern comfort. A one-stop service giving the best in lodging, food, auto service, and gift shop. Known from coast to coast. Located inside the city limits only a few blocks from theatre and shopping district." (Larry Roberts Antiques.)

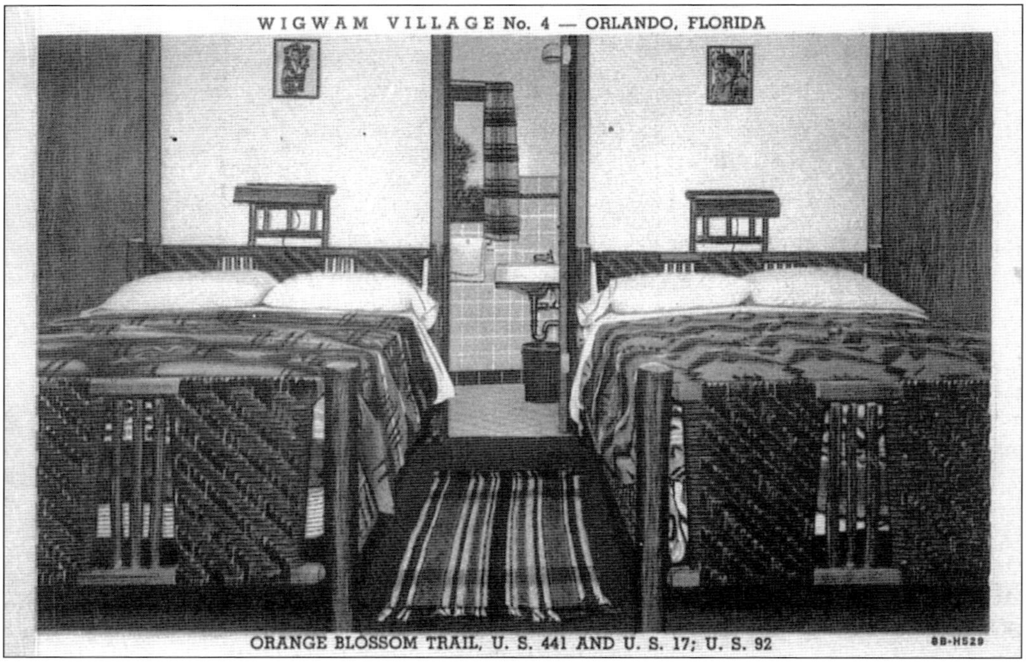

Surrounded by orange groves, Wigwam Village offered guests a chance to "EAT AND SLEEP IN A WIGWAM. A novel, unique, and modern motor court that offers an atmosphere of comfort, cleanliness, and refinement. A tile bath, radio, ceiling fan, and heater for each Sleeping Wigwam. All furniture of rustic, solid hickory wood. Fireproof." (Larry Roberts Antiques.)

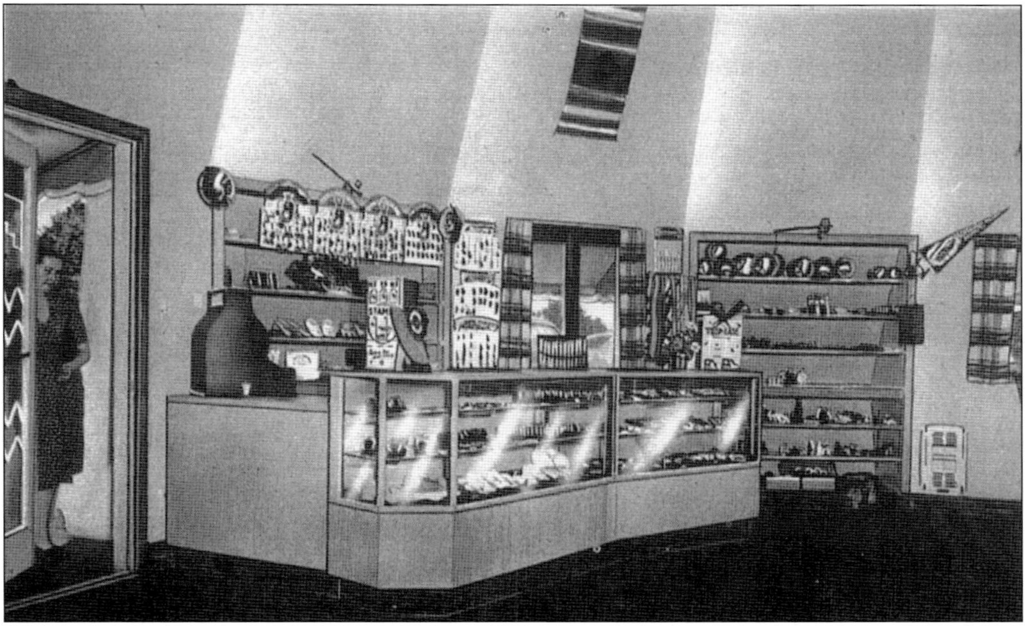

For a little refreshment, guests had to search no further than "THE WIGWAM GRILLE located inside a modern, air-cooled teepee, 50 feet tall and 40 feet across base. Latest type stainless steel kitchen for preparation of finest in steaks, seafood, and sandwiches. All citrus fruit and juices served fresh from the trees in our own Wigwam Grove." (Larry Roberts Antiques.)

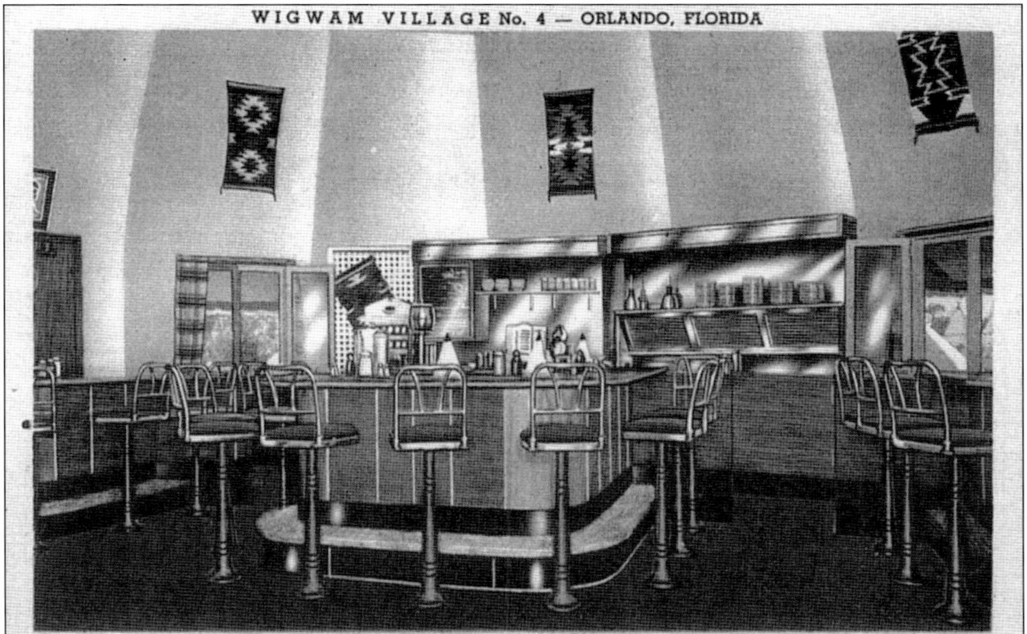

And of course, since no visit would have been complete without the purchase of presents for friends back home, the proprietors were quick to fulfill that need in the "WIGWAM GIFT SHOP. Here is found a large variety in genuine Indian-made jewelry and handiwork. Articles on sale from all of the leading Indian reservations in the United States." (Larry Roberts Antiques.)

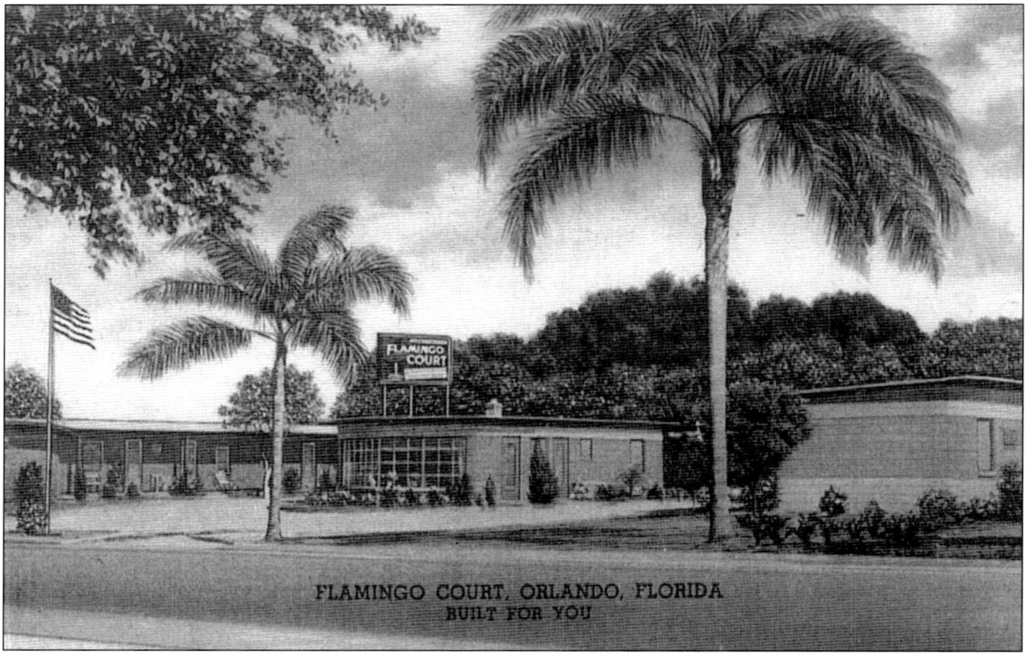

After World War II ended, along with its gas rationing, travel shortages, and dearth of new cars, more and more Americans began to take to the road. With an ever-improving network of highways, Florida quickly became the vacation destination of choice for thousands of people, including servicemen who fondly remembered the warm sunny weather and white sandy beaches they had experienced during their military training. For visitors traveling by automobile, motels proved to be a convenient, as well as less expensive, place to stay while en route. The Flamingo Court, owned by A.G. Barnhill, and Mr. and Mrs. Edward Hyder's Lake Tyler Motor Inn were two popular spots along U.S. Highway 17. (Larry Roberts Antiques.)

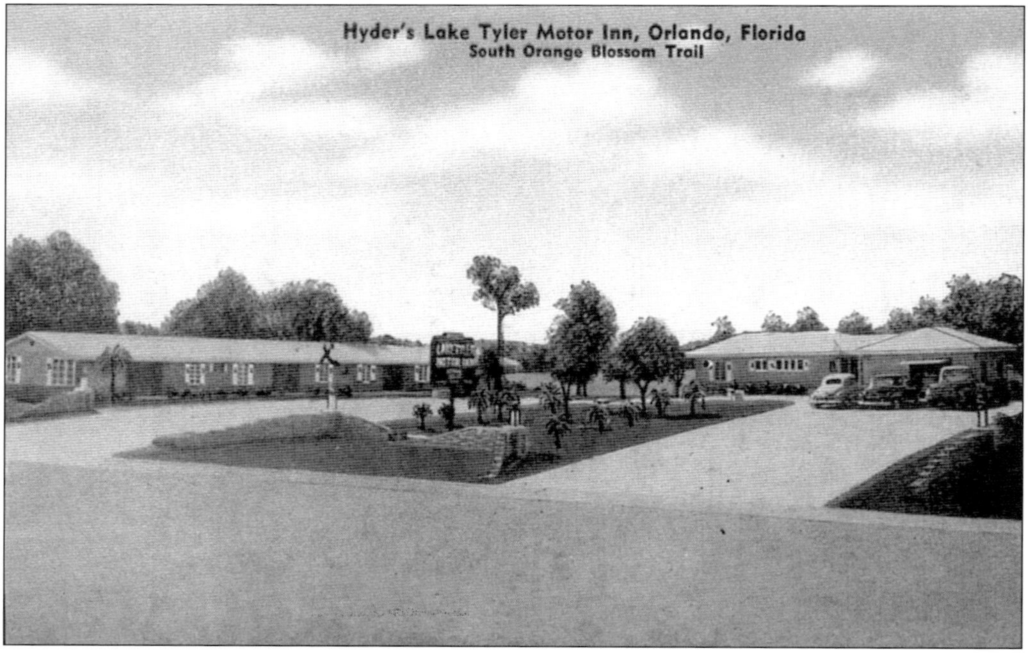

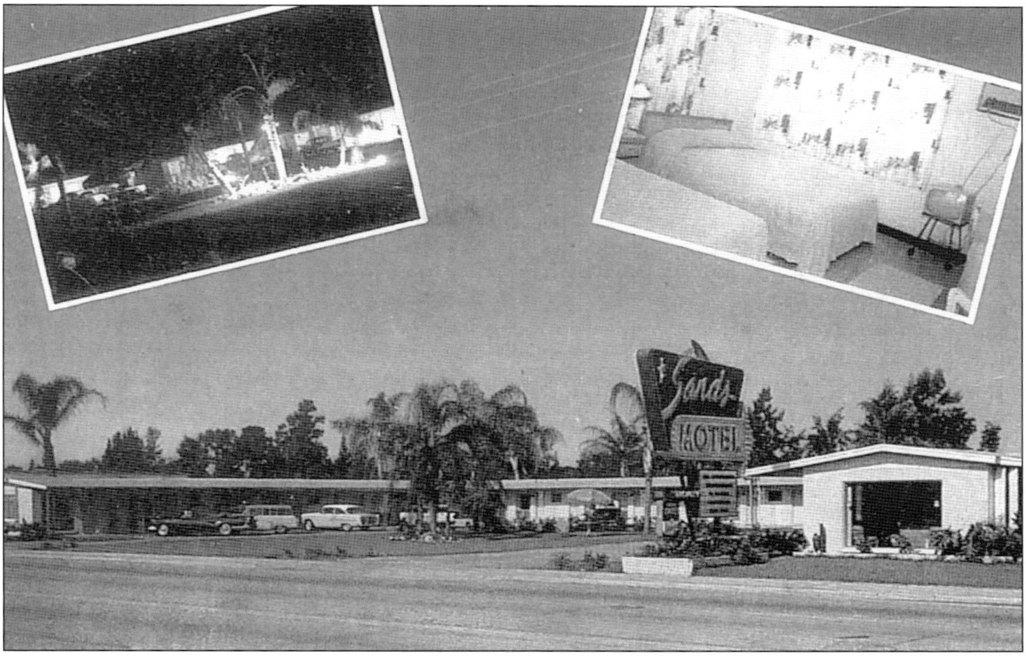

Located just five blocks apart on the Orange Blossom Trail, the Sands Motel and the Court Cadillac were two more establishments patronized by the traveling public. On glossy full-color postcards available at the front desk, both motels advertised ceramic tile baths, air conditioning, electric heat, room telephones, and free TV in every room. The Court Cadillac also catered to visitors by filling another need with its attached restaurant. Just as a point of local interest, until its renaming in November 1937 at the suggestion of the Greater Orlando Chamber of Commerce, Orange Blossom Trail had been known as Kentucky Avenue. (Larry Roberts Antiques.)

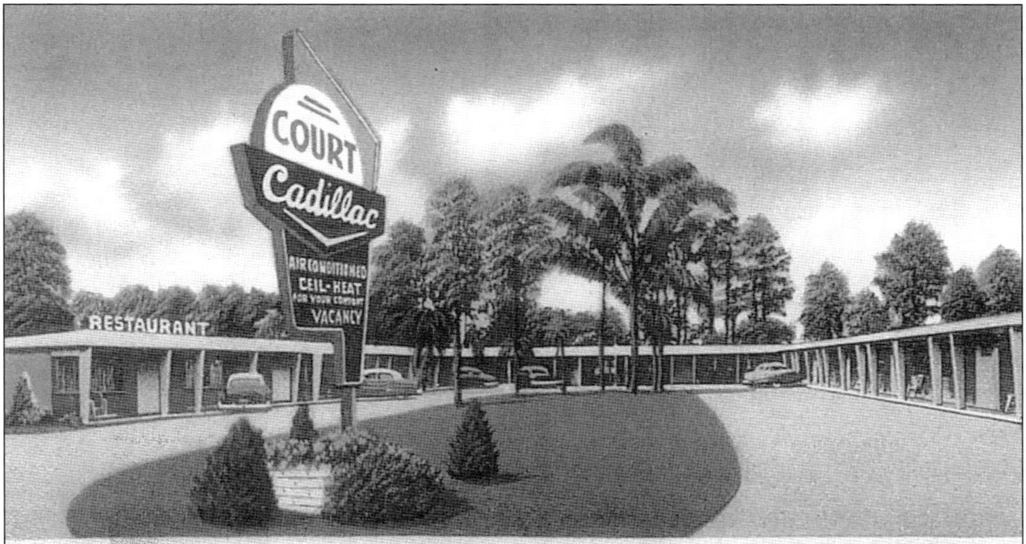

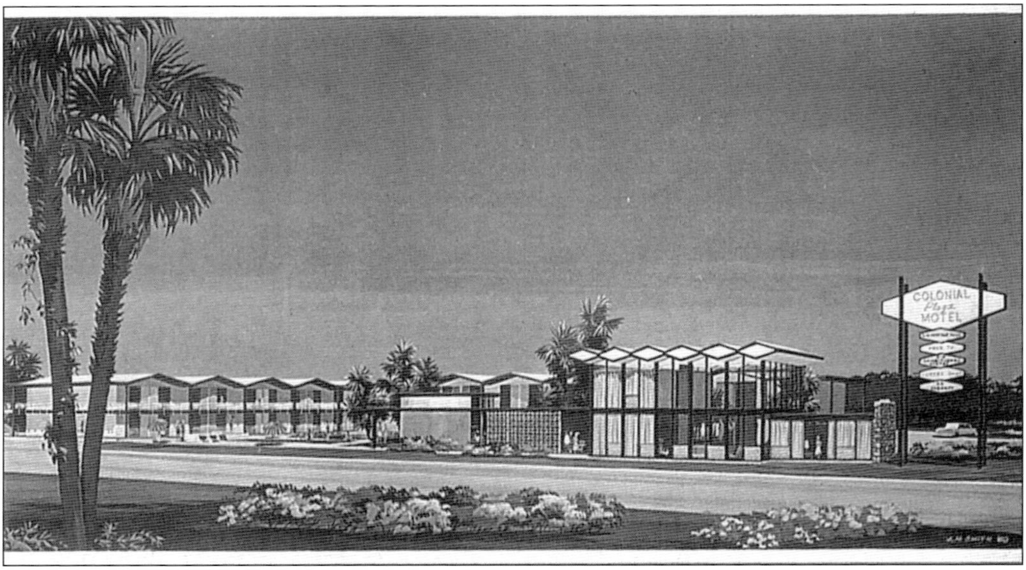

When the new Colonial Plaza Shopping Center opened for business in January 1956, it also opened an era of change for Orlando. Within a short period of time, downtown would no longer be the heart and soul of the business community. As major stores relocated to the new shopping center and its parking lot filled with cars, other developers recognized the trend and created their own shopping centers. Capitalizing on the name recognition, the Colonial Plaza Motel, at 2801 East Colonial Drive, opened as "Orlando's newest and finest motel, with 102 completely air conditioned, heated and TV equipped rooms. Beautiful coffee shop, snack bar, and heated swimming pool." Bucking the trend away from downtown, however, the 250-room Robert Meyer Hotel was built in 1963 on the site of the old Orlando High School on Lake Eola. The six-story hotel reportedly cost $4 million to build; a $1-million expansion followed three years later. (Larry Roberts Antiques and University of South Florida Special Collections.)

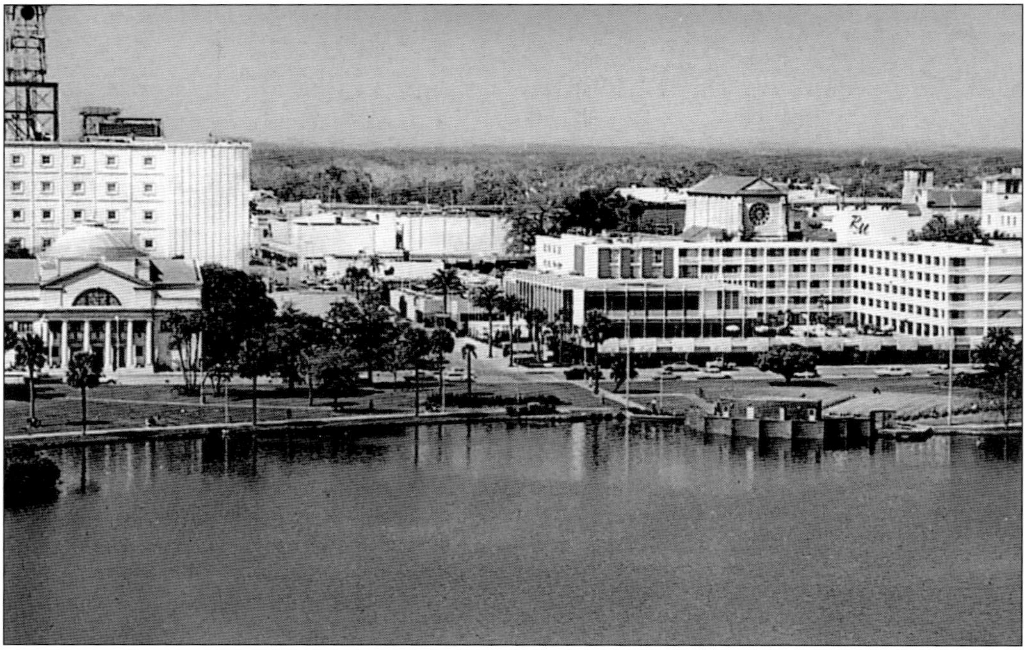

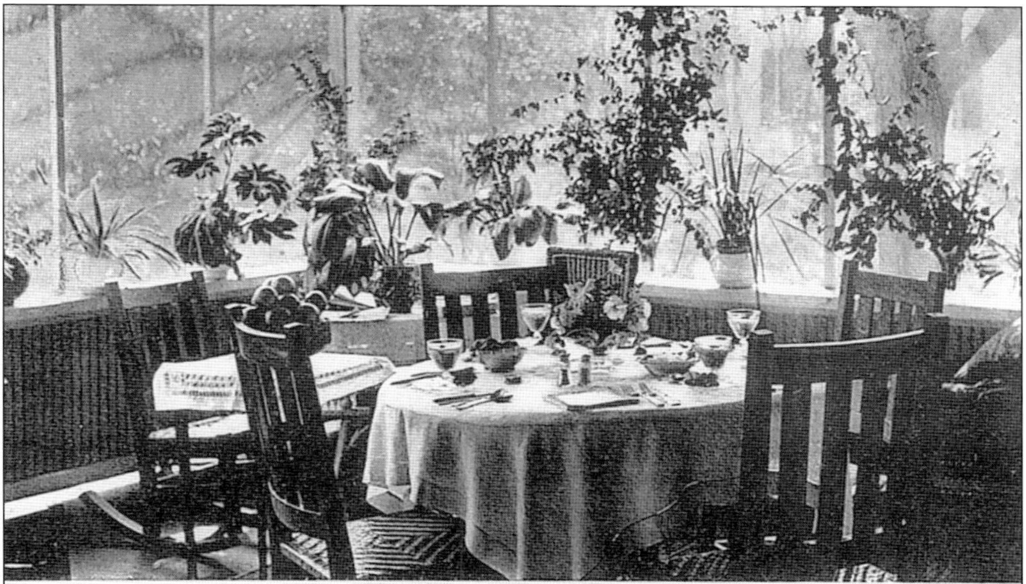

Open Air Dining Room, Orlando, Fla.

Both local residents and visitors to Orlando enjoyed going out to eat. A formal dining experience wasn't always required, however; tearooms and open-air dining rooms were quite popular for many years. The Little Tea Room called itself "an exclusive shop for ladies" in 1913; the following year, the roof garden on the fifth floor of the Yowell-Duckworth Company opened as a favorite dining spot. Luncheon and afternoon tea were available at the Polly Anna Tea Room, the Blue Bird Waffle Parlor, and the Primrose Tea Shoppe in the early 1920s. In 1937, Elizabeth Vick left the Latch String Tea Room on Magnolia Avenue for a new position as part owner of Paula's Restaurant. Ads during the 1940s talked of "delicious home-cooked food, country fried chicken, fresh vegetables, hot muffins, biscuits, honey, and blueberry cream pie" at the Lake Lawsona Tea Room as well as the Harmony Restaurant and Tea Room. (Larry Roberts Antiques.)

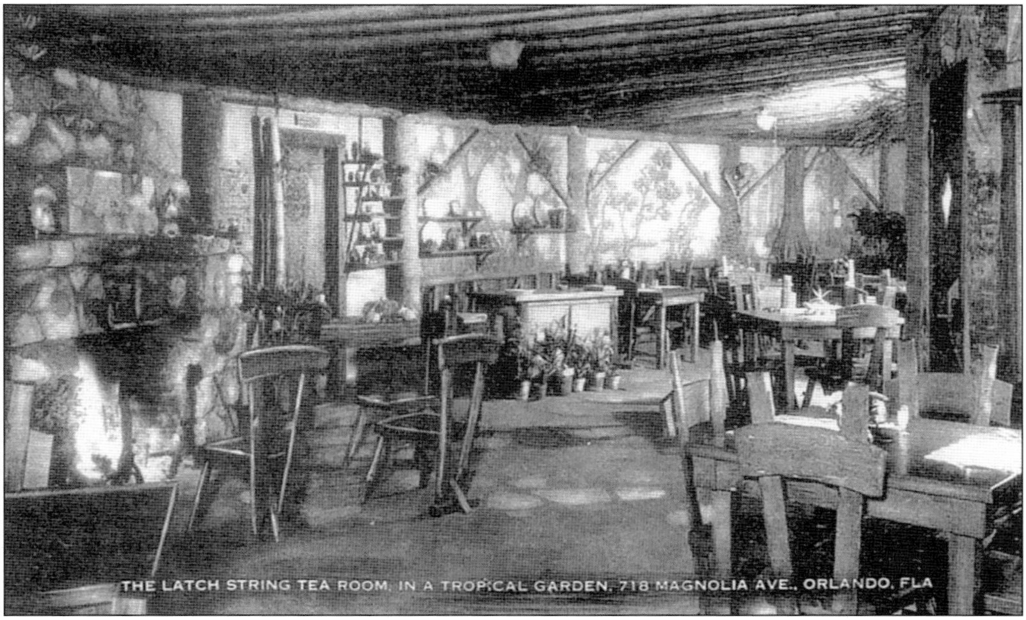

THE LATCH STRING TEA ROOM, IN A TROPICAL GARDEN, 718 MAGNOLIA AVE., ORLANDO, FLA

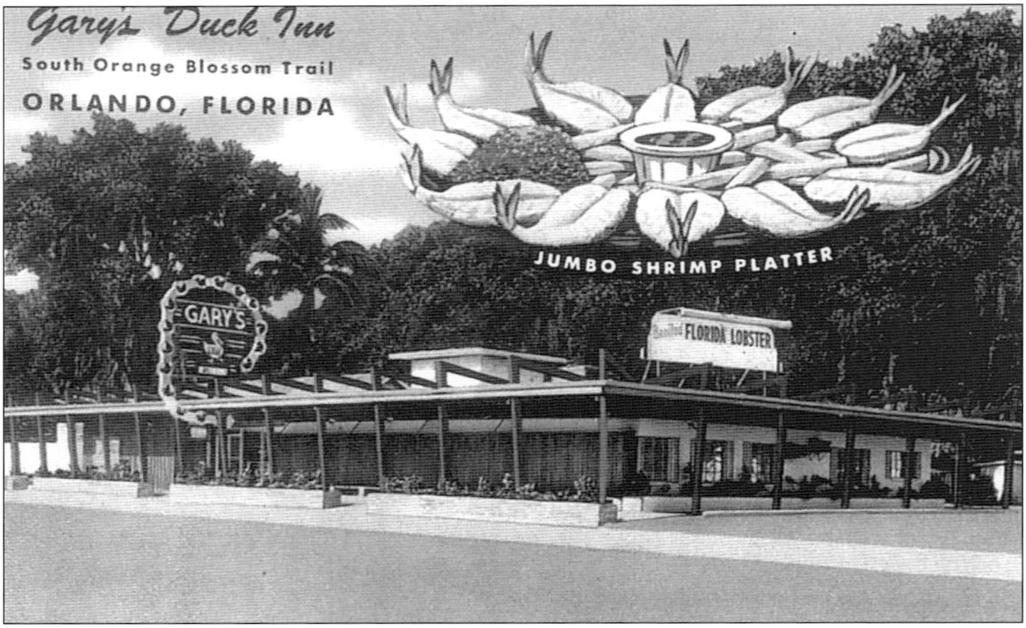

Slim (Sherman) Hoffman first opened his popular Duck Inn on North Orange Avenue in 1927, later moving his restaurant to the Empire Hotel. At that location, a record serving of 1,200 meals on January 3, 1936, led local merchants to believe that an economic recovery was underway. The establishment subsequently relocated to South Orange Blossom Trail and, under new ownership, became known as Gary's Duck Inn. In 1950, a broiled mullet dinner, complete with fries, coleslaw, hot biscuits, corn sticks, and hush puppies, cost $1.50; a mere $3.65 would buy all the lobster one could eat. Almost as popular were the area's drive-ins. Opening in 1934 and offering 24-hour curb service as well as steak dinners for 35¢, Goodbread's was Orlando's first drive-in restaurant. Other drive-in restaurants, including Steak 'n Shake, soon followed. (Larry Roberts Antiques.)

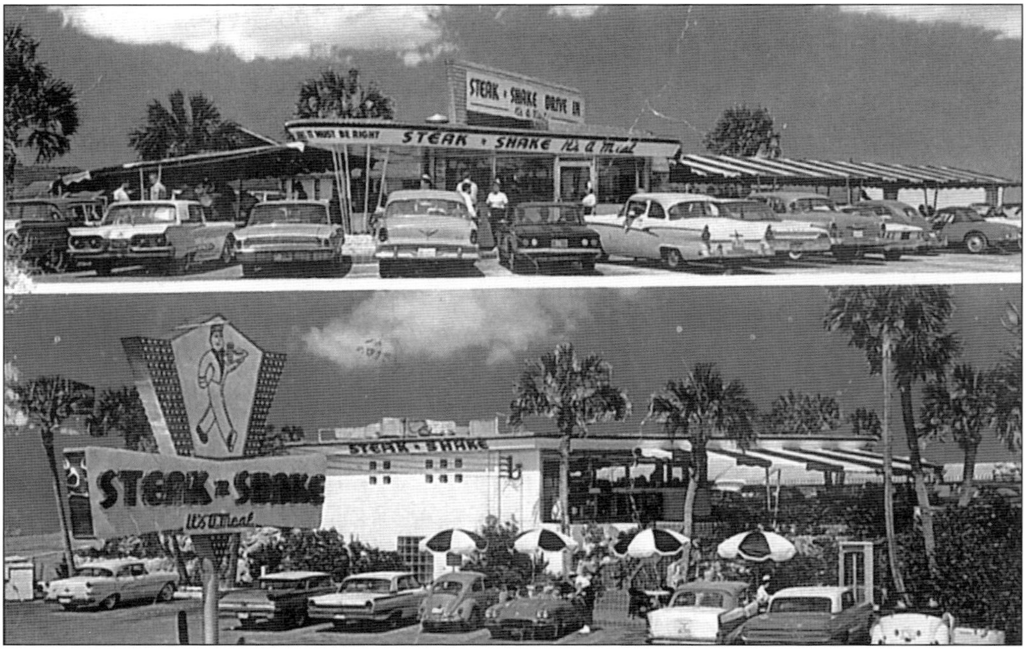

Five

LEISURELY LIFE

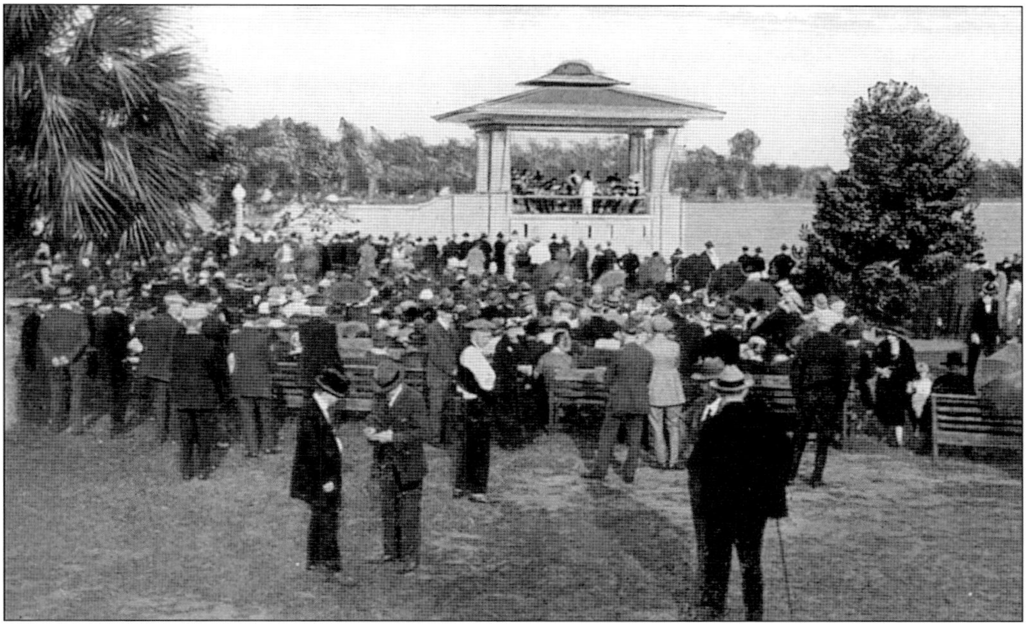

From the end of the 19th century until the mid-1960s, and with no reason to anticipate that the trend would not continue, Orlando's population increased steadily as more people settled in central Florida. At the same time, tourists, drawn by the weather and the many activities offered for their enjoyment, filled the city each winter. As a 1941 mail-away edition of the Orlando *Sentinel-Star* reported, "Band concerts are free. The Eola Park Bandshell is a three-minute walk from the heart of downtown Orlando. A multitude of bands plays here throughout the winter months. Here winter visitors may sit and enjoy delightful music, Orlando's flora, and a warm Florida sun. Benches seating nearly 2,000 persons are available. A combination of good music, often by the Orlando High School Band of more than 100 pieces which won top-ranking honors in the national contests this year, blue skies, natural beauty, and warm sun brings rest and relaxation in Orlando that is found nowhere else in Florida." (University of South Florida Special Collections.)

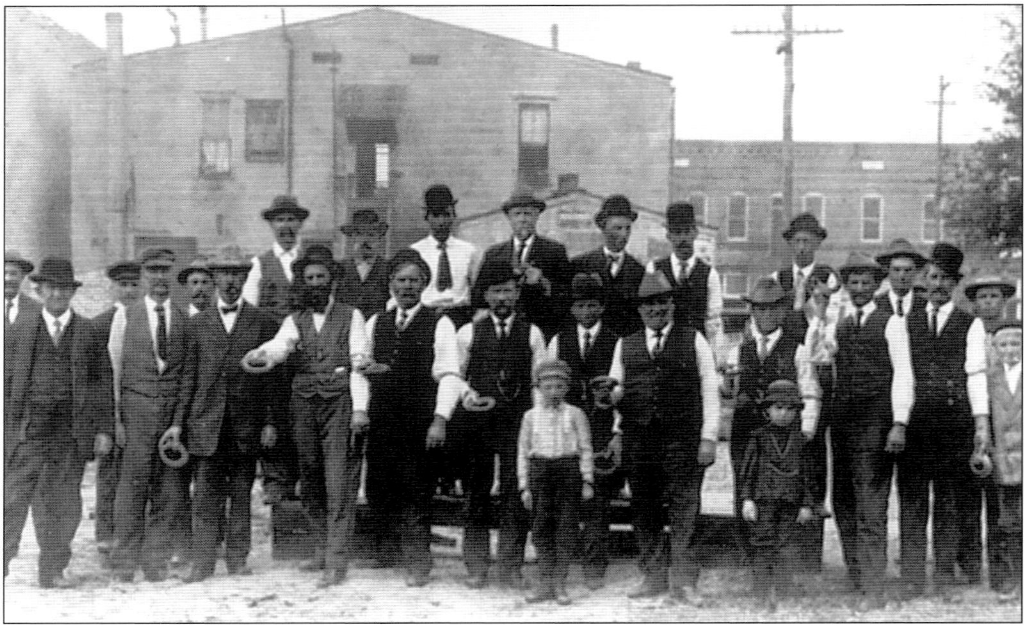

As early as 1912, clubs and organizations such as the Tourist Quoit Club offered recreational opportunities for visitors. In 1922, the Orlando Tourist Club, organized by the Chamber of Commerce, was given land at the corner of East Central and Main Streets for roque courts and a horseshoe-pitching field. The subsequent addition of seats and lights facilitated night play. Later moved to Livingston Street, these efforts marked the beginning of Sunshine Park, an aptly named setting for all types of sporting and social activity. "Sunshine Park, for winter visitors, is equipped for lawn bowling, roque, shuffleboard, and horse-shoes. Two clubhouses on the grounds. Sunshine Park teams have won high honors for Orlando, in Florida, and in international tournaments in northern cities." (Florida State Archives and Larry Roberts Antiques.)

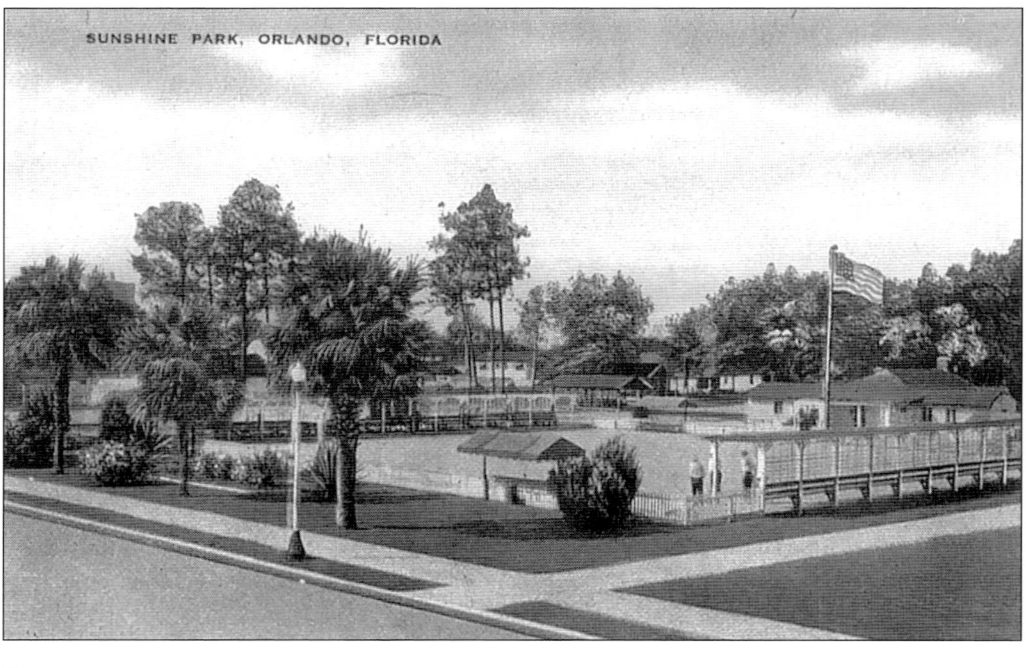

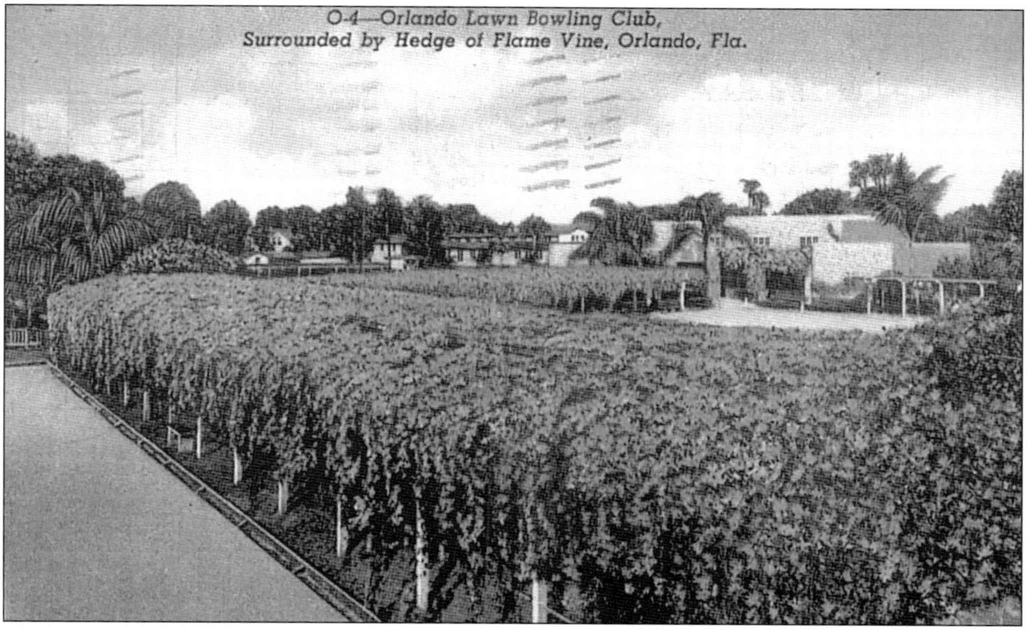

The local Chamber of Commerce boasted that "Orlando's winter temperature averages 64.2 degrees; the summer temperature a mild 77.5 degrees. Average rainfall and humidity are ideal. There are 415 acres of parks in Orlando, all entirely free; all beautifully landscaped with benches available everywhere." The flame vine in bloom along the lawn bowling lanes in Sunshine Park was just one more natural wonder for the visitors to enjoy. (Larry Roberts Antiques.)

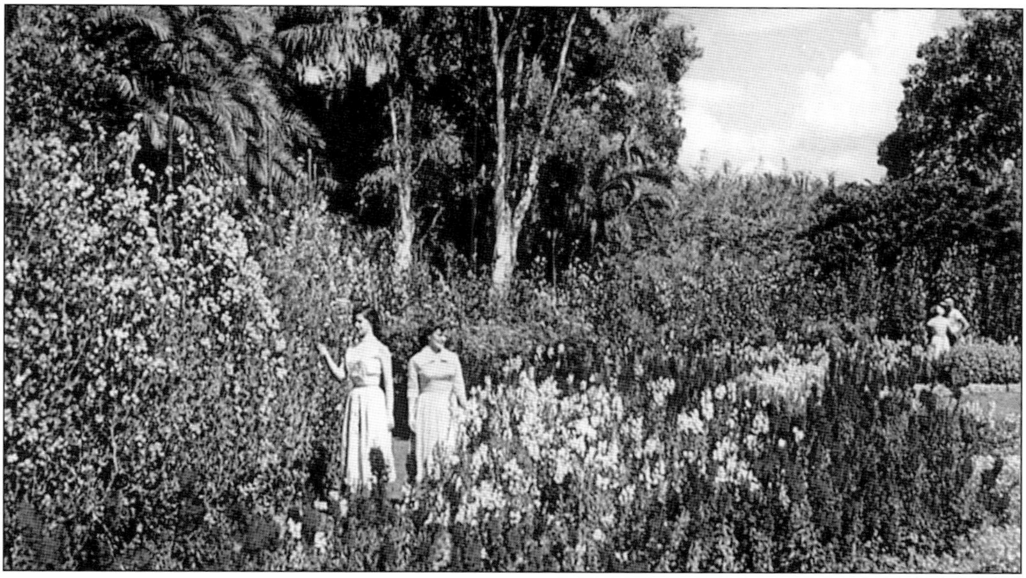

"Never before equaled is Orlando's famed sweet pea gardens that bloom profusely throughout the winter months in Lake Eola Park. Brilliantly colored by warm sunshine in the day, this solid wall of sweet peas makes visitors gasp in amazement. The blooms are equally splendorous at night under giant floodlights. This one garden spot, a part of the extensive lower gardens at Lake Eola Park, brings thousands of visitors to Orlando each year to marvel at their beauty." (University of South Florida Special Collections.)

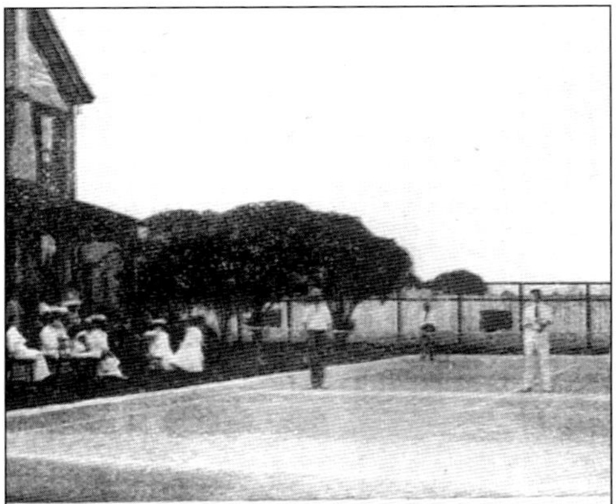

LAWN TENNIS.

Tennis was so popular that Orlando had already established a tennis club by 1908. Two tennis courts at the corner of Main Street and Central Avenue were built for tourist use in January 1921. For those less athletically inclined, nature beckoned. "The palm trees of Orlando are at their peak of verdure during the winter months and their gently swaying fronds lend an air of the tropics to 'The City Beautiful' and give a feeling of enchantment which makes Orlando a 'must' for all travelers." (University of South Florida Special Collections.)

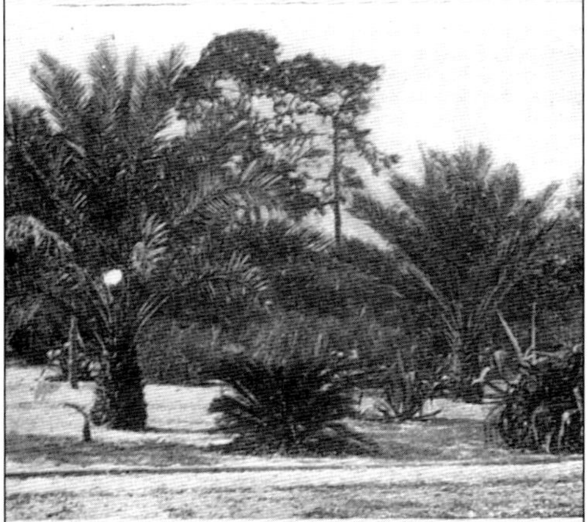

PALM GARDEN.

Settling in Orlando in the mid-1880s, the English Colony consisted of three groups of people—retired business professionals and military officers, second sons seeking to acquire fortunes, and the less affluent workers who served them. Along with their fondness for afternoon tea, the British brought polo, golf, and tennis to Orlando. By 1908, postcards proclaimed, "For those who enjoy golf and those who admire superior horsemanship, the opportunity is here presented." (University of South Florida Special Collections.)

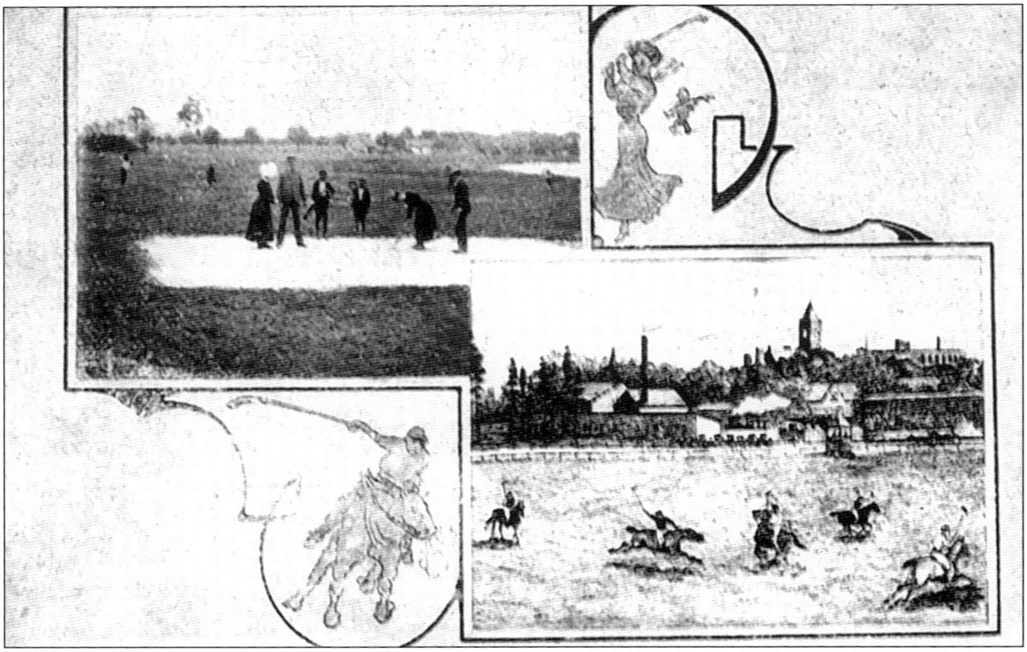

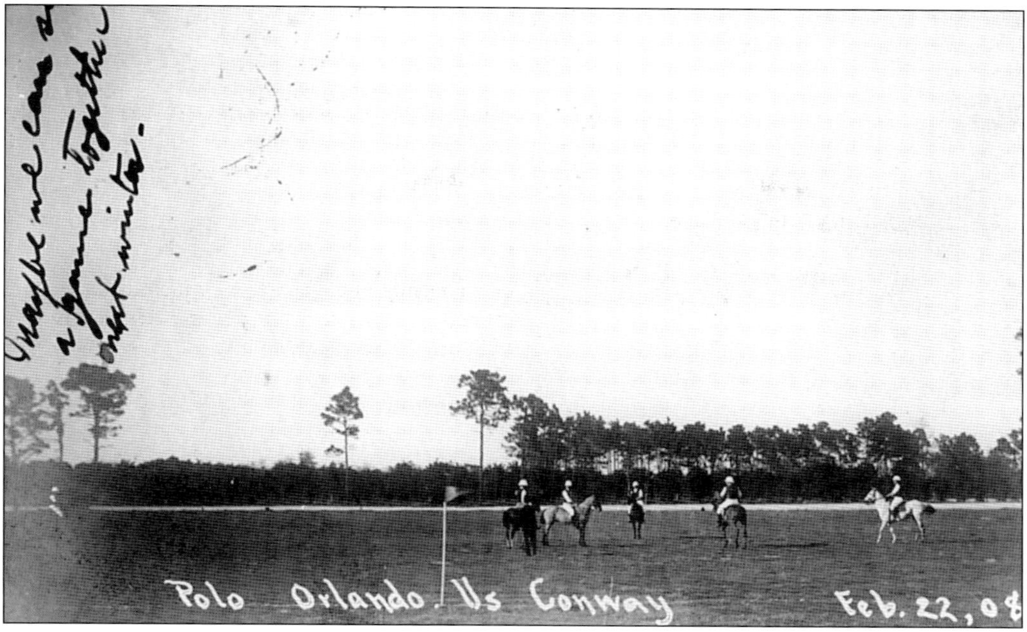

A former officer in the British Dragoon Guards allegedly originated the idea of a polo team in Orlando. Play began in 1888; the Orlando Polo Club was organized with more than 100 members two years later. Riding Florida cow ponies, the polo players quickly became a major attraction as they competed against teams from as far away as North Carolina. Everyone in Orlando turned out to watch the matches that were followed by afternoon tea. (University of South Florida Special Collections.)

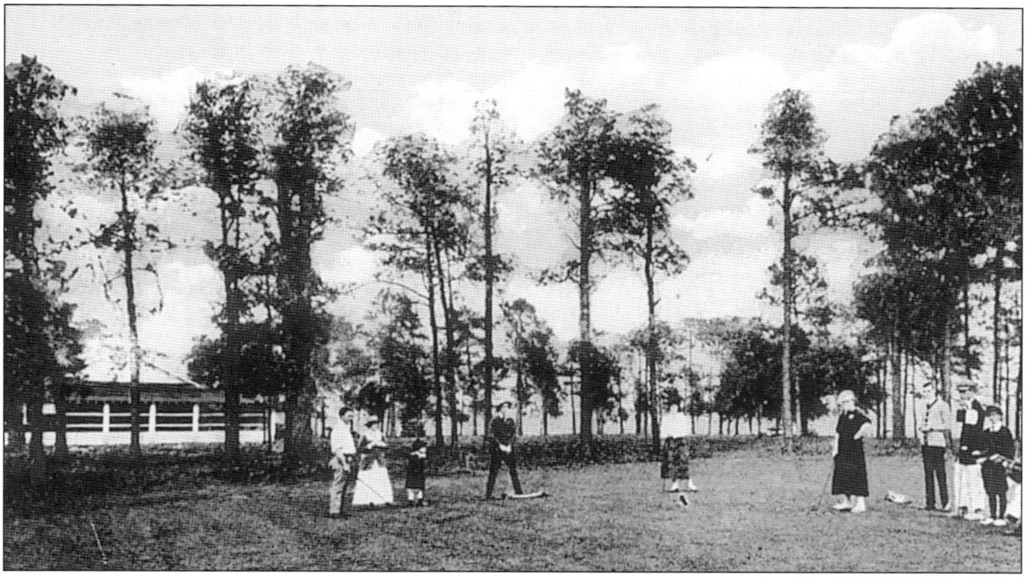

Depicting golfers at play, this postcard described Orlando in the most glowing terms. "A city of 6,000 souls. Finest climate. Best water. Good schools. Numerous churches. Driving park. Race course. Golf links. Polo grounds. Winter Chautauqua. Spring carnival. Good roads. Brick streets. Handsome residences. Fine hotels. Grand oak shade trees. Splendid lakes. Perfect sanitation. Health record unapproachable. No mosquitoes." (University of South Florida Special Collections.)

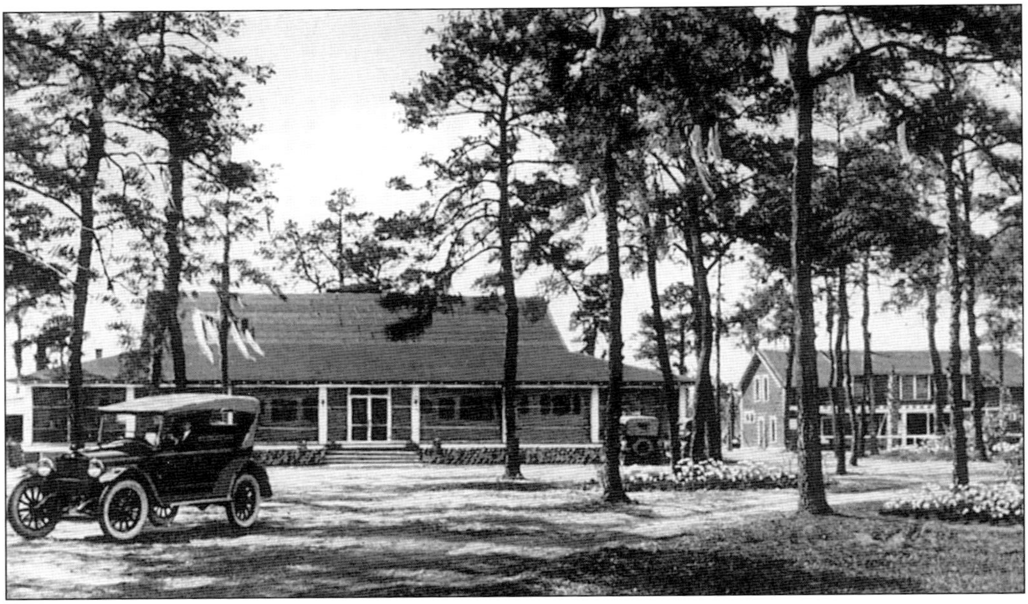

The English had also been responsible for the introduction of golf in Orlando. Leslie Pell-Clarke set up a nine-hole course along Lake Eola in the 1880s and soon convinced local residents of the merits of the sport. The Orlando Country Club created new golf links in 1911 on the north shore of Spring Lake; its clubhouse opened the following May. In 1916 the club spent $400 to purchase an additional 20 acres, giving the club an 18-hole course by the next March. In addition to golf, other club activities included card parties, dinners, and formal dances. Members built their new more elaborate clubhouse, complete with Mediterranean Revival elements including arched windows, barrel-tiled roof, and a bell tower in 1919, remodeling it in 1925. That building would last until replaced by a $300,000 clubhouse in 1954. (University of South Florida Special Collections and Larry Roberts Antiques.)

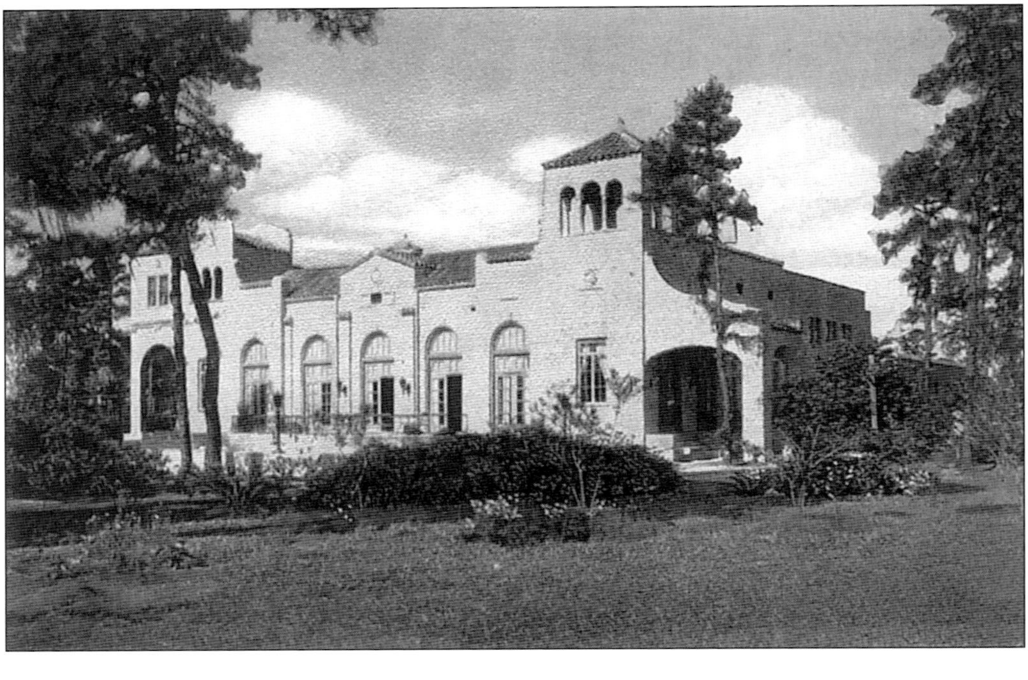

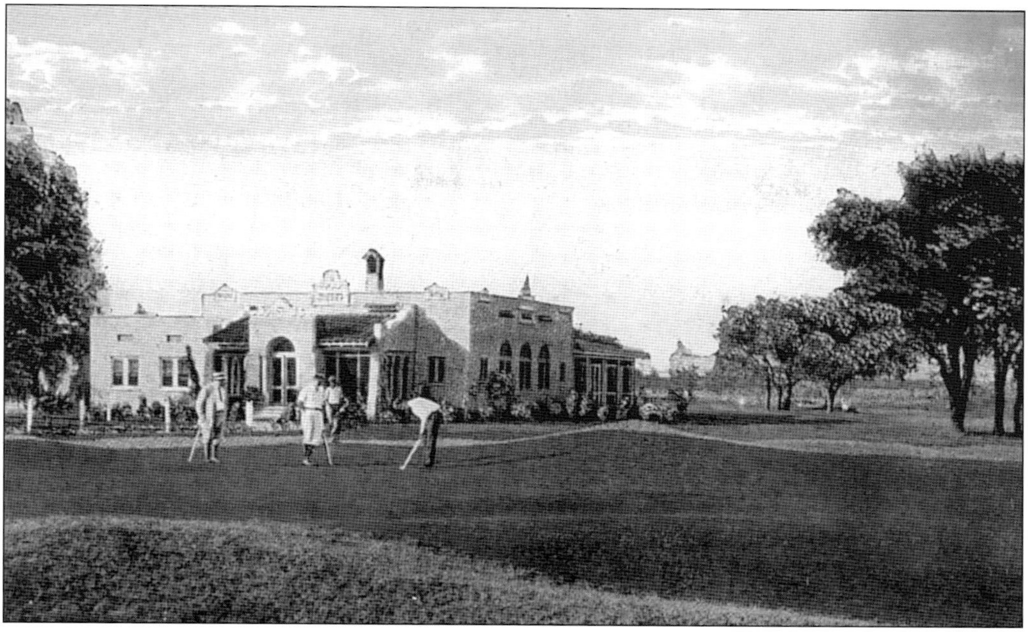

Competition for the Orlando Country Club occurred when Carl Dann, one of Orlando's strongest promoters, announced plans for a new golf and country club. A $40,000 project that opened in 1926, the popular new club was christened "Dubsdread." The unusual name was selected since the course was allegedly so difficult that unskilled players known as "dubs" dreaded playing it. Although damaged by fire eight years later, the clubhouse was quickly rebuilt. In 1941, headlines read, "Star Golfers at Dubsdread. Gerald Walker of the Cleveland Indians and Chick Harbert will team up in an exhibition golf match this afternoon at Dubsdread Country Club. The Walker-Harbert team will oppose Carl Dann and either Frank Stranahan, a Rollins student, or Lieutenant J.E. Fitzgerald of the Orlando Air Base." In 1944, Carl Dann sold the club to a South Carolina firm for $100,000. (University of South Florida Special Collections.)

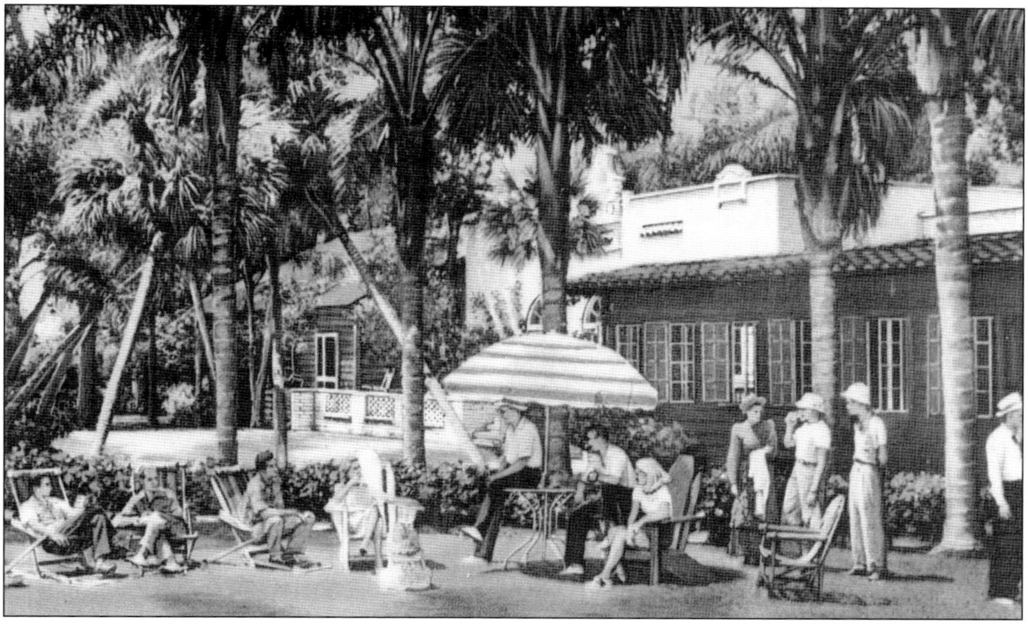

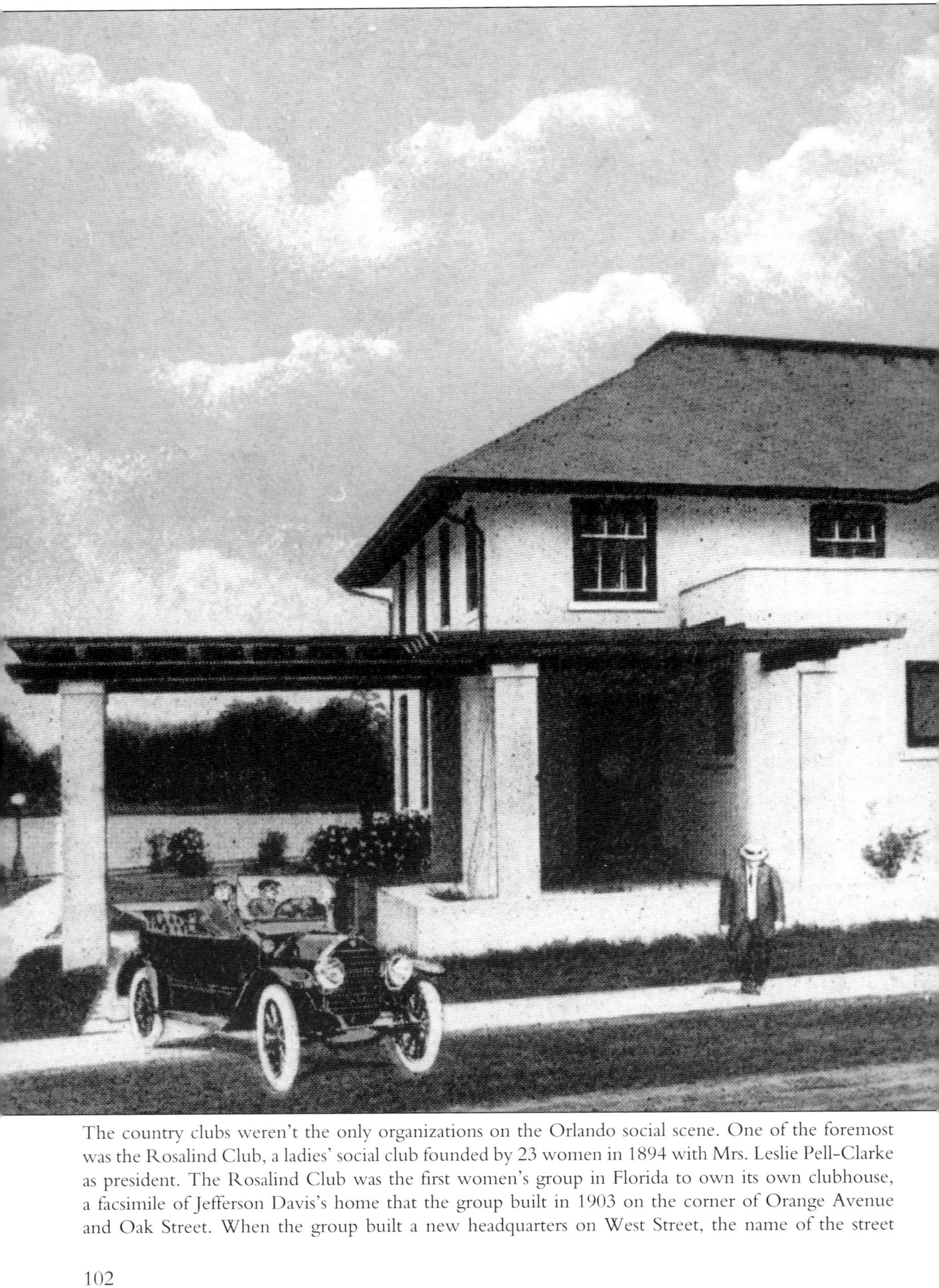

The country clubs weren't the only organizations on the Orlando social scene. One of the foremost was the Rosalind Club, a ladies' social club founded by 23 women in 1894 with Mrs. Leslie Pell-Clarke as president. The Rosalind Club was the first women's group in Florida to own its own clubhouse, a facsimile of Jefferson Davis's home that the group built in 1903 on the corner of Orange Avenue and Oak Street. When the group built a new headquarters on West Street, the name of the street

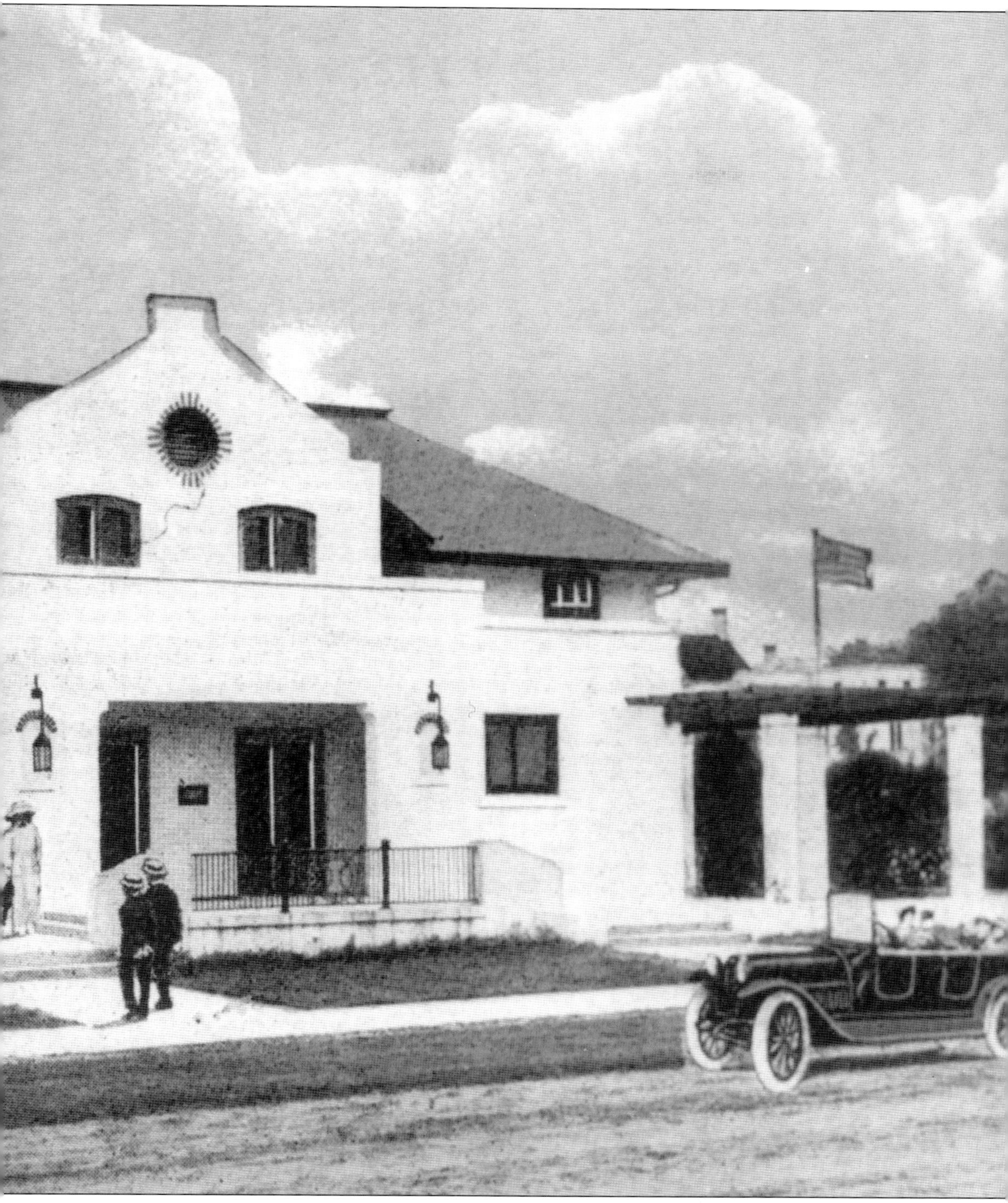

was changed to Rosalind Avenue at the request of the membership. While known for its card parties and other social activities, the annual New Year's Eve Ball became the organization's best-known event, replacing a New Year's Day afternoon reception to which non-member townspeople had been invited. (University of South Florida Special Collections.)

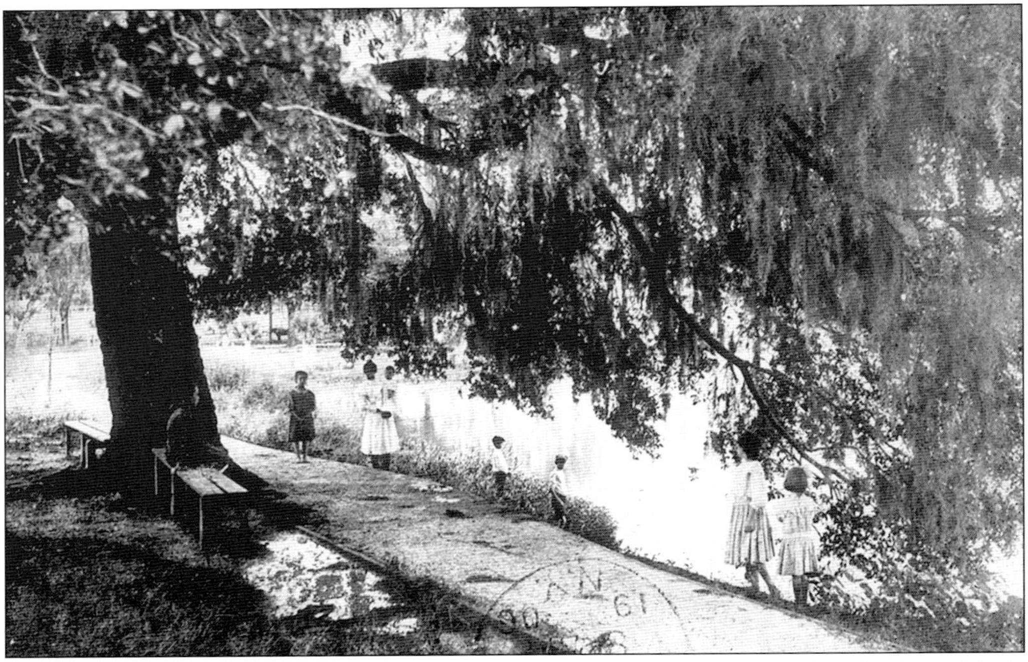

Visitors sometimes looked for less structured social or recreational activity. Orlando offered a multitude of opportunities—a picnic in a park, a quiet walk along one of the many lakes in Orlando, or a little bird watching. According to promotional literature, "There are 415 acres of parks in Orlando, all entirely free; all beautifully landscaped with benches available everywhere. Hundreds of miles of walks along lakeshores abound throughout the city. Mallards, blue bills, pin tails, and other wild ducks breed on the city's lakes and swim about with their goslings." The small wooden structure in the postcard view of Lake Lucerne provided a home for nesting waterfowl. (University of South Florida Special Collections and Larry Roberts Antiques.)

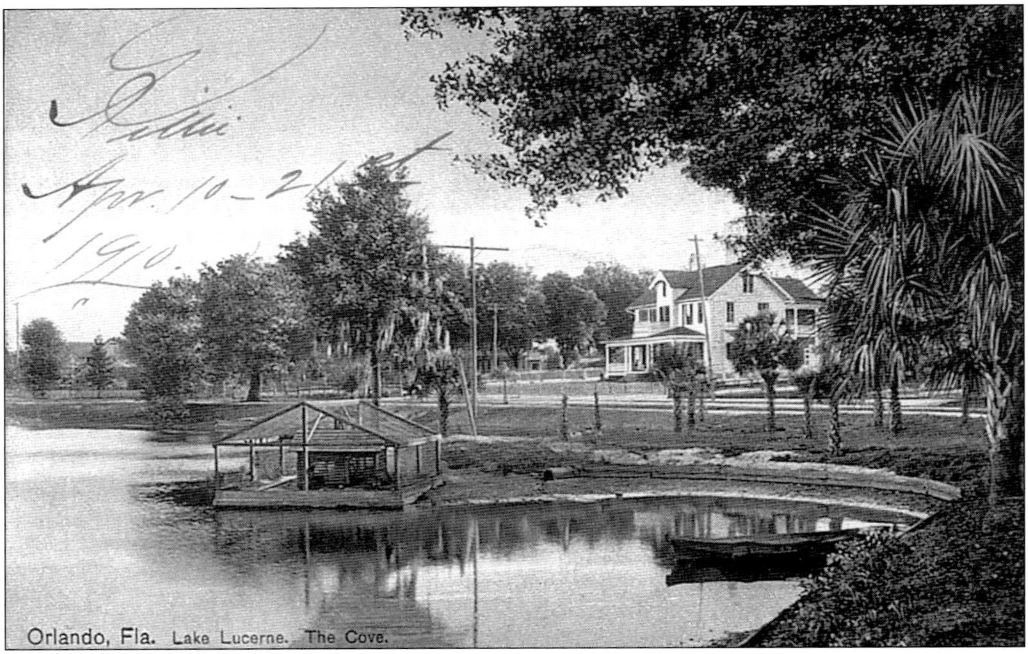

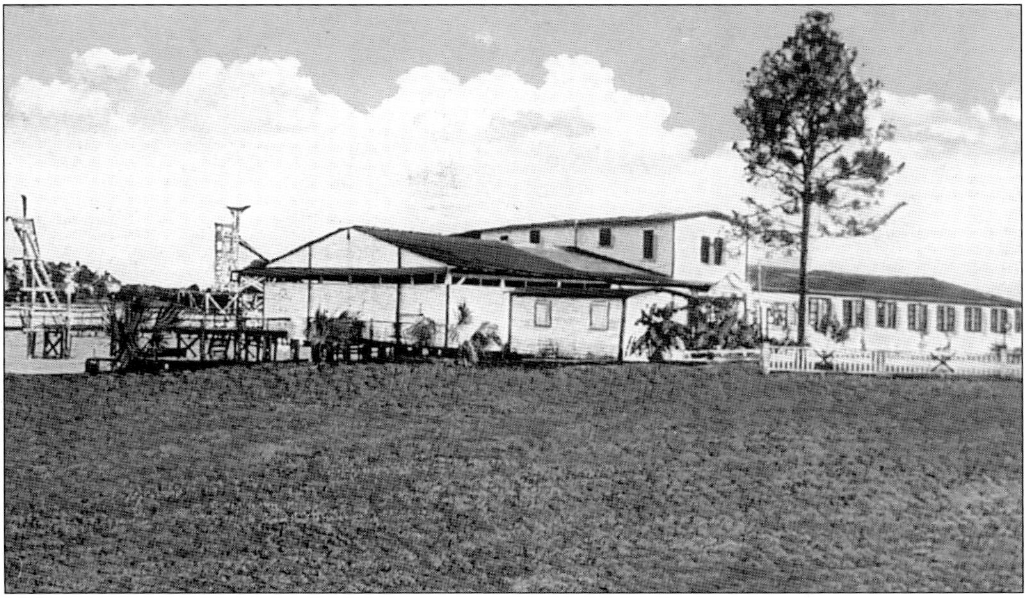

Russell's Point, owned by George Russell, was an amusement and recreation park on Lake Ivanhoe. The attraction, which soon came to be called Joyland, included all the amenities: "a pavilion and dock that had dressing rooms for swimmers, slides, a dance hall, meeting rooms, 50 boats for fishing or pleasure boating, a large picnic area, refreshment booths, and games of various kinds." Joyland was later demolished for a subdivision; Lakeside Park on Lake Conway took its place in popularity. (University of South Florida Special Collections.)

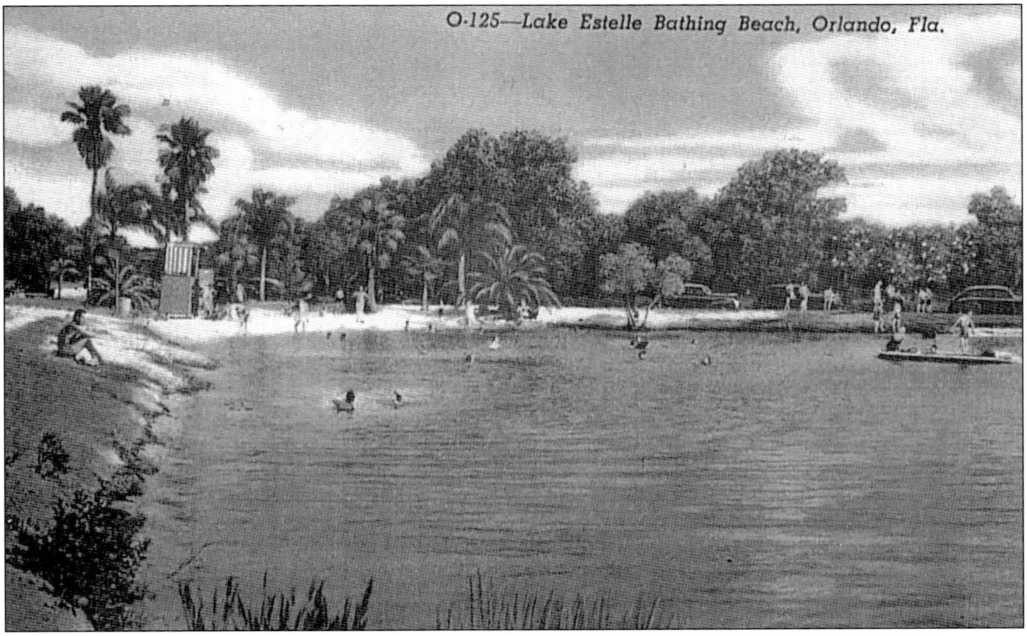

When a bathing beach and Spanish-style solarium was built on Lake Estelle as a WPA project in 1934, it caused an influx of aerial voyeurs. The result was the passage of a local ordinance prohibiting low-altitude flights by airplanes over the area. Even after the solarium closed in 1956, the bathing beach at Lake Estelle remained a popular spot for both visitors and local residents. (Larry Roberts Antiques.)

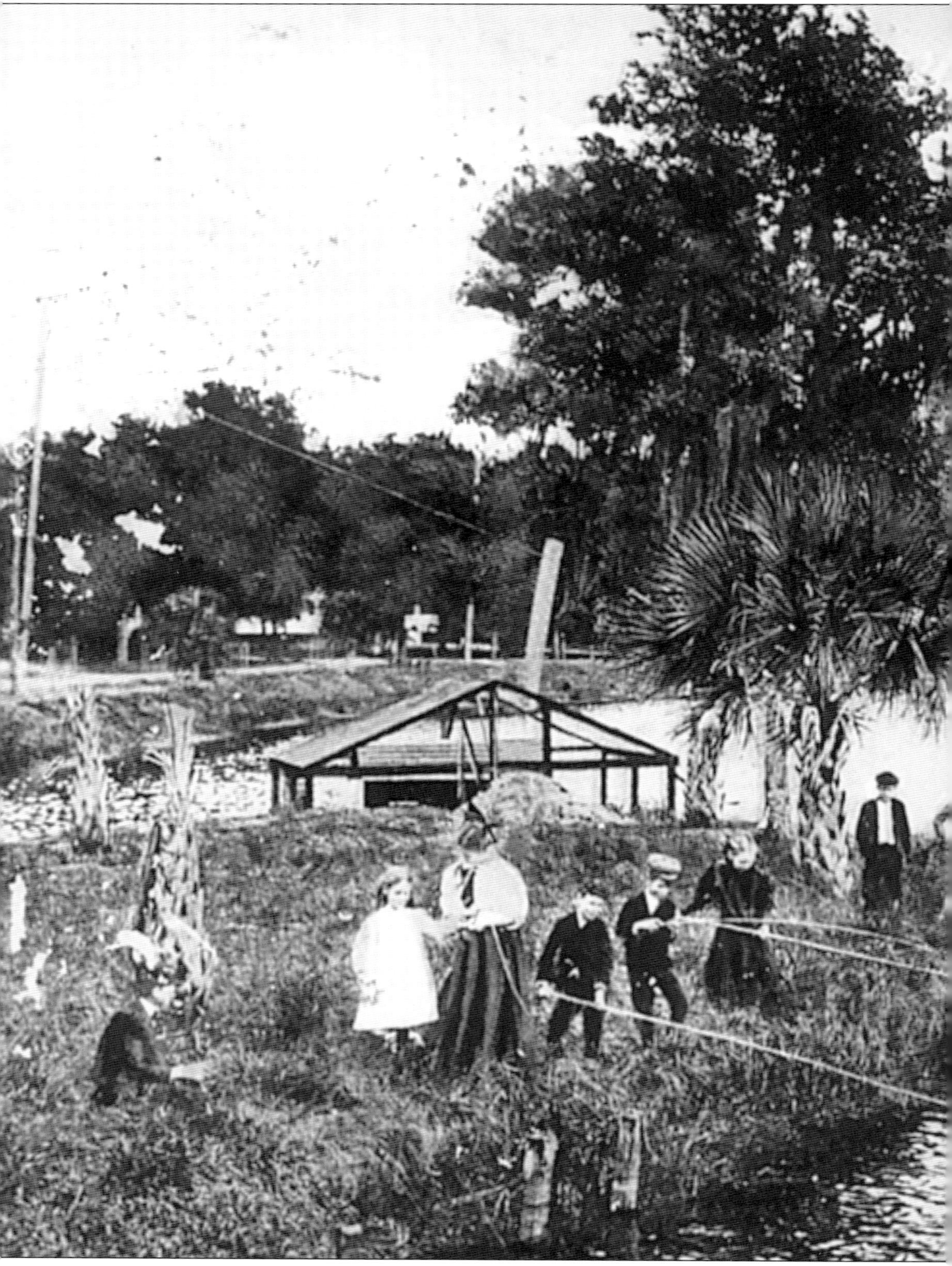

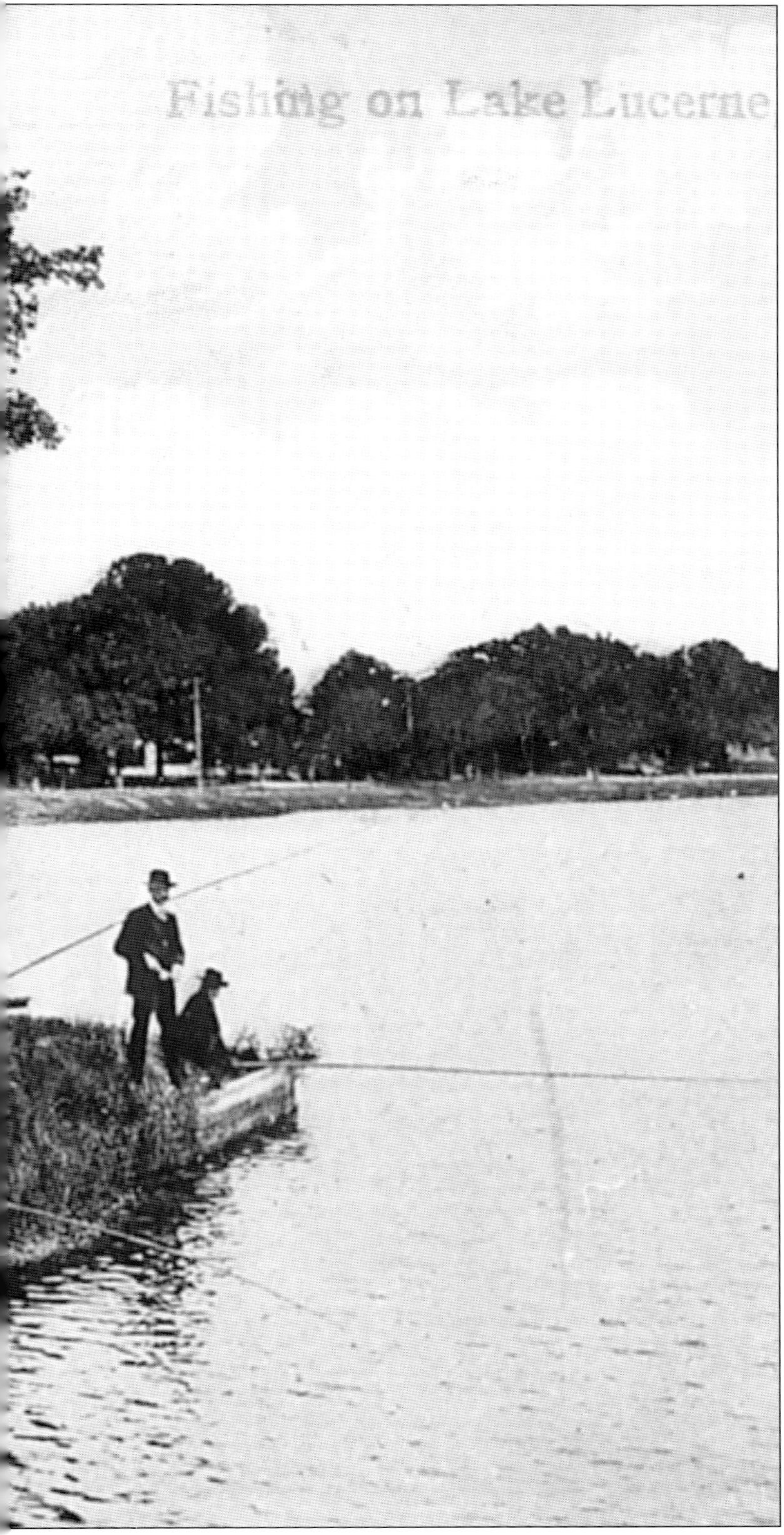

Judging from this turn-of-the-century postcard, fishing seems to be an activity that involved the entire family. Unless the rules had changed by 1941 when the *Sentinel-Star* offered the following information, the fishermen must have been local residents rather than tourists. "Ordinary people and millionaires rub shoulders together along the shores of Orlando's 33 mirrored lakes and Orlandoans are known as 'friendly people.' Large bass and other fresh water game fish swim close to shore and can be fed or jump playfully from the water providing never-ending interest for the visitor who likes to 'just loaf.' With the exception of Lakes Lucerne, Ivanhoe, and Eola, Orlando's other 30 lakes are open to fishing by visitors and contests are held with cash prizes for the big ones caught." (University of South Florida Special Collections.)

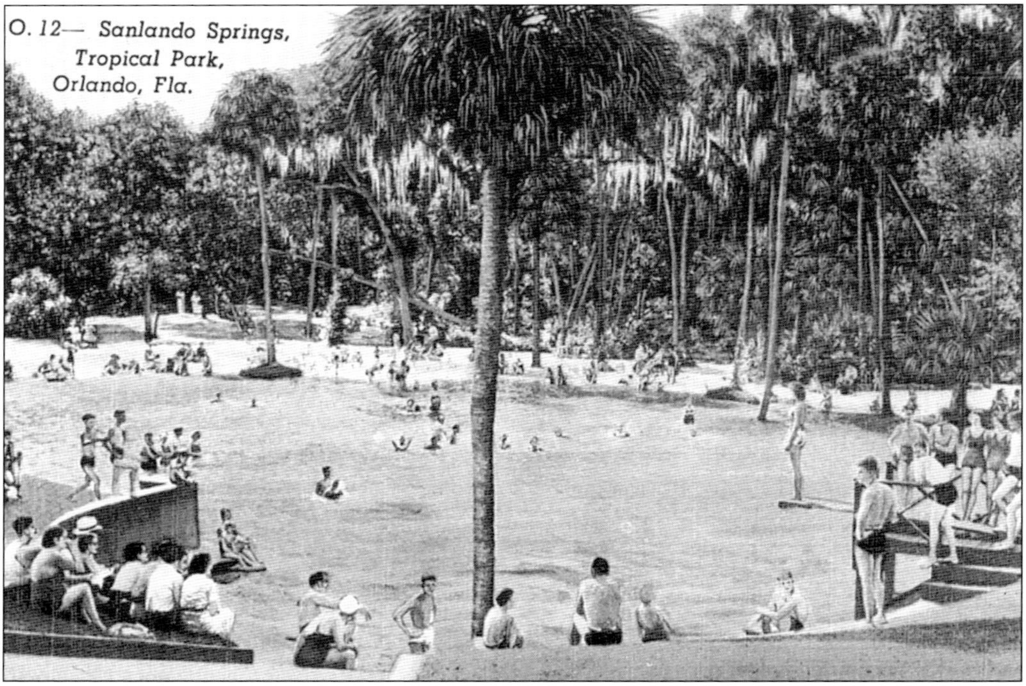

Sanlando Springs was described by the *Sentinel-Star* as "one of Orange County's most enchanting spots. It is only a 20-minute drive from Orlando over excellent highways through blooming orange groves. Sanlando Springs boasts the clearest and purest natural springs in all Central Florida. The water maintains a constant 72-degree temperature throughout the year. Even in the winter the water is as warm as the interiors of the homes in the North. Giant water oaks surround Sanlando Springs and other picnic grounds in Orange County. Their shade and mysterious looking Spanish moss draping from the boughs make picnicking a real delight for adults and a barrel of fun for children." (University of South Florida Special Collections.)

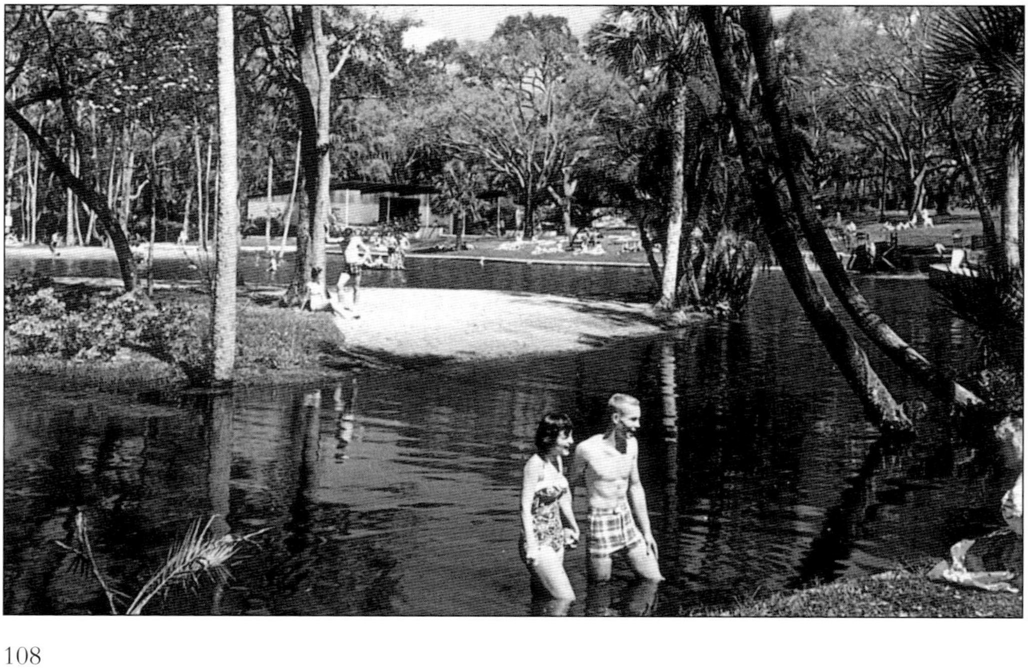

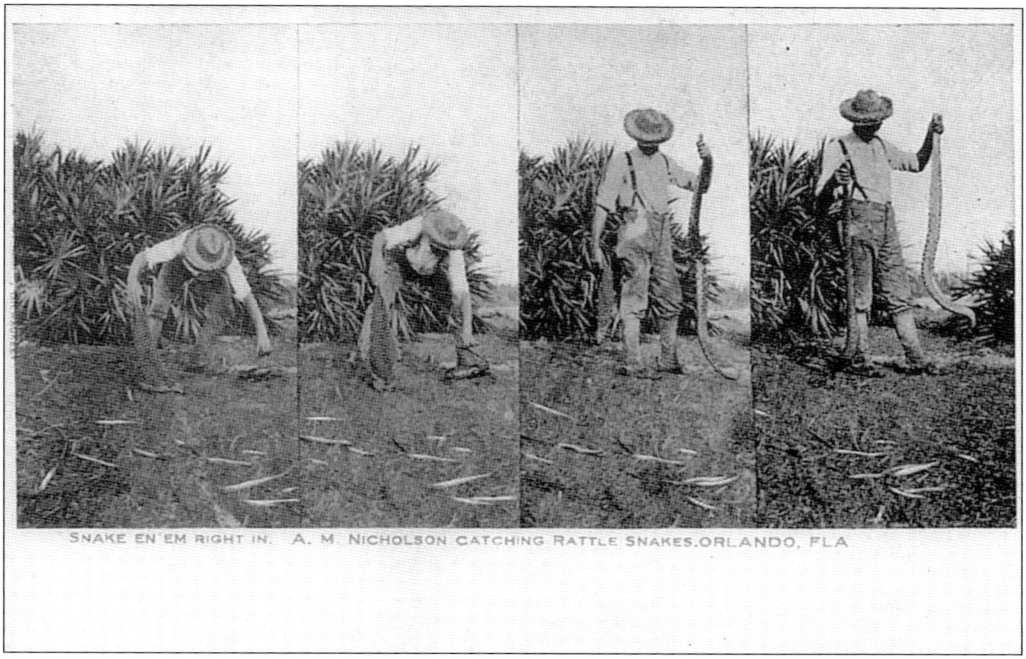

Snakes, snakes, and more snakes—some things never seem to go out of style! A.M. Nicholson exhibited his technique for catching rattlesnakes on a postcard dating from the late 1800s. As the city's first taxidermist, Nicholson had a thriving business dealing in birds, alligators, and snakes initially from a shop on West Church Street and later from his home on Division Street. Years later, another Orlando resident, Owen Godwin, gained national recognition as a big game hunter, world traveler, author, and lecturer. Wrapped in one of his Big Rock pythons from India, Godwin was photographed for this postcard at the Gatorland Zoo. (Larry Roberts Antiques.)

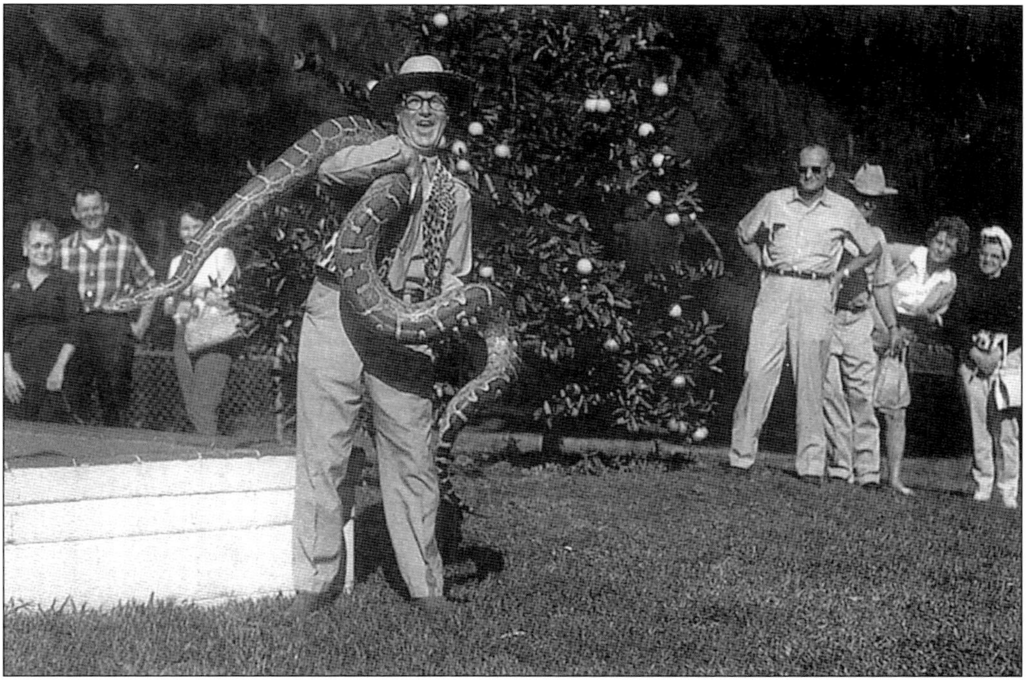

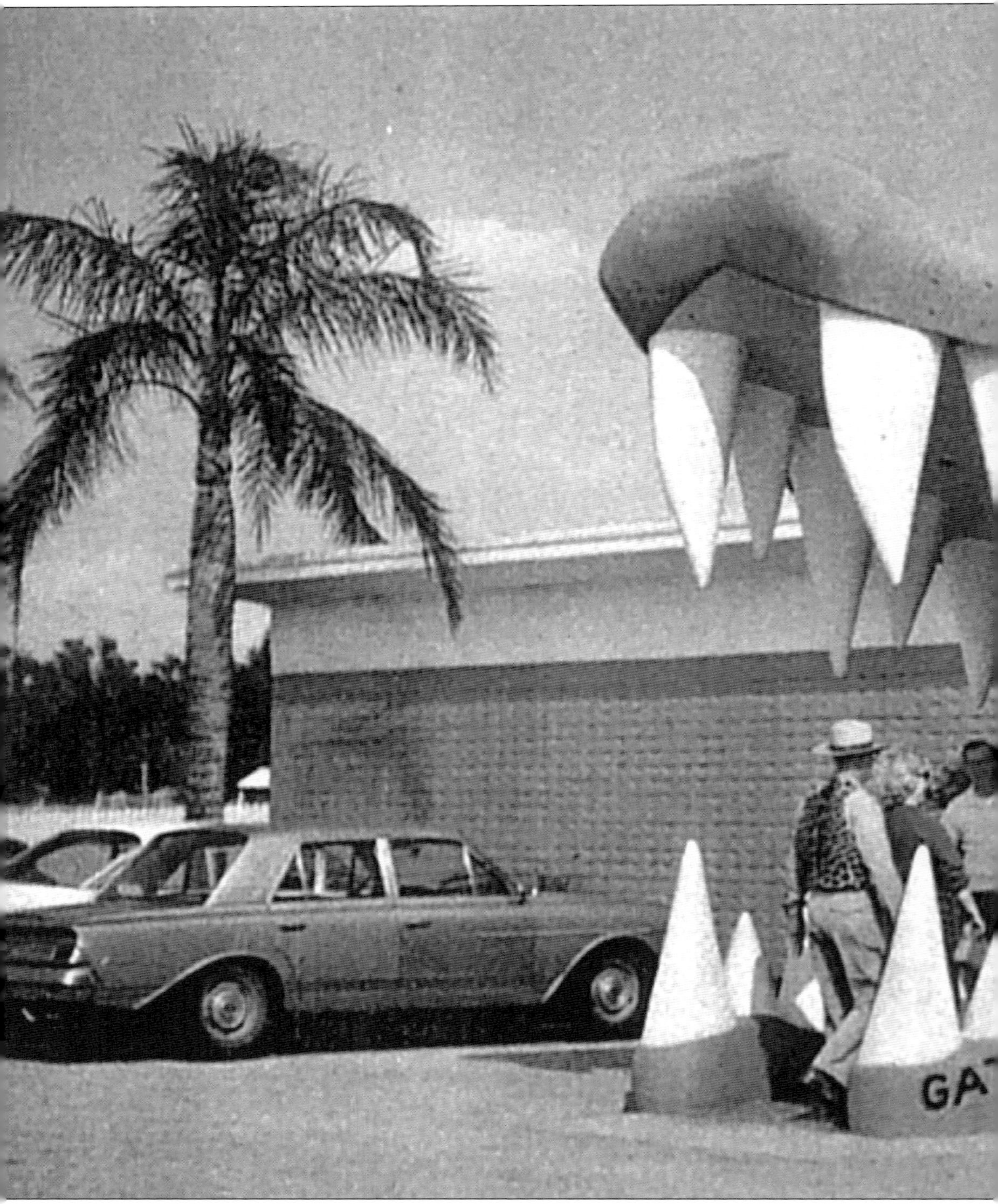

What could possibly be more "Florida" than a roadside attraction named Gatorland? One vacationing couple, John and Helen of East Orange, New Jersey, sent this postcard back to friends with the inscription, "Just been here and had an interesting time with snakes, gators, and all kinds of wild animals." Located on U.S. Highways 17, 92, and 441 between Orlando and Kissimmee, Gatorland

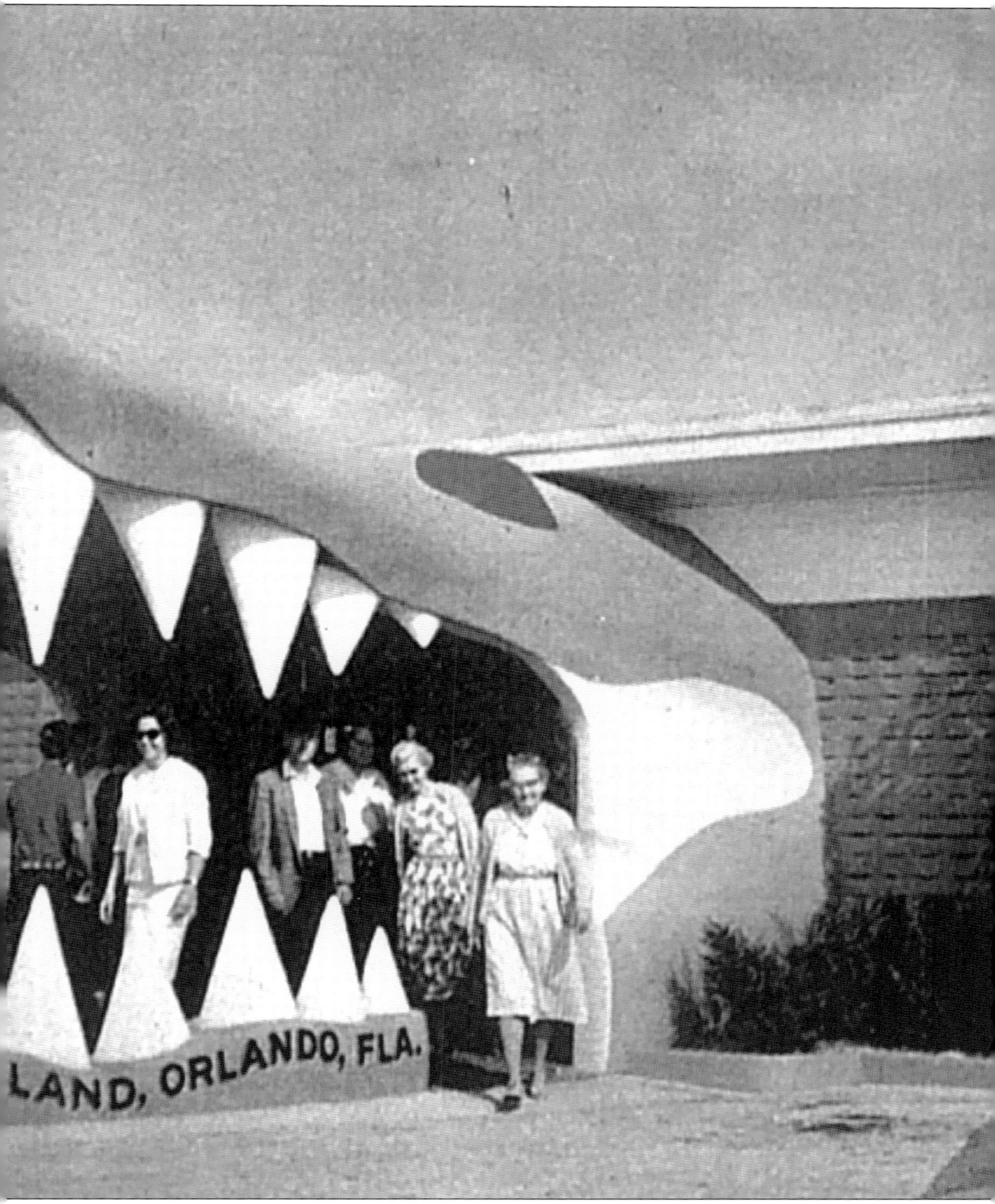

Zoo was a popular pre-Disney tourist destination. Visitors entered the zoo through 30-foot alligator jaws with menacing 3-foot teeth to see "hundreds of alligators and crocodiles in natural habitat and many other rare animals and birds from many parts of the world." (Larry Roberts Antiques.)

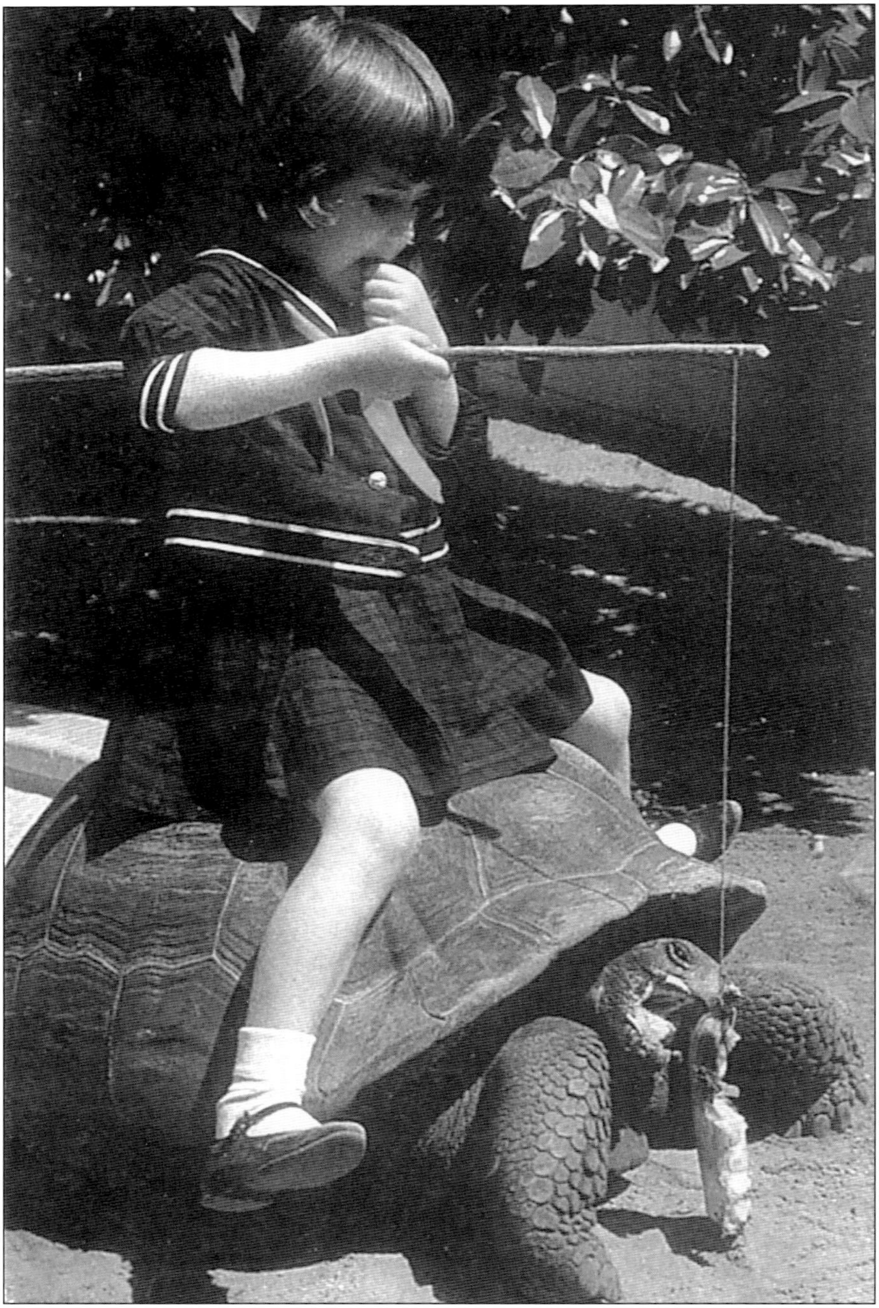

Although they lacked the glamour and glitz, as well as the size and admission prices of today's theme parks, roadside attractions of the 1930s, 1940s, and 1950s still drew thousands of tourists in search of entertainment and a chance to see sights not available back home. Operated by Owen Godwin, Gatorland Zoo presented a unique combination of wild animals and showmanship. While other Florida tourist stops, including Monkey Jungle, Dog Land, and Marineland, also featured exotic creatures of all kinds, Orlando's Gatorland Zoo was the only attraction to have Old Albert, a giant Galapagos tortoise. This postcard described Old Albert as "not very fast, but a lot of fun for a pretty little miss to ride." (Larry Roberts Antiques.)

Six

Business Endeavors

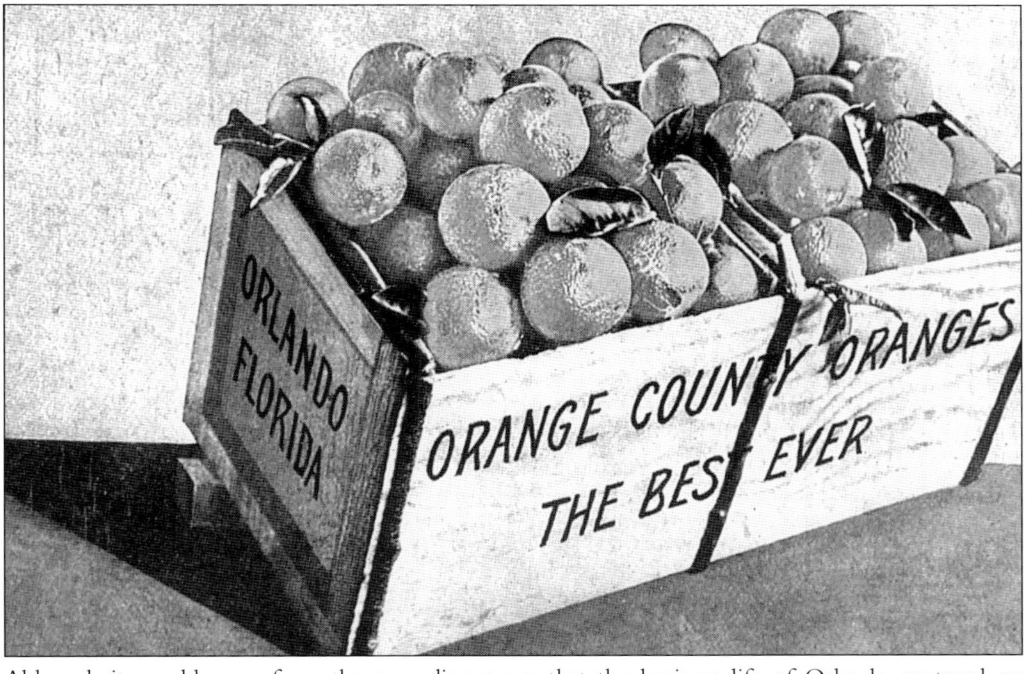

Although it would seem from the preceding pages that the business life of Orlando centered on tourists and the fulfillment of their every need, this wasn't always the case. For many years, Orange County, of which Orlando was the county seat, lived up to its name. Although a disastrous freeze in 1894–1895 devastated the citrus industry, forcing some growers to change occupations or to leave the area completely, those who had the financial resources to replant their trees and purchase additional groves at bargain prices saw the recovery of the industry. According to historian Jerrel Shofner, "Between 1910 and 1917, the amount of central Florida citrus acreage would double. The renewal of citrus culture brought with it improved methods of gathering and shipping the crops. Several new packinghouses opened. Despite a severe freeze in 1917 citrus had become a permanent part of the central Florida economy by World War I." (University of South Florida Special Collections.)

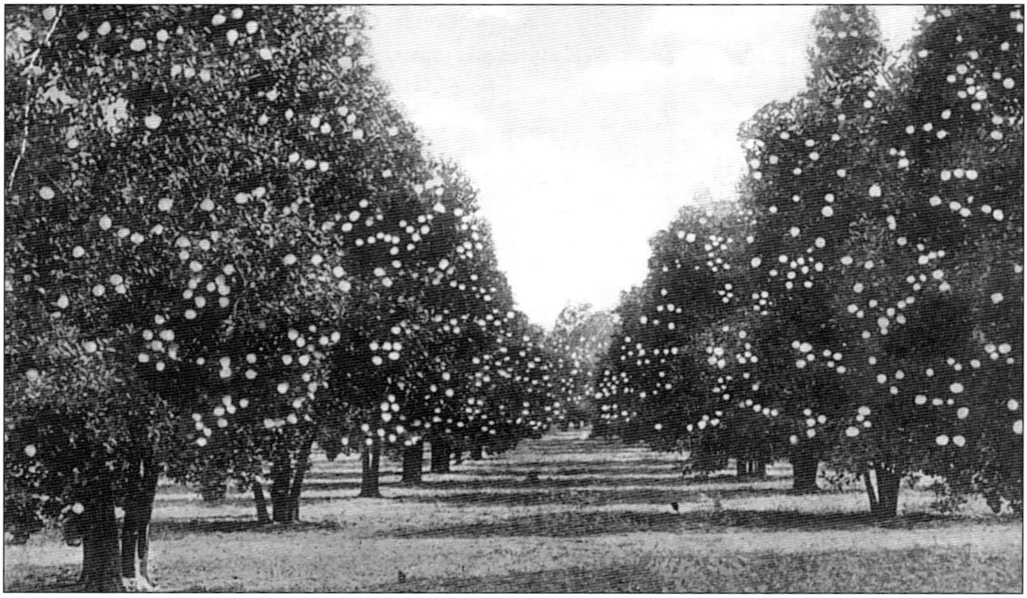

The Florida Growers and Shippers League selected Orlando, with its thousands of acres of citrus groves, as its headquarters in 1914. Four years later, the Orlando *Morning Sentinel* discussed citrus growers' opposition to a state law prohibiting work on Sunday, saying such regulations would be detrimental to the industry and would cause a loss of both fruit and profits. "The packers do not intend to lose their season's crop or any part of it and expect to fight the order should one come. The packers are optimistic over the fruit crop as a result of the recent low drop in temperature and all are unanimous in stating that there has been very little damage done to the citrus fruits." Periodic freezes and labor restrictions weren't the only problems, either. In April 1929, a Mediterranean fruit fly infestation was discovered in Orlando. Eventually spreading to six surrounding counties, the infestation was finally stopped through the efforts of W.W. Yothers, an entomologist widely recognized for his work in the Orlando area. (University of South Florida Special Collections and Larry Roberts Antiques.)

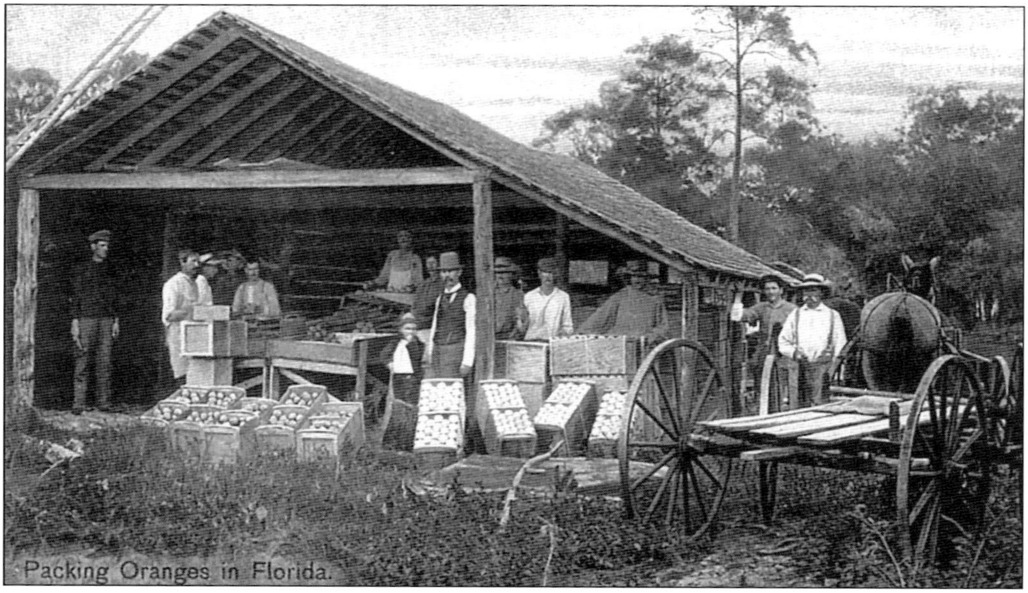

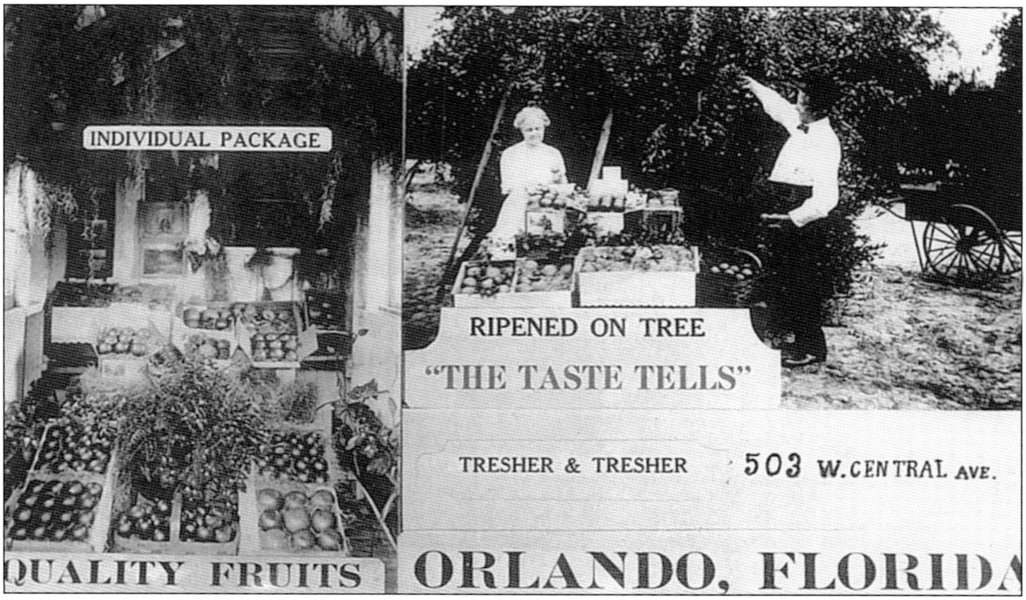

Tresher & Tresher was just one of many Orlando businesses engaged in the growing and shipment of citrus. According to the back of one postcard, "In packing oranges, boxes of light material are made, and each orange is wrapped separately in tissue paper. They are placed closely together in layers, so that there will be no rolling or sliding, and care is taken that only one grade is put into each box. According to the size of the fruit, a standard box will hold from 96 to 250 oranges." (Larry Roberts Antiques.)

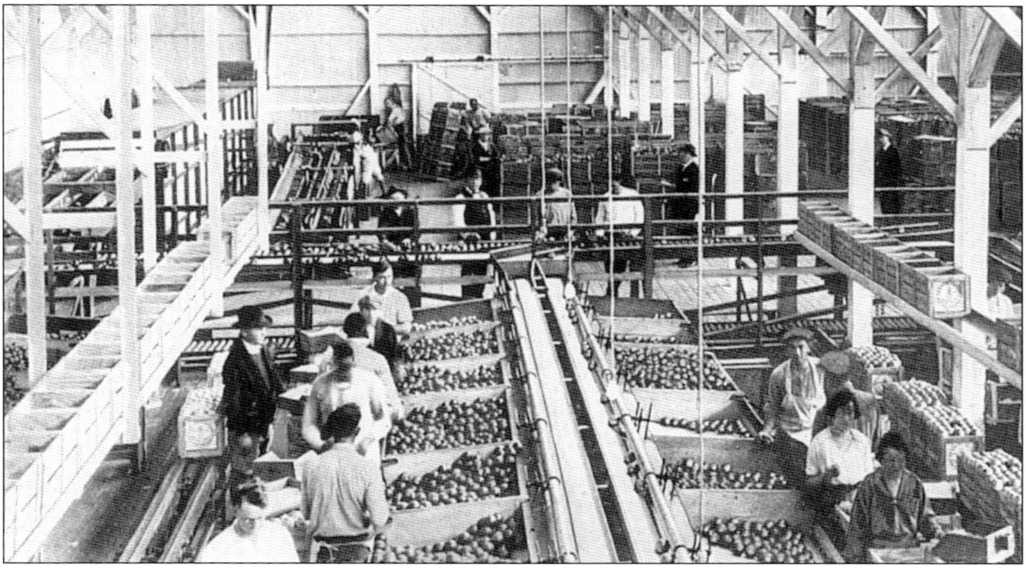

Using a patented process called "flash pasteurization," the Dr. P. Phillips and Company produced the first palatable canned orange juice in 1928. That same year the company also built the world's largest packinghouse, located just ten miles southwest of Orlando. With more citrus acreage than anyone in Florida, Dr. Phillips was considered to be the world's largest individual grower of citrus; in southwest Orange County, he owned the world's largest tangerine grove. (University of South Florida Special Collections.)

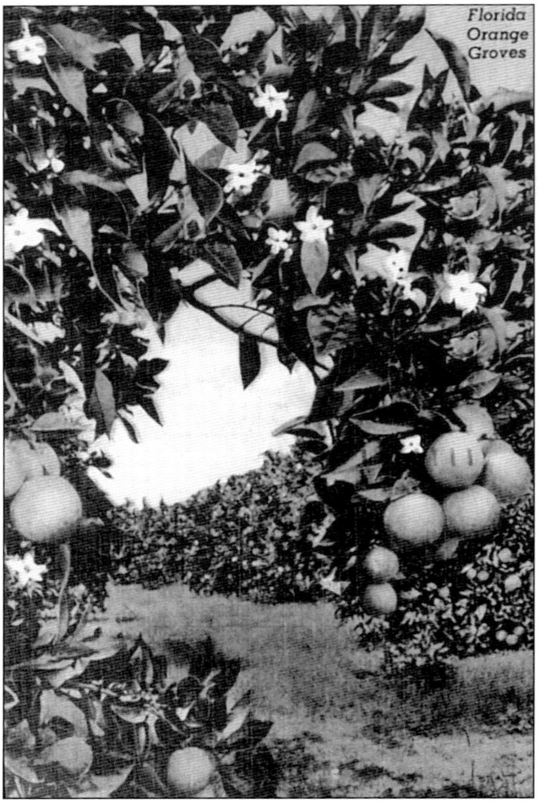

Always the entrepreneur, Dr. Phillips hired Edna Giles Fuller, Florida's first woman legislator, to give lectures in northern cities to promote his grapefruit. His canned juice was the first to receive the American Medical Association's seal of approval. The reign of citrus as economic ruler wasn't to last, however. Although millions of citrus trees once perfumed the Orlando air with fragrant blossoms, the smell would become fainter with the passage of time. Land that sold for $50 per acre in 1918 became more valuable as home, commercial, and industrial sites. Even the Dr. P. Phillips and Company would succumb; in 1954 all of the company's citrus holdings were sold to a subsidiary of Minute Maid, all non-grove land was developed into commercial sites and the planned community of Bay Hill. The fruit from the grove sale provided the crop for the world's first frozen concentrate plant. (Larry Roberts Antiques and University of South Florida Special Collections.)

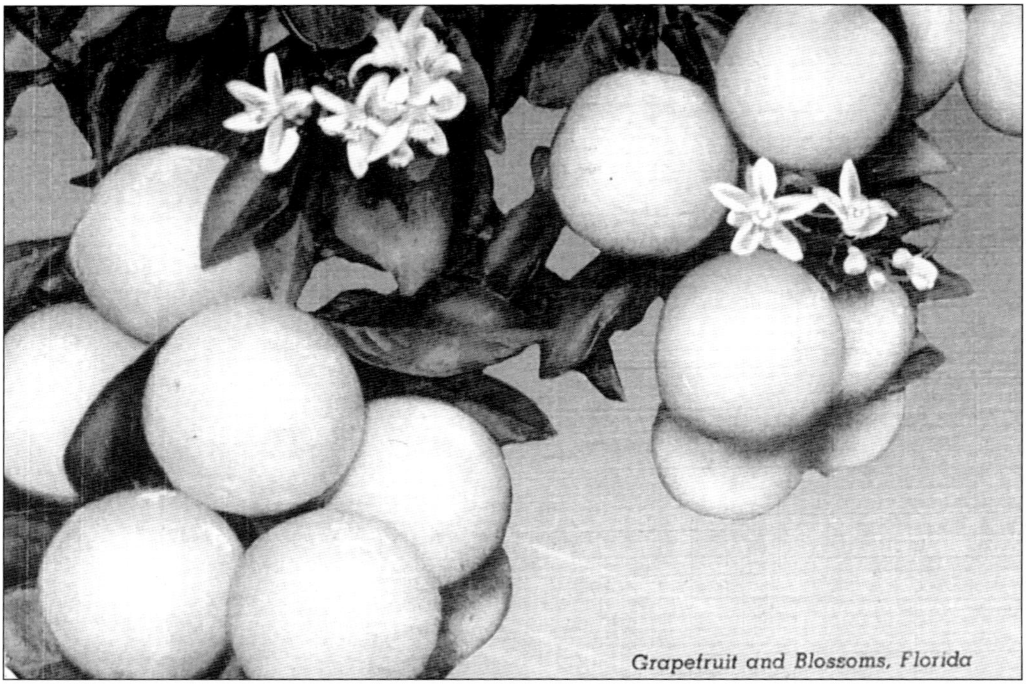

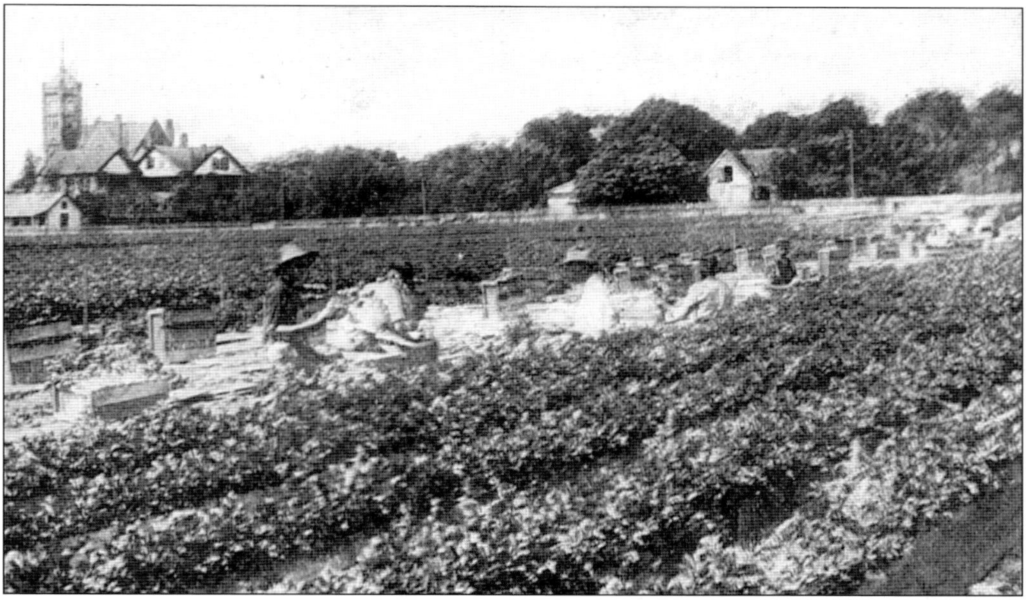

The devastation of Orlando's citrus industry in 1894–1895 led to diversification into other agricultural areas. This 1908 postcard proclaimed, "Orange County has become as famous as Kalamazoo for its celery. It is grown during the winter and marketed in the early spring. It is the most profitable truck farming crop grown. Orlando offers attractive inducements for market gardens. This particular field is on the shore of Lake Eola in sight of the courthouse." (University of South Florida Special Collections.)

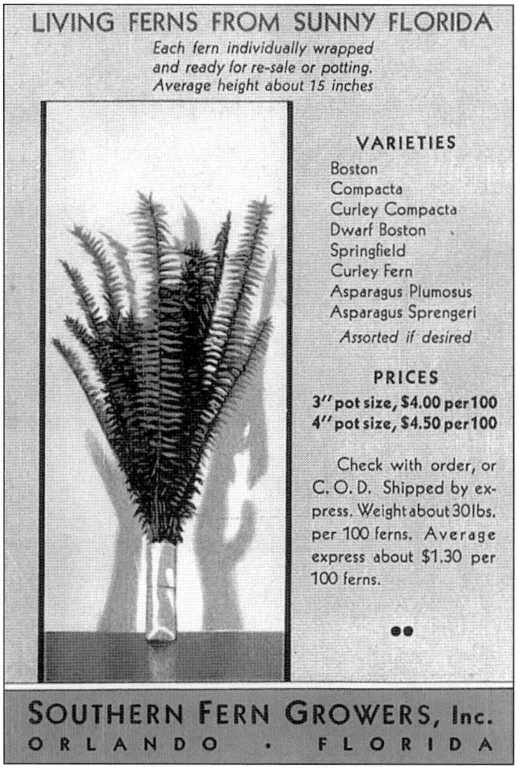

Southern Fern Growers, Inc. of Orlando shipped "Living Ferns from Sunny Florida," individually wrapped and ready for resale or repotting, to destinations across the country. Priced at just $4 or $4.50 per 100 plants, depending upon their size, varieties included Boston, Compacta, Curley, Asparagus, and Springfield, or any assortment thereof. (Larry Roberts Antiques.)

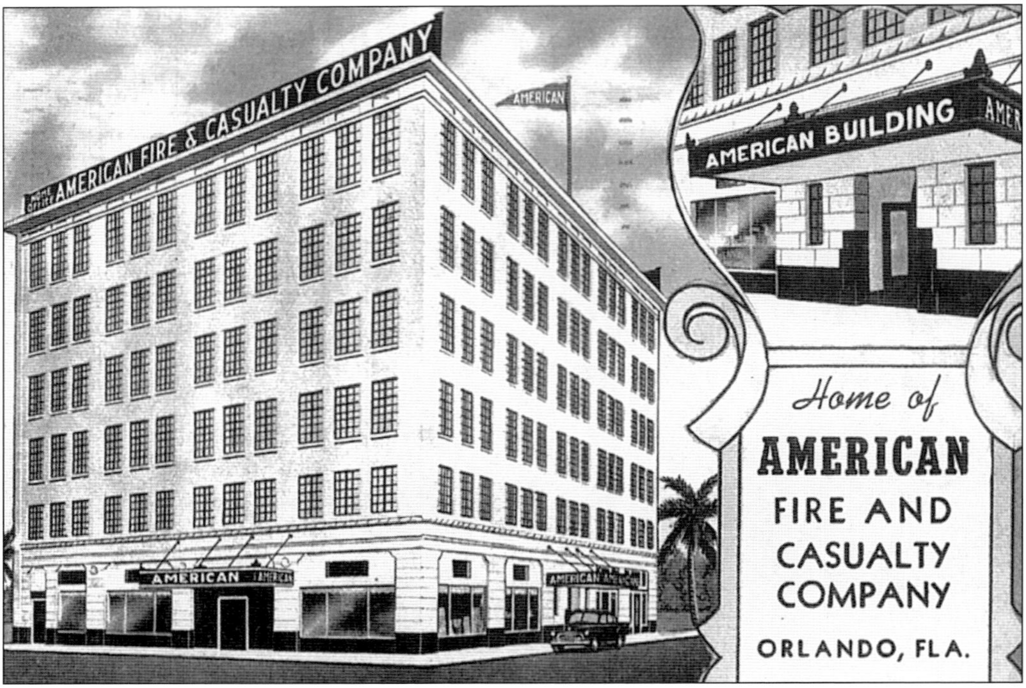

Touting itself as "One of the nation's most complete insurance companies, writing fire and allied lines, all forms of casualty insurance (including automobile and aviation), fidelity and surety bonds," the American Fire & Casualty Company had offices in downtown Orlando's Exchange Building for many years. Finally, in 1946, the company became owner rather than tenant when it purchased the structure on the corner of Orange Avenue and Jackson Street and renamed it the American Building. (Larry Roberts Antiques.)

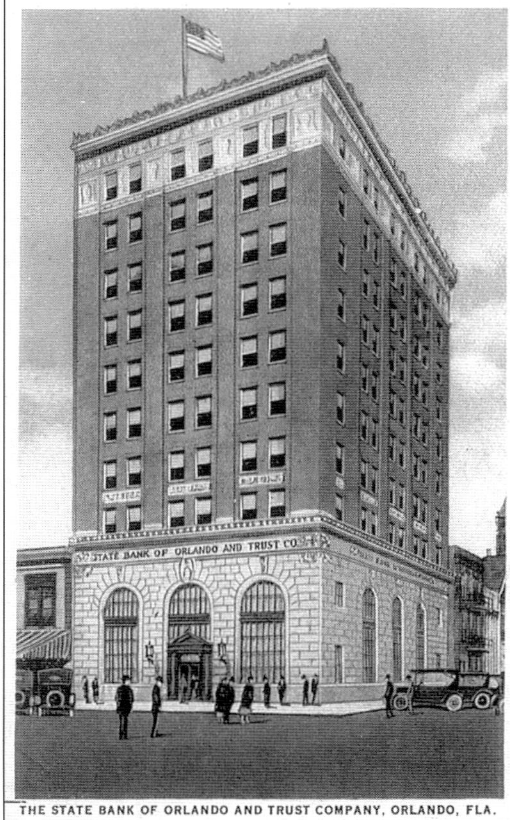

THE STATE BANK OF ORLANDO AND TRUST COMPANY, ORLANDO, FLA.

A long-term Orlando institution dating from 1893, the State Bank of Orlando & Trust Company constructed its beautiful new 10-story Beaux-Arts bank building in 1923–1924 on the corner of Orange Avenue and Central. Soon to be a casualty of the Depression, however, the bank was placed in receivership in August 1929, after a failure to meet customers' withdrawals. Finally, in 1933, Florida Bank of Orlando purchased the building. (Larry Roberts Antiques.)

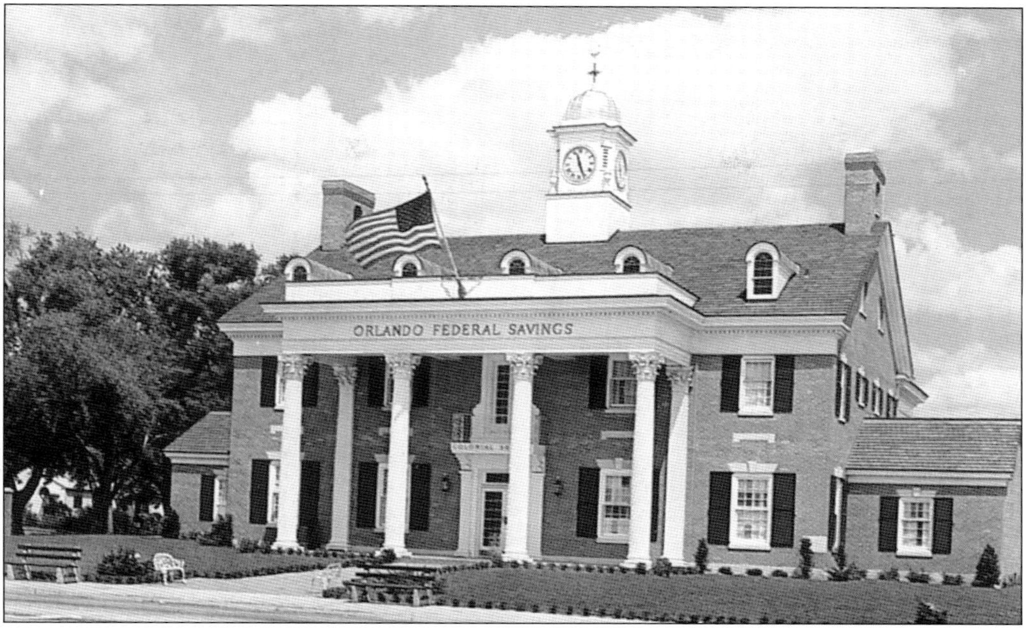

Orlando Federal Savings & Loan received its charter in 1949 and opened a bank at the corner of Magnolia and Robinson Avenues. Six years later, it moved into a new Colonial Revival–style building on Livingston and Magnolia. Obviously printed and distributed by the organization, this particular postcard, mailed to Little Valley, New York, touted the benefits of the architectural style and decor. "A warm and friendly atmosphere is created by the authentic Williamsburg Colonial architecture of the Orlando Federal Savings Building so finely expressed in the spacious lobby." Branch banks of similar architectural design opened on Colonial Drive in 1962 and in Pine Hills two years later. (University of South Florida Special Collections.)

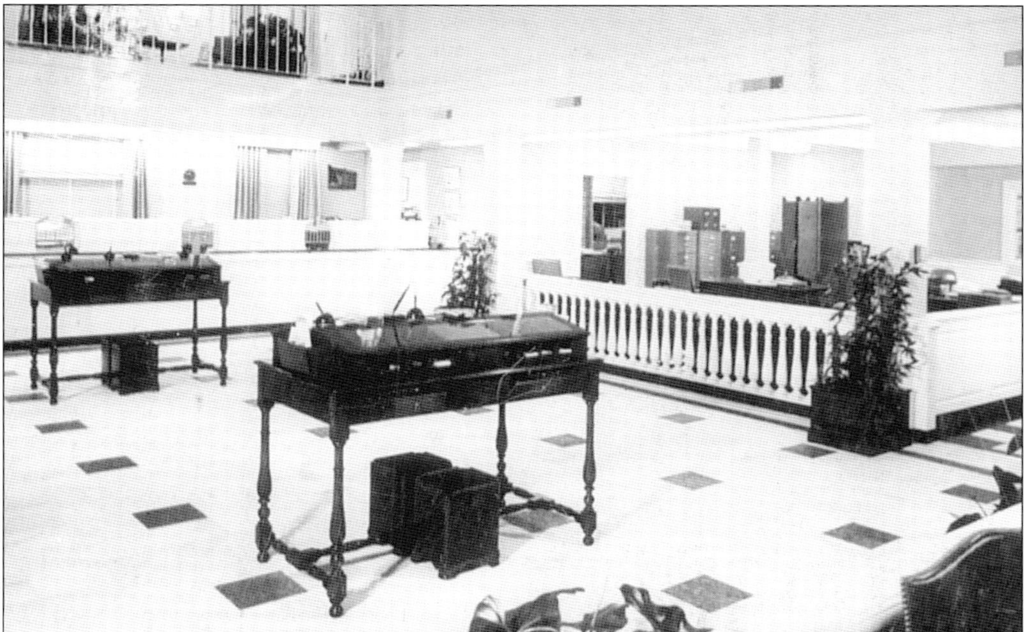

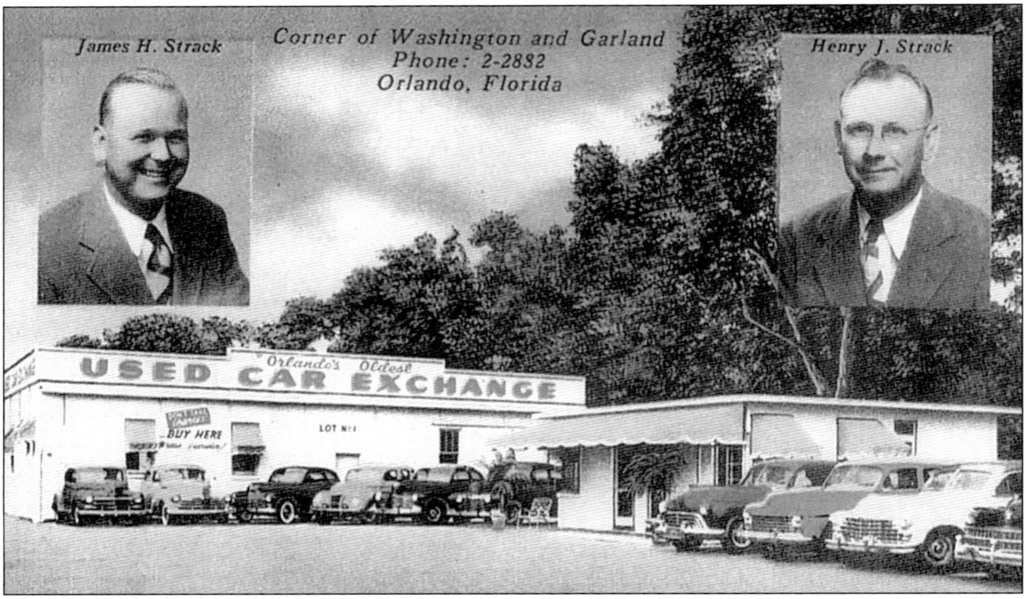

Orlando in 1915 bragged of being "The Automobile City" with reputedly one car for every 14 citizens. Six years earlier, everyone in Orlando owning a car had posed for a photo at Lake Lucerne—a glorious total of nine cars. By the 1940s, however, the Used Car Exchange was just one of many automobile businesses. Proclaiming its expertise, the business stated, "Men in our organization represent 110 Years of Automobile Buying and Selling." (Larry Roberts Antiques.)

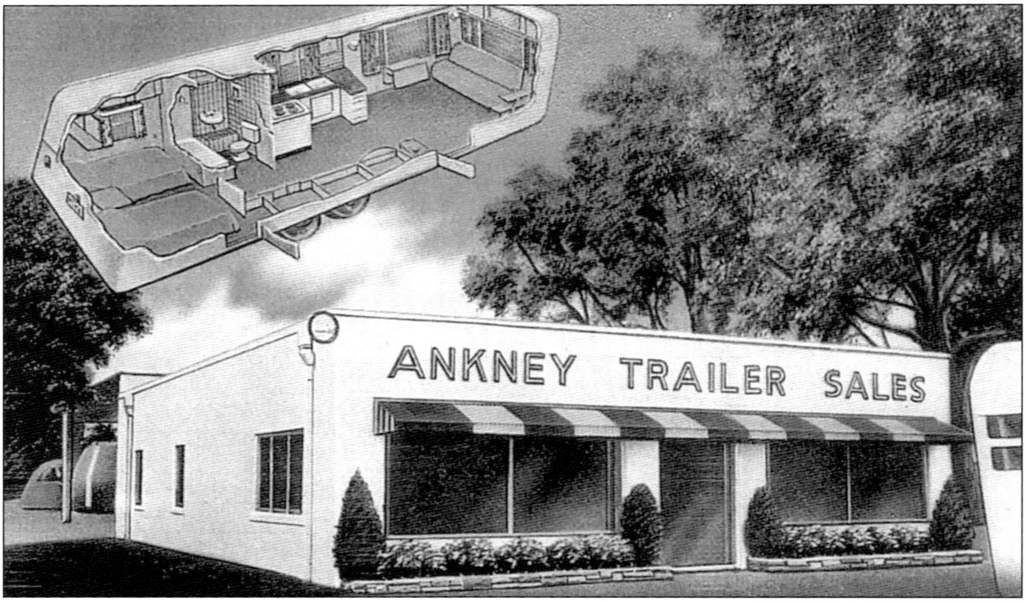

In 1918 the local newspaper reported, "A party of five in two Fords and one trailer arrived in Orlando yesterday. They left Minneapolis, Minnesota, on October 18 and have traveled 3,327 miles since then. They had only one blowout during their journey. Their trailer was the most completely equipped of any that has arrived in Orlando. It contained two beds equipped for four, two gas stoves and a refrigerator." Years later, Ankney Trailer Sales continued to furnish trailers for travelers. (Larry Roberts Antiques.)

Orlando was no different than other cities, needing companies to provide services to both residents and visitors. Even though the Greater Orlando Chamber of Commerce bragged of warm winter temperatures, Woods Fuel Oil Company had a thriving business supplying fuel oil and kerosene to both residential and commercial customers. Located on Lake Ivanhoe, Fairchild's provided "smooth riding, two-tone green Cadillac ambulances that make up the Fairchild fleet. Immediately dispatched by three-way radio to meet any emergency. Ready to go anywhere, anytime." (Larry Roberts Antiques.)

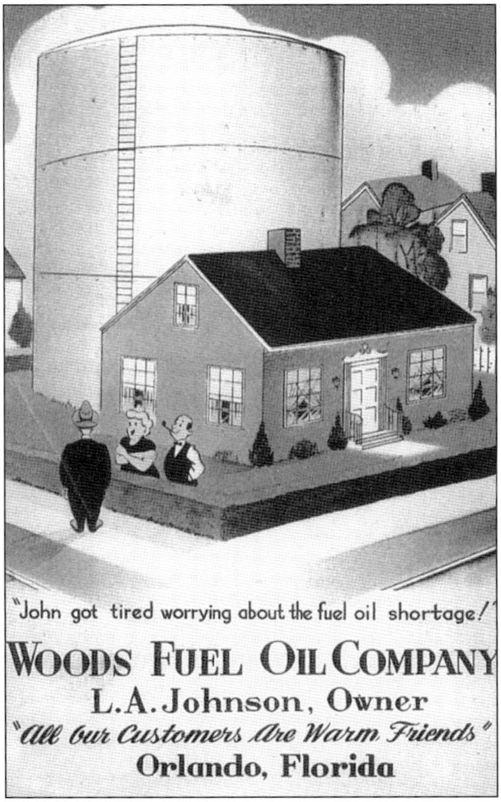

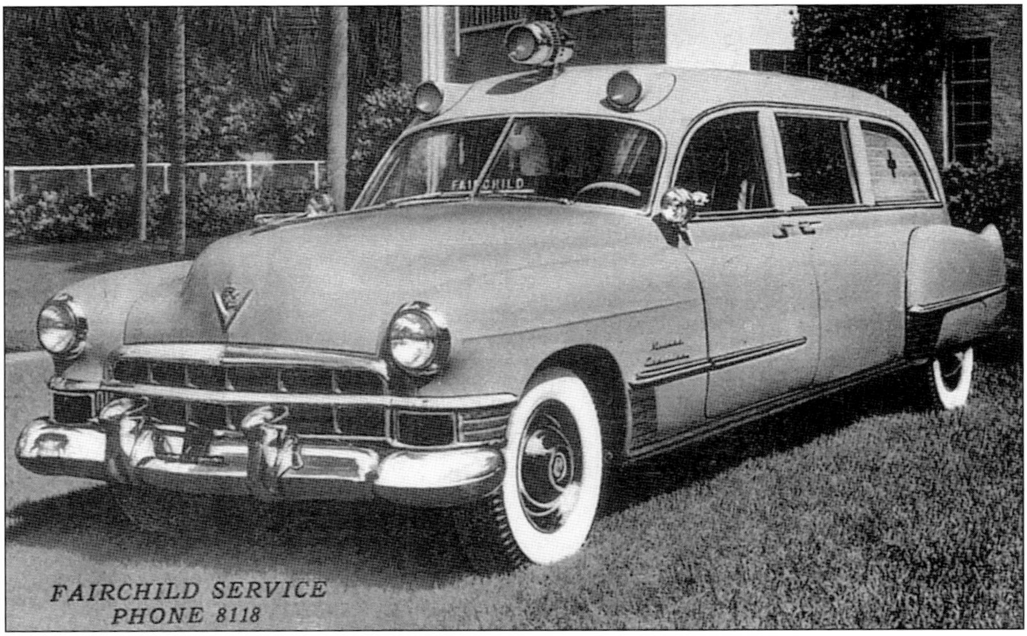

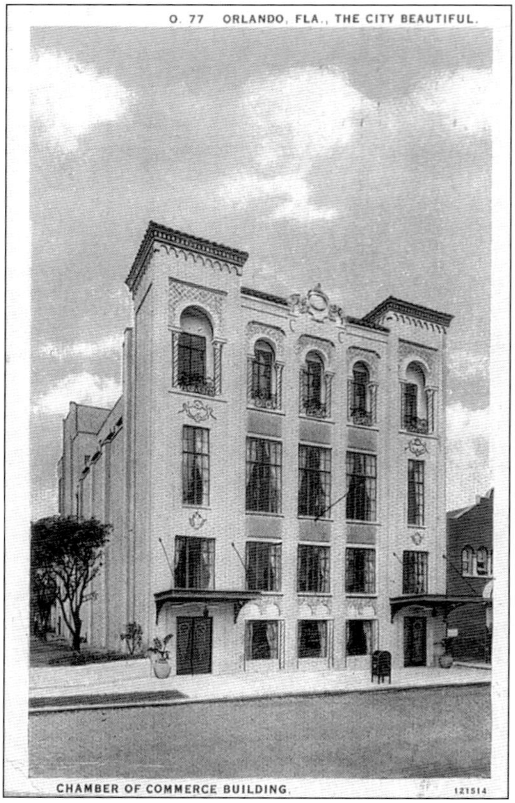

Christened as the Chamber of Commerce in 1920, the organization had its beginnings in 1886 as the Board of Trade. Renamed the Greater Orlando Chamber of Commerce in 1933, the group, regardless of its title, consistently had one purpose—to attract visitors and businesses to Orlando. Completed in 1927, the Chamber's new building on East Central Avenue would serve as the organization's home until 1968. (Larry Roberts Antiques.)

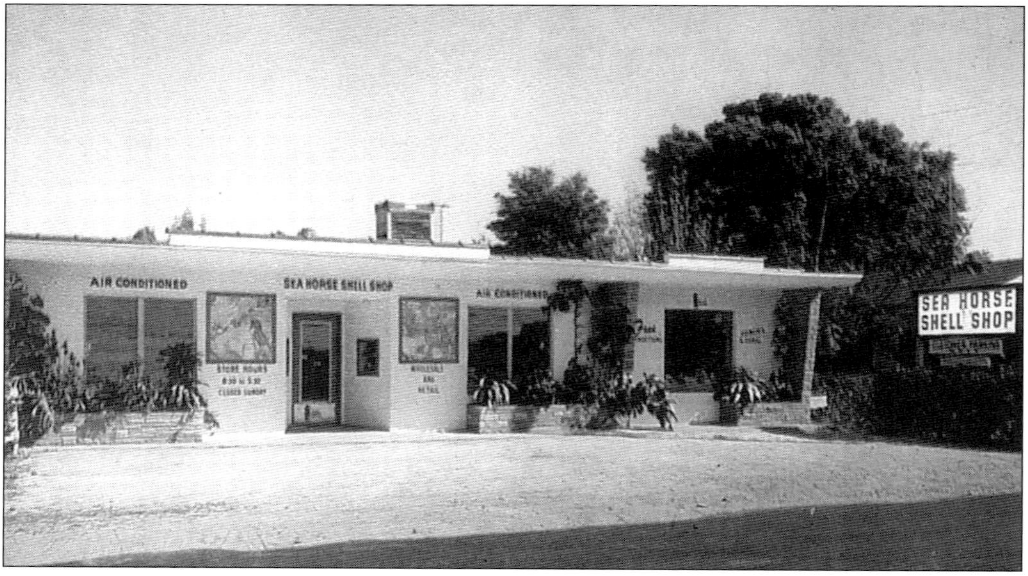

While there were thousands of businesses that catered to every need of Orlando's visitors, a shop selling Florida seashells seemed to personify the idea of tourism. From its location at 1225–1227 Twenty-ninth Street, the Sea Horse Shell Shop offered hobby and craft supplies that included shells, coral, and driftwood. The shop also offered shell jewelry, shell craft supplies, a large selection of woven bags, gift items, and souvenirs. (Larry Roberts Antiques.)

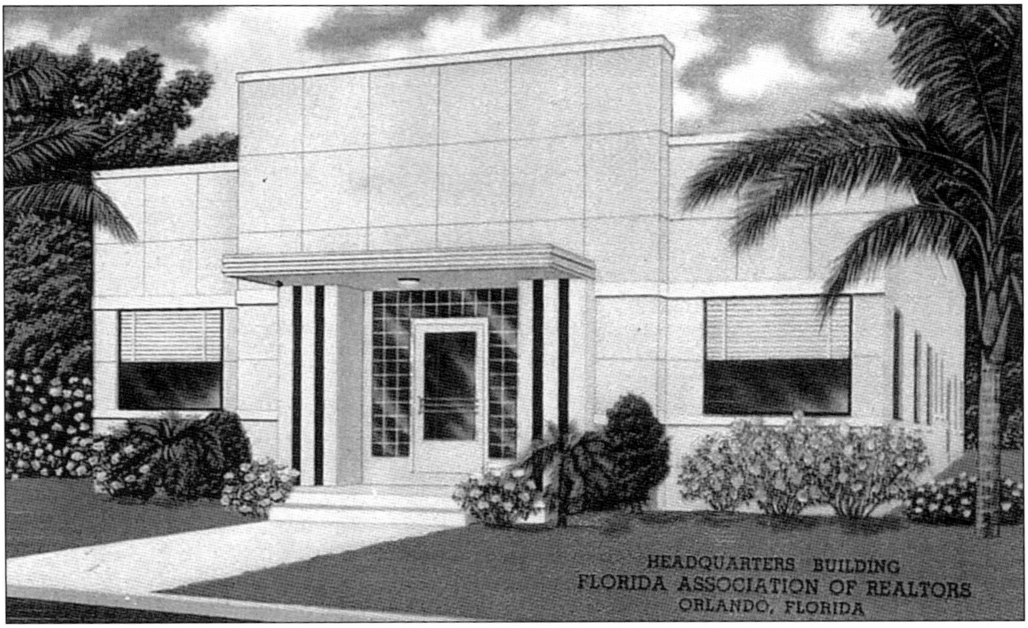

As early as 1920 the Orlando Chamber of Commerce realized the need for a diversified economic base rather than one dependent solely upon either citrus or tourism. To that end, the organization mounted an ongoing campaign that sought to attract both corporate headquarters and branch offices to town. Two examples of its success were illustrated by the presence of the state headquarters of the Florida Association of Realtors and the Florida Nurses Association. The Florida Association of Realtors proudly identified its Orlando facility as the only state realtors' building in the United States to be built entirely through contributions by members and affiliated groups. (Larry Roberts Antiques and University of South Florida Special Collections.)

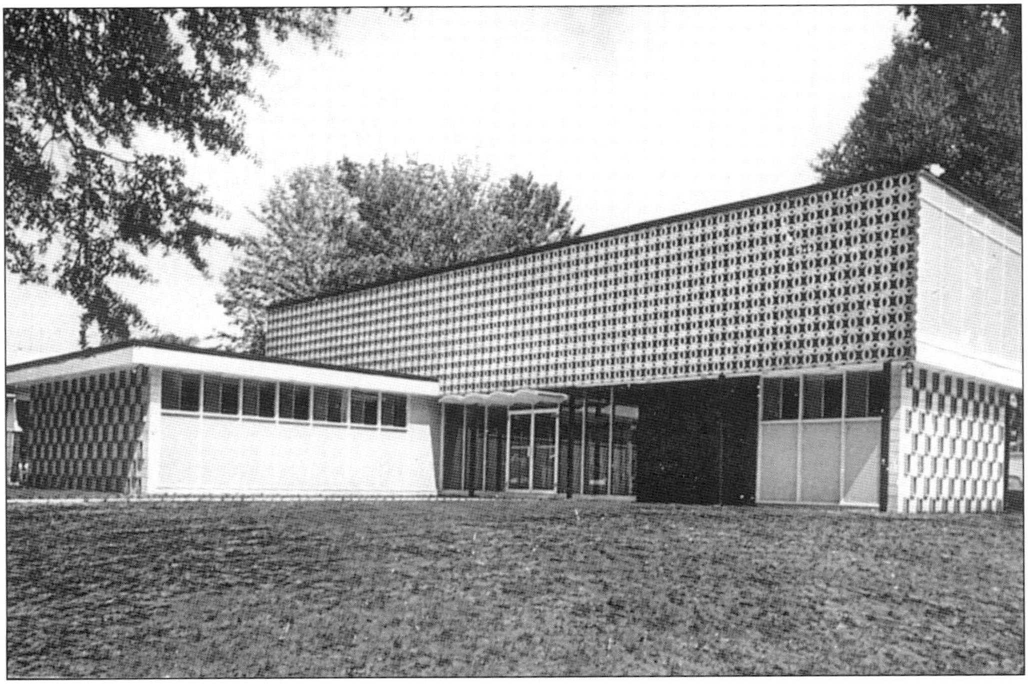

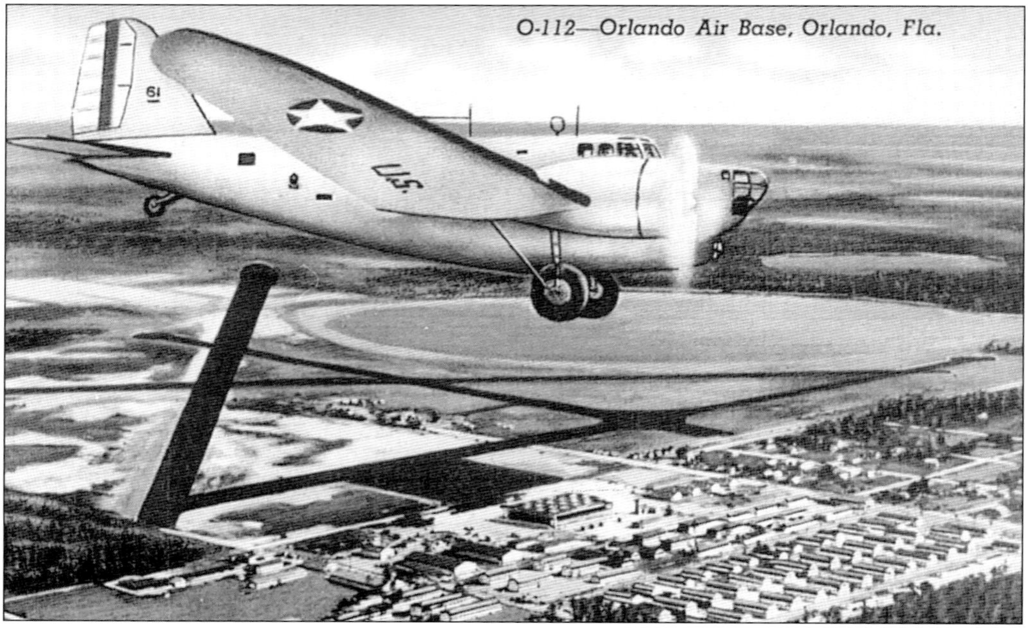

Although Orlando had been quite involved in World War I, the community would play an even more active role in World War II. In addition to personnel serving in the armed forces and dollars contributed to bond drives, volunteers donated thousands of hours to the Red Cross and other worthwhile causes. By 1940, as it became apparent that America would soon be at war, the federal government chose Orlando Municipal Airport as the site of a pilot training facility, the Army Air Corps Center. It also took a 25-year lease on adjacent land for military housing; Robinson Avenue was converted into an access road for the base. The officers' mess hall was just one of hundreds of quickly built structures on the base. The day after the attack on Pearl Harbor, newspapers reported that a second field would be built just south of the city. Costing more than $500,000, Pine Castle Air Base would be constructed on 24-hour shifts. Several aviation companies also opened facilities in the area to fill military contracts. (University of South Florida Special Collections.)

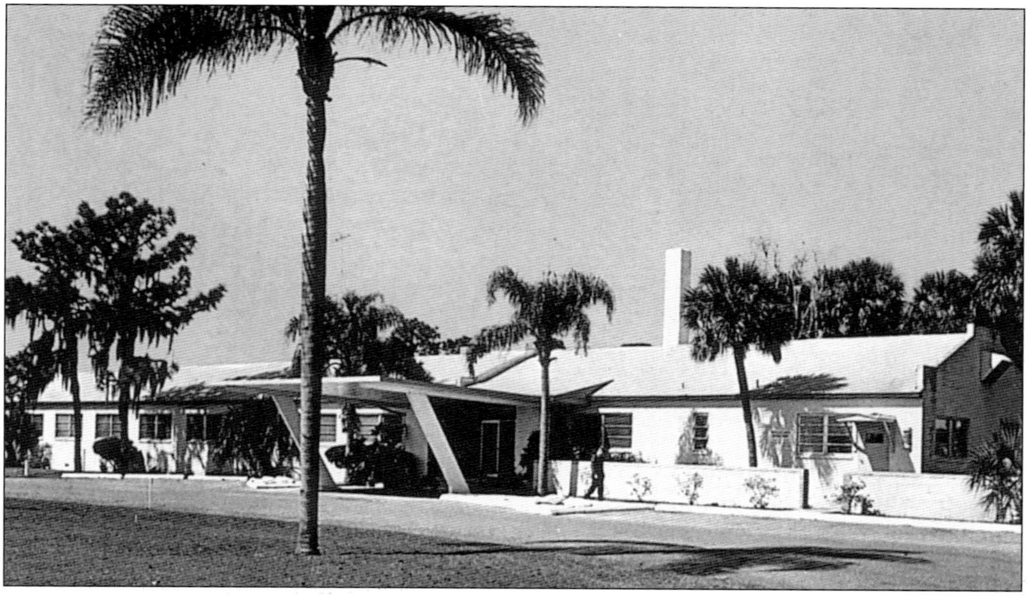

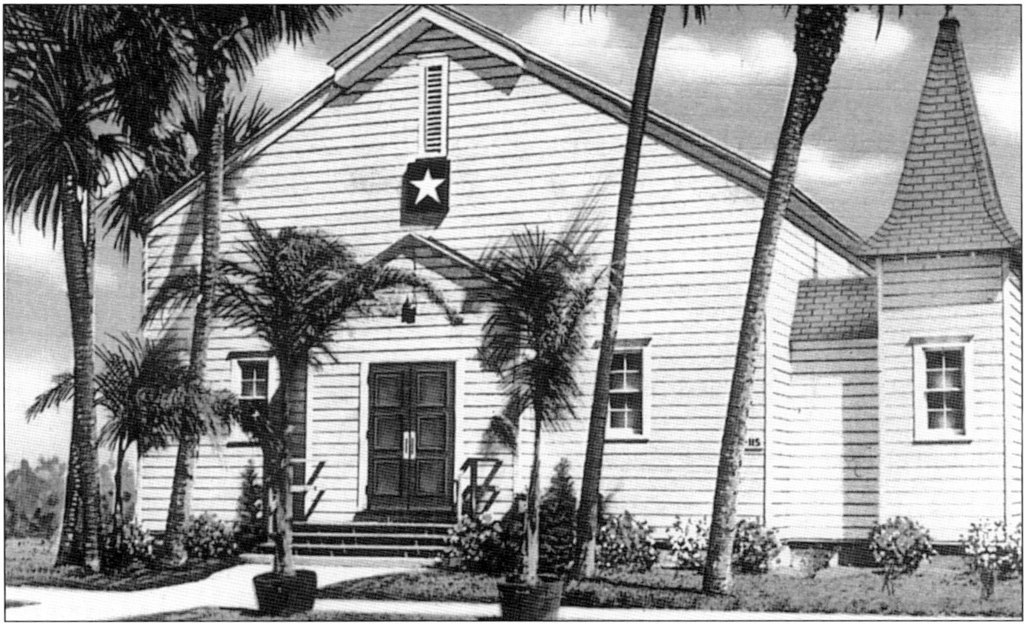

The post chapel was another of the buildings constructed at the former municipal airport. Stationed at Orlando Air Base were units of the Twenty-third Composite Air Group, including a headquarters squadron, fighter and bomber aircraft, a radio detachment, and a weather division. On standby after the war, both bases were reactivated during the Korean Conflict, with Orlando Air Force Base expanding to larger quarters on Bennett Road. (University of South Florida Special Collections.)

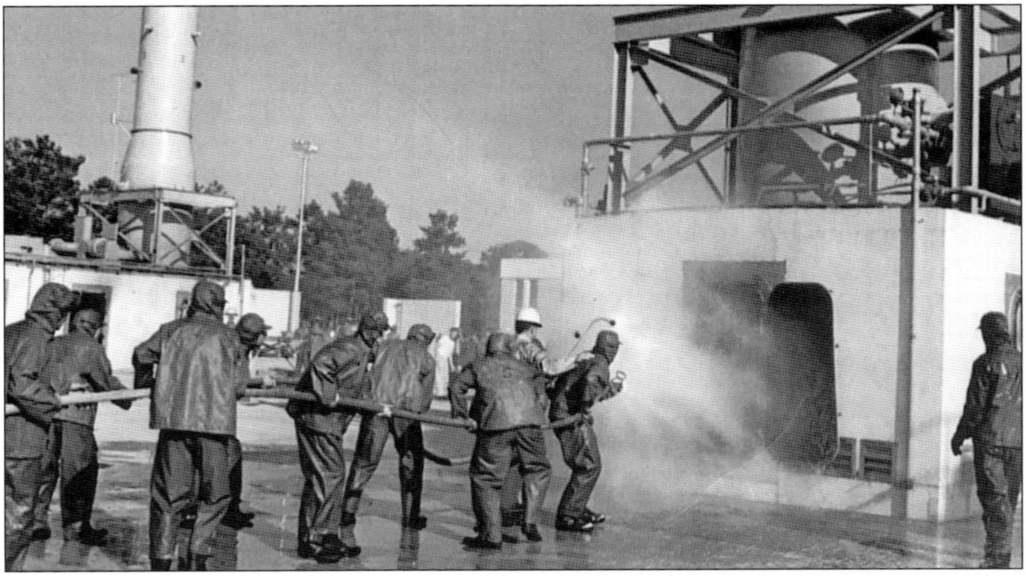

The U.S. Navy also had a major effect on the Orlando economy when it officially took over the former Orlando Air Base as a training facility in 1968. Bringing with it more personnel and a bigger payroll, the $14.9-million, 1,229-acre Naval Training Center also acted as a contracting and procurement agency for the Navy, benefiting many of the high-tech companies that had moved into the Orlando area. (University of South Florida Special Collections.)

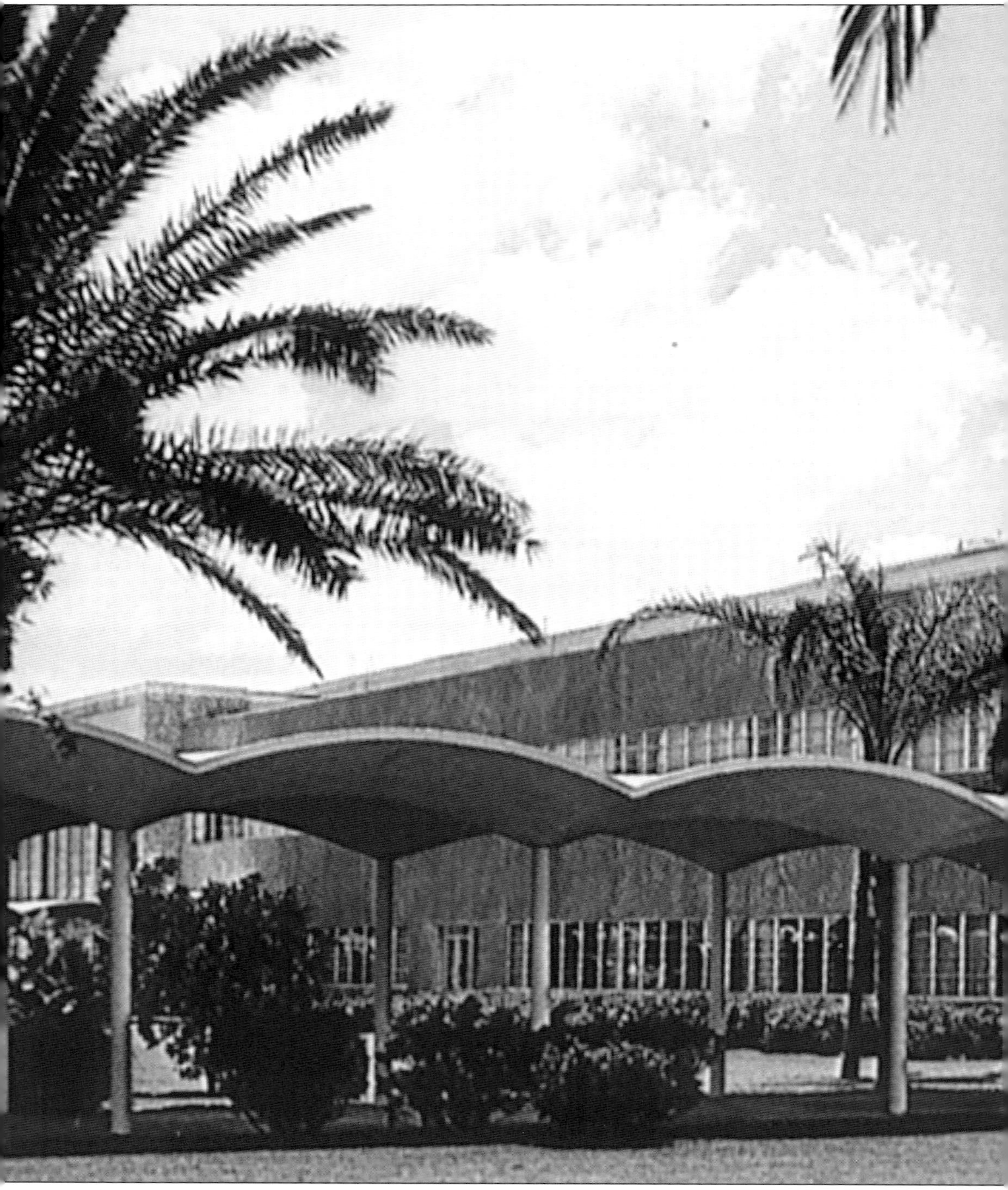

The 1950s saw a technological revolution in America, as computers, space exploration, and the Cold War dominated the news. Orlando was no exception, as the Glenn L. Martin Company, builder of the Matador missile, spent nearly $2 million in 1956 to purchase 7,300 acres of land along the Orange Blossom Trail just south of Orlando. According to historian Jerrel Shofner, "Land was suddenly more valuable for urban or industrial use than for agriculture." Later known as Martin-Marietta Orlando

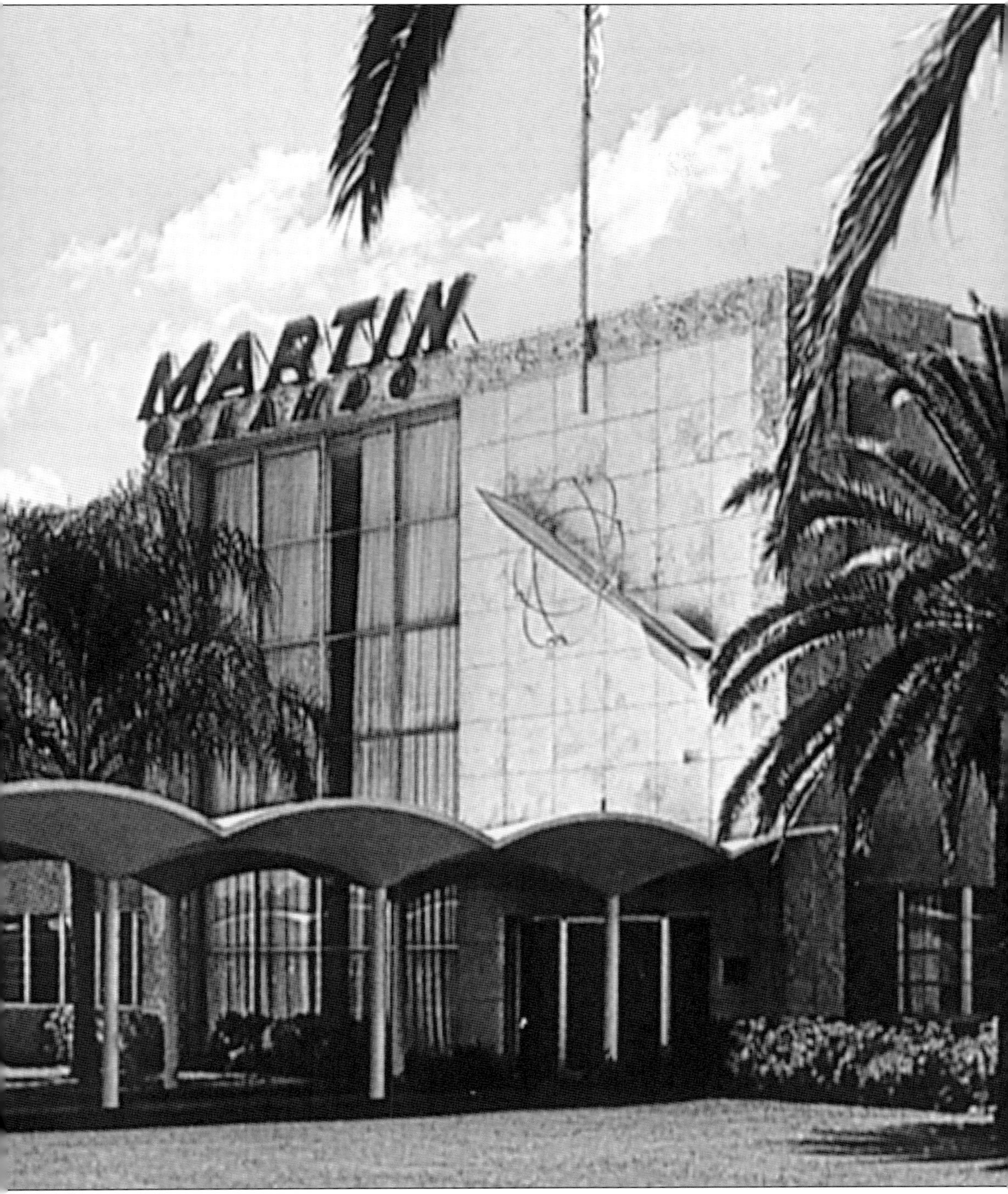

Aerospace, the company employed as many as 8,000 workers on the development and production of high-technology weapon systems and associated equipment. The Pershing missile was just one of the products designed at the Orlando plant whose presence also brought other related industries. (University of South Florida Special Collections.)

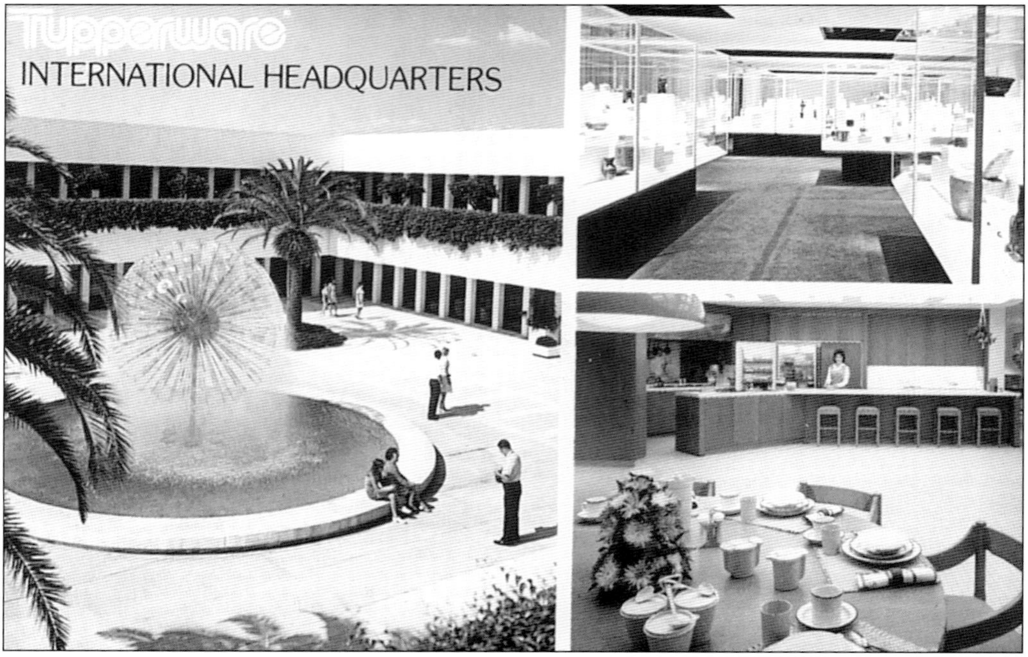

The Martin Company's massive land purchase was located in the same general area as one that had occurred just four years earlier. In 1952, the Tupperware Company of Farnomsville, Massachusetts, bought 1,000 acres for its national headquarters. With a $250,000 annual payroll, the manufacturer of plastic containers was welcomed to the community with open arms. (University of South Florida Special Collections.)

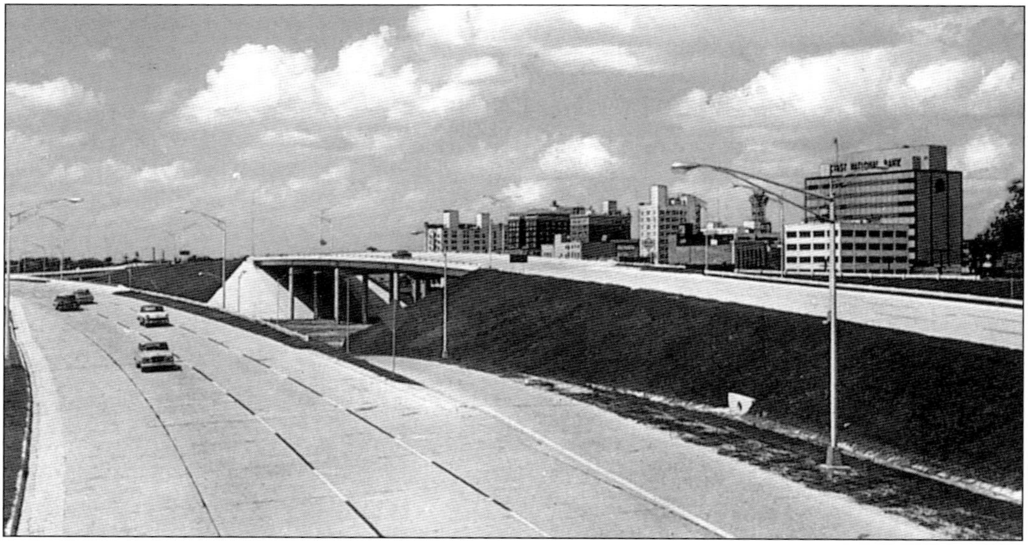

The Orlando Chamber of Commerce ushered in the 1960s with a new promotional slogan—"The Action Center of Florida." The growing system of expressways, turnpikes, and interstate highways that would be completed during the remainder of the decade would inextricably link Orlando with the rest of Florida. They would also facilitate travel by the millions of visitors who would soon be visiting Orlando to see a certain mouse. An era had ended—another was about to begin. (University of South Florida Special Collections.)